D0867257

*f***P**

A PERSONAL ODYSSEY

THOMAS SOWELL

THE FREE PRESS

NEW YORK   LONDON   TORONTO   SYDNEY   SINGAPORE

THE FREE PRESS
A Division of Simon & Schuster Inc.
1230 Avenue of the Americas
New York, NY 10020

THE FREE PRESS and colophon are trademarks
of Simon & Schuster Inc.

Designed by Kyoko Watanabe

Manufactured in the United States of America

10 9 8 7 6 5 4 3 2 1

Library of Congress Cataloging-in-Publication Data

Sowell, Thomas, 1930–
A personal odyssey / Thomas Sowell.
p.   cm.
1. Sowell, Thomas, 1930–   2. Afro-American intellectuals—Biography.
3. Intellectuals—United States—biography.   4. Afro-Americans—intellectual
life—20th century.   5. Afro-Americans—Civil rights—History—20th
century.   6. Charlotte (N.C.)—Biography.   7. Southwell family.
I. Title

E185.97 .S69   2000
975.6'7600496073'0092—dc21
[B]   00-033853

ISBN 0-684-86464-9

To Mary Frances,

who came to look for me.

Contents

A PERSONAL
ODYSSEY

Preface

One of the few compensations for growing old is accumulating memories and sharing them with others. This is the stage of life that Disraeli called "anecdotage."

These vignettes are not an autobiography, for they do not try to cover a continuous lifespan or to tell an exhaustive story. Unlike some memoirs which "tell all" (or perhaps more than all), these reminiscences are as selective as memory and as prudent as required by a concern for other people's feelings. Some names have been changed. Moreover, I promise not to bore the reader with my love life.

Personal memories may have more than purely personal implications, especially when they span more than one-fourth of the entire history of the United States—years of great social change, seen from radically changing personal circumstances, and accompanied by evolving changes in personal perceptions and visions.

In retrospect, even my misfortunes were in some ways fortunate, for they taught me things that would be hard to understand otherwise, and they presented reality from an angle not given to those, among intellectuals especially, whose careers have followed a more straight-line path in familiar grooves. I lived through experiences which they can only theorize about.

Once, when I had listened to about as much advice from my daughter as I could stand, I asked her:

"How do you suppose I managed to make it through this world before you were born?"

"Luck!" she replied.

The following pages may suggest that she had a point, at least partly.

1

Carolina in the Morning

Henry was about to become a father again—if he lived that long. He probably knew he was dying, though he may not have known exactly what he was dying of. Black people in the South did not always go to doctors when they were sick, back in 1929. In any case, when Willie became pregnant, Henry went to his Aunt Molly to ask if she would take the baby to raise. There were four children to take care of already and there was no way that Willie could take care of a new baby, all by herself, while trying to earn a living without Henry.

Aunt Molly was the logical person to turn to. Her own children were grown and she had recently tried to adopt a baby boy, but the baby's mother had changed her mind and returned after a few months to take him back. It was an experience that may have left a lasting mark on Aunt Molly. But she was willing to try again. Willie's new baby turned out also to be a boy—and Henry was dead before he was born.

Willie had little choice but to go through with the arrangements that Henry had made with his aunt. Feeding four children and herself on a maid's wages turned out to be very hard, even after she gave the baby to Aunt Molly to raise as her own. Still, Willie managed somehow to visit the little boy regularly, even though Aunt Molly lived 15 miles away. These visits had to be carefully managed, as if Willie were visiting Aunt Molly, so that the boy—"little Buddy," she called him—

would never suspect that he was adopted, much less that Willie was his mother. This was in fact managed so well that he grew up to adulthood with no memory of the woman who came by unobtrusively in his early years, supposedly to visit with the adults.

Willie could see that her son had a better material life than she could give him. He wore better clothes than her other children and had toys that she could not buy them. He was also loved, and perhaps even spoiled, in his new family. Aunt Molly's youngest child was a 20-year-old girl named Birdie, who was especially fond of him. Still, Willie sometimes returned home in tears after a visit and spoke wistfully of someday being able to go get little Buddy and bring him back. But it was not to be. Willie died in childbirth a few years later.

Aunt Molly was very possessive of the boy, perhaps in reaction to having had the other little boy taken away from her after she had become attached to him. Whatever the reason, when she eventually moved away from North Carolina to New York, some relatives said that she did it to put distance between the boy and those who knew the family secret that he was adopted. Though there were in fact other, more compelling reasons to move to New York, it is significant that those who knew her could believe that she would do it to preserve her secret. In any event, she severed all links between the boy and his past. His brothers and a sister in North Carolina all knew of his existence, but he did not know of theirs, and they heard about him as he grew up in New York only through the family grapevine.

His original family continued to refer to the boy as Buddy, but he never heard that name as he grew up, for his new family renamed him in infancy. Birdie prevailed upon Aunt Molly to name him after her boy friend, Thomas Hancock. Aunt Molly's legal name was Mamie Sowell.

● ● ●

My earliest memories were of Mama and Daddy, and Birdie and Ruth. Daddy was my favorite—and I was his. He was a construction worker, a short man, and an elder in the church until I came along. One of the scenes that came down in family legend was his standing up in front of the congregation, with me in his arms and a baby bottle in his pocket, explaining that he now had new duties to take the place of those he was resigning in the church.

Daddy had a certain gruffness about him but was usually good-natured with people and was extremely patient with me. However, he became angry whenever he thought anyone was not treating me right. He would fuss with Mama if he found out that she had spanked me while he was at work. (I was, of course, the usual source of this information.) Once he almost got into a fight with a man on the street, who inadvertently frightened me by pointing his walking stick in my general direction while trying to give another man directions. Mama was more enigmatic, with changeable moods. A woman with very little education—she wrote her name with painful slowness—she was nevertheless shrewd and even manipulative, but she was also emotional and subject to an unpredictable sentimentality which sometimes brought her to tears over small things.

Birdie and I were very close in those early years, and remained so on into my teens. She taught me to read before I was four years old. We read stories in the comics together, so some of the first words I learned to spell were words like "pow" and "splash." Birdie also read to me some of the usual children's stories. One story that I found sad at the time, but remembered the rest of my life, was about a dog with a bone who saw his reflection in a stream and thought that the dog he saw had a bigger bone than he did. He opened his mouth to try to get the other dog's bone—and of course lost his own when it dropped into the water. There would be many occasions in life to remember that story.

Birdie gave me most of the mothering I received in these early years, with Mama being more concerned with teaching me practical things and maintaining discipline. But Mama also put some of her practical responsibilities on Birdie or others. One summer, when I was playing outside barefoot, as Southern kids did then, I stepped on some jagged glass and suffered a bad gash on the bottom of my foot. As I came running up the long back stairs, crying and yelling and trailing a stream of blood, Mama came out on the back porch, took one look at the scene and seemed to turn sick. She said, "Oh, Gosh!" and went back inside to lie down on the sofa, sending Birdie out to take care of me. Birdie soon had me calmed down and comforted, and my foot bandaged up.

Ruth was a few years older than Birdie and was a more reserved person, with an occasional enigmatic smile and a more worldly air about her. But she was softer and warmer than her more sophisticated exterior would suggest. However, to me Ruth was always an adult, while Birdie and I sometimes played rough-house together, as if we were both kids.

A fifth person who entered my life so early that I was unaware of a time when I did not know him was Birdie's new boy friend, Lacy. He was a debonair young man with a gift for words and a way of jauntily tilting his head as he strode along. In later years, after he and Birdie were married, he would recall that the first time he saw me, I was swinging on the front gate, with my diapers very much in need of changing.

Lacy was to become a major influence in my formative years, especially after Daddy and Mama broke up and we moved to New York. Though it would be many years later before I would understand Lacy's background, he had himself been adopted and had not always been treated well. He not only took a special interest in me, but was also quick to speak up if he thought I was being unfairly punished or even unfairly criticized. Over the years, he many times charmed Mama out of punishing me.

A more remote figure was Mama's oldest child, Herman, who was married and lived in the country on his own farm. Herman was a dignified, even stuffy, individual. He also owned a car, which to us was a sign of prosperity well beyond our reach. He was not a fan of mine nor I of his. We seldom saw each other, however, and showed no sign of suffering from each other's absence. Herman's wife, Iola, was an attractive woman with a certain genteel quality, and she had several children from an earlier marriage. One of them, Gladys, was about three years older than me. One Sunday, when I fell asleep in church, Gladys picked me up and held me on her lap. When I woke up, I was outraged at the indignity of having a mere girl holding me like a baby. I tore loose from Gladys' embrace and punched her. Apparently this shocked even Herman's low expectations of me.

By this time, Birdie was in her mid-twenties, Ruth was around thirty, and Herman was in his early forties. This meant that Mama was already elderly when I was a small child—more like my grandmother than my mother. My grandmother was in fact her sister. They were part of the first generation of our family born after slavery.

The first house I remember our living in was a wooden house at 1121 East Hill Street in Charlotte, North Carolina. It was near the bottom of a tall hill on an unpaved street, like most of the streets in the black neighborhoods. Daddy put a paved walkway in our yard and made a little window in the kitchen door in the back. Both were marks of distinction in which we took pride.

Like most of the houses in the area, ours had no such frills as electricity, central heating, or hot running water. There was a living room, a kitchen and two bedrooms. In the kitchen there was a wood-burning stove, with the brand name "Perfection" on it. They said it was the first word I spelled. The toilet was a little shed on the back porch. To take a bath, you heated water on the kitchen stove and poured it into a big metal portable tub. For heat in the winter, we had the stove, a fireplace in the living room, and a kerosene heater. For light at night, we had kerosene lamps.

It never occurred to me that we were living in poverty, and in fact these were some of the happiest times of my life. We had everything that people around us had, except for a few who had electricity and one lady who had a telephone. Once I tagged along with Ruth when she went to her job as a maid in the home of some white people. When I saw two faucets in their kitchen, I was baffled and said:

"They sure must drink a lot of water around here."

When Ruth showed me that there was hot water coming out of one of the faucets, I thought it was the most amazing thing.

We grew flowers in our front yard, but there was no back yard, just an alleyway. On the side of the house, however, there was a space fenced in, where we kept chickens. I can still remember the shock of seeing a chicken's head chopped off and watching the headless body running frantically around the yard, until it collapsed in the convulsions of death. But all that was forgotten when it reappeared hours later at dinner, completely transformed into beautiful and delicious pieces of Southern fried chicken.

Here and there I encountered white people—usually grocers, peddlers, or occasionally policemen. But white people were almost hypothetical to me as a small child. They were one of the things that grown-ups talked about, but they had no significant role in my daily life. That remained largely true until after we left Charlotte, when I was almost nine years old, and moved to New York. Then it came as a shock to me to be told that most of the people in the United States were white. Most of the people I had seen were black, everywhere I went. In reading the Sunday comics, I was not bothered by the fact that the characters were almost always white, but I could not understand why some of these characters had yellow hair. I had never seen anybody with yellow hair, and doubted that there were any such people.

• • •

The only books I remember seeing in our home during those early years in North Carolina were the Bible and books of the children's stories from which Birdie read to me. Daddy read the newspaper and the grown-ups sometimes talked about things that were happening in the world. There was a war going on between the Ethiopians and the Italians, and I knew that we were on the side of the Ethiopians, though I am not sure that I knew why or what color either of them were. However, I did know that there was a young black boxer coming along and that we were all very proud of him—as a man, as well as a fighter. Some said that he was going to be a champion someday. His name was Joe Louis.

One news story that got Mama emotionally involved was the kidnapping of the Lindbergh baby. For reasons unknown, she became convinced that the convicted kidnapper, Bruno Richard Hauptman, was innocent. She cried when he was executed. Some time later, after we had moved and Daddy and Mama had split up, we got a big white dog, who was given the name Bruno—even though it was a female dog. Later, Bruno had pups.

Daddy did not stop seeing me after he and Mama broke up. He came back regularly and once took me to where he was now living. He asked me if I wanted to come and live with him and I said "yes," but nothing came of it. A couple of years later, he and Mama reunited for a while, but it was not to last. I have no idea what their differences were.

Whenever I think of Daddy, I think of the joy of riding on his shoulders as a child. In fact, whenever I see a child riding on his father's shoulders, I still think of him. He was a good man, but it would be many years later before I would fully realize how good.

• • •

When Birdie and Lacy were courting, they often sat in the swing out on the front porch in the evenings. It was very romantic—just the three of us. They often let me sit in the swing beside them. I was fond of Lacy and looked up to him, but somewhere I had heard that he would take Birdie away, so I had mixed feelings, and I think they let me sit with them for reassurance.

Birdie and Lacy were high-spirited young people and even drank, despite Mama's disapproval. From them I acquired an early taste for beer.

One day, while Mama was away, I asked them for some beer. In order to discourage me, they said that I could have some only if I also drank some whiskey—which they knew I didn't like. However, I took them up on it and quickly downed some whisky and then claimed my beer. This combination was pretty potent stuff for a five-year-old, so I became woozy and they became alarmed, fearing a scene when Mama returned. They had me lie down and I slept it off before she came back home. But I don't recall having any more taste for any form of alcohol for many years and, even in adulthood, I never became a really enthusiastic drinker.

• • •

Bruno's pups were growing and I became very fond of them, as I was of Bruno. One day, however, I was puzzled as she began walking away from the pups when they wanted to nurse from her. She was of course starting to wean them, but I had no idea what she was doing. To me, it seemed like a mean way to treat the little puppies, who looked so pitiful as they ran after her, yelping and trying vainly to keep up, with their short legs scrambling.

Finally, I pounced on Bruno and held her, so that the pups could catch up and get some milk. Fortunately, the grown-ups saw what was happening and explained to me one of the lessons of life, that pups must be weaned for their own good. That experience was also one that came back to me many times later, in my adult years.

• • •

Beginning about the age of four or five, my world began to contract painfully. The first loss was when Daddy and Mama separated, for though he came back to see me, it wasn't the same as having him there all the time. Then Lacy went north to New York City, to look for work and a better life. Once he had a foothold, he sent for Birdie and they were married in 1934 in New York. They returned in 1935 but, after a few months, they went back to New York again, for good. A year later, Ruth followed in their footsteps. By the time I was six, only Mama and I were left and we lived in a smaller place. To make matters worse, I came down with mumps and whooping cough, so that I couldn't go to school until I was seven. None of the kids my age were around anymore on school days, so it was a lonely time.

There was a pretty little girl in our new neighborhood. She used to walk by our house around sunset and pat me on the back as she passed by, saying, "Hi, Tom."

I was tongue-tied and flustered, but Mama told me that just meant that the little girl liked me. Since I liked her too, I decided to show her in the same way. One day I turned and enthusiastically pounded her on the back as she passed. She collapsed like a house of cards, got up crying and ran home. She never spoke to me again and I was heartbroken. It was not the last time I was baffled by the opposite sex, nor perhaps they by me.

Another unsettling episode of this period was the only time that Ruth ever spanked me. I cannot recall what it was for, but it had something to do with her being up on a ladder. I cannot believe that I would have tried to pull the ladder out from under her, but it is hard to imagine Ruth's spanking me for anything less. At the time, however, I was highly indignant.

. . .

We moved again before I began school in September 1937. There was a house at 1212 East Brown Street, owned by some of our more prosperous relatives by marriage. It had acquired a reputation as a place where Sowells died, shortly after moving in. They were usually of advanced years when they decided to settle down there to retire, so it is not all that surprising that they died there. However, in a place and time where superstition was a force to be reckoned with, not many Sowells wanted to move into that house, which was considered haunted. But we were too poor to be able to afford superstition, so that was where we went.

It wasn't a bad house and it even had electricity. I remember listening to Bing Crosby on the radio there. The backyard was large enough for us to grow a considerable amount of vegetables, and there was a large tree that gave us apples. Someone planted a cotton plant, apparently for my benefit, so that a Southern boy should not grow up without knowing what cotton looked like. I remember Ruth's living there for a while and Daddy's living there for a while.

Bruno got into the habit of going off by herself on long excursions by a stream in the area. We would watch from the house until she disappeared around a bend. She would usually return much later. But one day she didn't return at all. To me, it was as if someone had died. It was part of a melancholy time, when I seemed to be losing a whole happier world of earlier years.

. . .

There was a knock on our door one day, but when Mama went to answer it, there was no one to be seen. Later, we learned that one of the young Sowell women had decided to brave the haunted house (after much teasing) and come to visit us. However, after she knocked on the door and saw Mama's silhouette coming down the hall—looking just like the silhouette of her dead Aunt Alma—she fled fast enough to be out of sight by the time the door was opened.

We enjoyed many a laugh recounting this incident to others, and it had a lasting effect in making me consider all superstition ridiculous.

· · ·

A white fruit-and-vegetable peddler came by the neighborhood regularly in his horse-drawn wagon. One day he had his little girl—about my age—riding beside him. She decided to get down off the wagon and come join me where I was playing in the yard alone, while her father made his rounds on the street. We hit it off wonderfully, had a great time playing together, and waved happy good-byes when the time came for her to leave. But when I turned to Mama to enthuse about my new playmate, I found her unsmiling and even grim.

"You've just taken your first step toward the gallows," she said.

From then on, whenever the girl and her father came around, there was always some excuse why I was not available to play with her.

· · ·

Another chapter of my life opened when I finally entered school in September 1937, a year older than the other kids in my class because of my year out with illness. Mama did not take me to school herself, but instead paid one of the older girls in the neighborhood to take me with her. Mama often tended to avoid confronting situations where she would feel awkward and out of place.

I went along quietly enough with the girl—until we were out of sight. Then I told her in no uncertain terms that there was no way I was going to have some girl bring me to school. She conscientiously insisted, but when I discovered that words were not enough, I resorted to throwing rocks—and arrived at school in splendid isolation.

It was an attractive little building and I was fortunate enough to have a pleasant teacher. My memories of the first grade include nothing that I learned. I already knew how to read and count before going to school. My only memories are of fights, being spanked by the teacher, having crushes on a couple of girls and the long walk to and from school.

The next year, in the second grade, I encountered one of those mindless educational routines, which happened to work to my advantage in this case. During the reading period, a child would be asked to read aloud until he or she made a mistake, after which the book would then be passed on to the next child. (There was no such thing as issuing a book to each child.) Because I had already been reading for some years, I could go straight through one of these books without making a mistake—and when I did so, I was simply handed the next book in the series and told to continue. Within a couple of weeks, I had done all the reading for the term.

One day, when the rest of the kids were acting up, the teacher said in a pique that this was a silly bunch for me to be stuck with, and arranged to have me promoted immediately into the third grade—only a few weeks after the beginning of the term. Suddenly I was with kids my own age.

One of these kids was a boy named Henry, whom I knew from the days when we lived on East Hill Street. Henry and I looked so much alike that Mama had once mistakenly called to him to come to dinner. He was also the toughest kid in the class, which came in very handy. Apparently I had rubbed one of the other boys in class the wrong way and he decided to beat me up—but he jumped on Henry by mistake. It was not a mistake that anyone wanted to repeat, so I had relatively little fighting to contend with in the third grade.

Academically, there were some difficulties at first, partly because I lacked everything that I was supposed to have learned in the second grade. For example, I had to learn division in the third grade without having stayed in the second grade long enough to learn addition and subtraction. However, I was soon at or near the top of the class. It was a nice feeling, but of course I had no inkling as to what it might mean for my future.

● ● ●

Somewhere in 1938 or 1939, Mama and I—there were now just the two of us—moved again, this time to 1123 East Hill Street. It was next door to the house we had lived in several years earlier. We were now living at the end of the street, so we had neither a back yard nor a side yard. We no longer had electricity—and now I missed it, especially when some of the other kids talked about hearing a new radio program called "The Lone Ranger."

Like most of the other houses in the neighborhood, ours did not have a paved walkway like the one Daddy had built next door. Seeing that walkway was just one of the painful reminders of happier times, when Daddy, Birdie, Lacy, and Ruth were all part of my world.

To make matters worse, the family living next door was awful and their children were brats. When one of them started a fight with me one day, I beat him up. This brought his parents over to our house, making threats against Mama and me. Fortunately, it wasn't long before we moved to New York. For all I know, that may be what prompted the move. In any event, there had been talk before about our going to New York, and now we did it. We left before the school year was out, on Mother's Day, 1939.

My last day in Charlotte was spent at Herman's house, while Mama went off somewhere to make the last-minute arrangements. Herman was now living in town, not far from us, in a bigger and nicer home. I wasn't happy with the idea of going to spend the day at Herman's, and he probably wasn't overjoyed at my being there, but it went better than either of us might have expected. Eventually, Mama returned and we headed for the train that would take us to a new life.

2

In Old New York

After a long and exhausting train ride, we finally arrived in Penn Station, New York, and suddenly I was wide awake and filled with wonder. The station was so much bigger and grander than the station we had left back in Charlotte. Above all, it was wonderful to see Birdie, Lacy, and Ruth again. The gleaming station and then the subway—clean and sleek in those days—were a breath-taking sight for an eight-year-old kid from the South.

My first glimpse of New York above ground was a fire escape hanging from a building next to the 146th Street exit of the 145th Street subway station on St. Nicholas Avenue in Harlem. We lived just across the street, in a five-story building that seemed so tall—and so imposing. Harlem still retained some of the appearance of the middle-class neighborhood it had once been.

That first day, Lacy also took me for a walk over to Riverside Drive, a very lovely place in those days, to see the Hudson River. It was the first time I had ever seen a river or a ship. There were many things to see and do for the first time in New York, and Birdie, Lacy, and Ruth took turns showing me where things were in the neighborhood, or took me sightseeing on the double-decker buses which regularly drove up and down St. Nicholas Avenue.

We lived on the top floor of our building at 720 St. Nicholas Avenue. The front room, looking out on the street, doubled as a living room and as Birdie and Lacy's bedroom. The furniture was new and looked to me so impressive and modern. I was amazed to hear sound coming from one of the end tables. It was a radio as well. We had electricity again—and a gas stove, hot running water, and a built-in bathtub, all for the first time. The back room was for Mama and me. The middle room was supposed to be for Ruth, but she worked as a live-in maid, as she was to do for many years, so we did not see as much of her.

Mama and I spent a lot of time comparing things in New York to what they were like in Charlotte, always to the disadvantage of Charlotte. To have mentioned any touch of homesickness would have been like treason. But, when all was said and done, I was still a new kid in a strange town, where I knew no other kids—and where the other kids were still in school while I hung around the house all day. It would be a long summer before I would join them in school. Moreover, I was

Here I was about nine years old, shortly after arriving in New York.

not allowed to hang out in the streets, where I might fall in with the wrong crowd or get into the many new troubles and dangers of a big city. Mama was very strict and Lacy warned me not to associate with "roughnecks."

Even crossing streets was something they did not want me to do by myself at first, since I was not used to the kind of traffic in New York, and had not dealt with traffic lights before. Fortunately, the block on our side of the street was a long one, stretching from 145th Street all the way up to 150th Street, so I could take quite a walk without crossing a street. There was a grocery store and a news stand on our side of the street, so I could also be sent on errands, which I liked.

With all this, however, time still hung heavy. One day, as I was looking out the front window at other kids playing across the street, I began to cry and Mama relented to the extent of letting me go downstairs to bounce a ball against our building—but not across the street, where the other children were. I was also limited to how long I could stay outside, usually no more than an hour, and Mama hung out the top floor window, keeping an eye on me.

Along with a concern for my physical safety, there was another, longer-range concern in the family that I heard, especially from Lacy, Birdie, and Ruth. They had never had the opportunities that I would now have in New York, including an opportunity for a good education, and they wanted me to make the most of those opportunities. All this was a little vague to me at first, but it was a theme I would hear again and again over the years. Even before I arrived in New York, Birdie and Lacy had picked out a boy they wanted me to meet—a slightly older, more genteel, and more knowledgeable boy named Eddie Mapp. They obviously wanted me to become more like him and to choose such company, rather than the "roughnecks" Lacy warned me against.

These ambitions of theirs were only partly fulfilled. I met Eddie Mapp and we saw each other from time to time, but we didn't have enough in common to become close buddies. He played classical music on the piano, for example, which put him in another world, as far as I was concerned. However, he also introduced me to Chinese checkers and to comic books, and showed me a store where you could trade comic books after you read them. Most important of all, he took me one day to a kind of place where I had never been before and knew nothing about—a public library. Impressed but puzzled as to why we were in a building with so many books, when I had no money to buy books, I found it all difficult to understand at first, as Eddie patiently explained to me how a public library worked. Unknown to me at the time, it was a turning point in my life, for I then developed the habit of reading books.

No one in the family read books except Birdie, who read detective stories. Lacy, however, was an avid follower of current events in the newspapers, and he would listen to a couple of hours of news broadcasts every night, at a time when news broadcasts were only fifteen minutes long. After a while, I became familiar with the names of all sorts of newscasters—Elmer Davis, Gabriel Heatter, Stan Lomax (sports), and eventually the greatest of them all, Edward R. Murrow. Every Sunday, Lacy would send me down to the news stand to buy two newspapers, which was considered something of an extravagance. However, this not only gave me something to do, it provided me with two sets of comics to read.

• • •

I was astonished one day when a grocer asked me if I were from the South. "How could he have known?" I wondered. It never occurred to me that I had an accent. However, with the passage of time, there was not only a natural and gradual adoption of the ways of New York; there was a concerted effort on all sides to get me to become a New Yorker. Mama became Mom, for example.

Lacy, especially, liked to take me around to places like Central Park or down to Washington Square on the double-decker bus, explaining things as we went along. It took me a long time to get used to seeing so many white people in New York. Some of them even had yellow hair. One day, Lacy rented a bicycle and put me on the handlebars as he came down the long hill on 145th Street. It was a wild ride that we both laughed about many times in later years.

Lacy was a cook for a wealthy family called the Whitneys. He must have talked about me on the job because Mrs. Whitney asked him to bring me to work with him someday, so that she could meet me. What I most remember about the visit was seeing Lacy make butter balls in the kitchen. I had never seen butter balls before—and was far more impressed by that than by a piece of furniture in the living room that seemed to have a tiny movie in it. It was one of the earliest television sets. Mrs. Whitney and I sat in the living room talking about whatever nine-year-old boys and middle-aged ladies talk about.

Birdie, Lacy, and Ruth all worked in white people's homes and all at one time or other discussed me with their employers. A family that Ruth worked for, for a number of years, had a boy and a girl who were slightly older than me. All sorts of toys, books, and games that they outgrew found their way to me, giving me a sort of second-hand middle-class lifestyle. When I was just a baby, I received a baby carriage that way from one of Birdie's employers. What also found its way to me through Birdie, Lacy, and Ruth were tidbits of middle-class culture in such things as table manners and vocabulary.

As my world began to expand in New York, I slowly but steadily began to move beyond Mom's world, which seldom stretched beyond a radius of about five blocks, and never reached into the realms of books, ideas, or current events. She became, and remained over the years, ambivalent about my progress—proud of my advancement and yet resentful of being left behind, inconsistent in word and deed, tenaciously determined to assert her authority, however arbitrarily, and yet with a premonition that our relationship—never the strongest—was completely unravelling. Sometimes she recalled a song that said, "Oh, where is my wandering boy, tonight," and wondered out loud whether someday she would be singing that song. Occasionally it brought tears to her eyes.

* * *

In September 1939, I was enrolled in Public School 5 in Harlem. Again, it was not Mom who took me. This time it was Birdie, who was working part-time. There was a question as to what grade I would be put in. The school back in Charlotte had promoted me to the fourth grade, even though I didn't stay to finish the term, but there was no reason to assume that the promotion would stick in New

York, where black children from the South were routinely put back a grade.

As the bureaucratic process of registration dragged on, the time for Birdie to go to work was fast approaching. Her main concern was whether I could find my way back home and, when I assured her that I could, she left me there to finish enrolling by myself. When a school official told me that I would be put back to the third grade, I asked to see the principal.

After a long wait, I was brought into the principal's office. He was a sympathetic man and was favorably impressed that I had the spunk to bring this matter to him. When I told him that I thought I could do fourth grade work, he gave me a few arithmetic problems to solve and then, after I finished them and we had some further discussion, the principal was willing to let me try it. I was assigned to class 4A3, the A meaning the first term in the fourth grade and the 3 designating the third-best class at that level.

Birdie was astonished that night to learn that I had not been put back. As it turned out, I probably should have been. From being at the top of my class back in Charlotte, I suddenly found myself at the very bottom and hopelessly confused as to what was going on. It was a very painful experience. Many unhappy afternoons were spent agonizing over my homework, and sometimes crying.

Social adjustments were no easier. Although we were all black kids in Harlem, I was from the South and talked "funny." Besides, everybody "knew" that Southern kids were "dumb"—and reminded me at every opportunity. In addition, fighting was more frequent, more fierce, and more important than it was back in Charlotte—and was more likely to involve gangs, rather than just individuals. At one point, getting home for lunch safely became such an ordeal that a friend would lend me his jacket as a disguise, so that I could get away before anyone could spot me.

Somehow, both the social and the academic adjustments were slowly made. At the end of the term, I received a commendation card from the principal as the "most improved student" in the class, though at that point I stood no higher than midway in the class. I was promoted to 4B4—the *fourth* best class in the second half of the fourth grade.

. . .

Somewhere during 1940 our family split up again, at least in the sense of no longer sharing the same apartment. I don't know exactly why, though it had something to do with a quarrel that developed while Lacy's relatives were visiting. Birdie and Lacy remained together in a new and smaller place but Mom, Ruth and I now had lasting differences in our living arrangements. For the next couple of years, Mom and I were rooming in other people's apartments—not an uncommon way of living in Harlem in those days, but definitely not like having your own place. Ruth, as a sleep-in maid, was less affected.

Although I no longer had daily contact with Lacy, I had already picked up enough of his pattern of keeping up with current events to continue doing so on my own. This was the year when the Nazis' bombing of London was at its worst—and when Edward R. Murrow's broadcasts from the scene made vivid not only what was happening, but also its fateful significance for the rest of the world. I talked about such things with Lacy when I saw him and Birdie on weekends.

Although I was beginning to take an interest in serious things outside of school, in the school itself I was beginning to retrogress somewhat. My social adjustment was a little too complete, in that I was now hanging out with a mischievous bunch. We didn't do anything terrible—certainly not by today's standards—but we were full of pranks and were disruptive in class. Once we went around the neighborhood, tearing down Wendell Wilkie's 1940 election posters. This was probably my idea, as the only one in the gang interested in politics.

Academically, I cannot remember learning anything in 4B4. The teacher was kept busy trying to maintain order, which often meant keeping after me and my classmates to be quiet, sit down, come back into the room, etc. This class, incidentally, was in a newly built school—P.S. 194, a few blocks from P.S. 5. If anyone thought that an attractive, modern building was going to have a favorable effect on student behavior, he was sadly mistaken.

Normally, students from 4B4 would be promoted to 5A4, but I was promoted to 5A3, perhaps to break up our little band of trouble-makers. There were a couple of really tough kids in 5A3 who made life miserable for the rest of us. However, we were all sufficiently mischievous to make the classroom a bedlam anytime the teacher left the room. Although teachers in the New York school system were not supposed to use corporal punishment, some of them did anyway, and the teacher in 5A3 was one of them. He was white, as were virtually all the other teachers in the school at that time.

One day, he returned to class to find that some mischief had been committed while he was away. Convinced that I had done it, he grabbed a long ruler and took after me, with anger written all over his face. I dodged and skipped across desk tops, with him in hot pursuit, until I tripped and fell on my back across a couple of seats. As I lay there, he gave me a whack across my arm that later raised a large welt from my elbow to my wrist. He came after me again, and this time I kicked him as hard as I could in the lower belly—only because my aim was bad.

He doubled over in pain and threatened to take me to the principal, which I dared him to do. By this time, I knew that teachers were not supposed to do anything they felt like. It was a standoff, and afterwards we were both very wary with each other. Yet, strangely enough, this man must have seen some sign of promise in me, for the next term I was promoted to 5B1—the first time I was put in with the best students.

• • •

The teacher in 5B1 was a West Indian black woman—the only black teacher I had during all the years I spent going through the New York City public school system. Aside from being black, she was a remarkable person in a number of other ways. Although a little austere and distant, she was plainly dedicated to getting the most out of the black kids she taught, and was openly critical of the low expectations and low standards of the white teachers. She had the cultivated bearing of a lady, but she could also be a very aggressive, no-nonsense lady when the occasion demanded it.

When we were preparing to put on the class play, she insisted to everyone that there were footlights in the stage of the school auditorium, even though no one had ever seen any, and a number of people—including the principal, I believe—tried to tell her that there were no lights there. But she was adamant and eventually someone was dispatched to get the tools to open up whatever it was that she saw on the stage. When the little doors in the stage floor were opened up, there were the footlights.

She also managed somehow to get the mothers of the children in her class to sew costumes, so that they could put on a first-rate play. How she got those mothers, with either large families of their own or a job in some white family's kitchen, to sew costumes at home in the evenings I will never know, but she did it. She took pride in the fact that every year her class play was always the best by far, and sometimes the only play that was more than a perfunctory gesture toward fulfilling a requirement. Yet she was not really satisfied. Once she remarked that, in some white schools, they did Shakespeare.

This was my first experience with a class that was serious about its studies. Fighting was much less frequent and discipline in general was less of a problem. I was in fact myself one of the few disruptive elements in the class, having only partly shed the habits I had formed in my three previous classes in Harlem.

One episode may have been especially important in putting me in bad with the teacher. She was out of the room one day when her son, who was in the class a year ahead of this one, came by to see her. Having nothing better to do while waiting, he went around the room popping kids behind their ears with his fingers as they sat at their desks. As he neared me, I told him that he had better not do it, and when he did it anyway, I was on my feet throwing punches. As we were going at it, his mother walked in. She was instantly convinced that this guttersnipe had attacked her child.

That term my subject grades were fair—I did not apply myself steadily enough to do well—but my conduct grades were all bad. At the end of the term, I expected a promotion but instead found myself assigned to "5B-6A op." This was a so-called "opportunity" class. Euphemisms were fashionable even then, but everyone knew what it meant—that you were a dumb kid who didn't belong in a regular class.

● ● ●

In the summer of 1941, some other roomers—a couple named Mr. and Mrs. Anderson—were visited by Mr. Anderson's niece Shirley, who was about my age. Shirley was a very pretty girl, but was also very tomboyish—the latter being as important as the former, for getting our friendship under way. Shirley and I put on boxing gloves and she decked me. It was virtually love at first sight.

I saw Shirley only sporadically over the years, for she lived in New Jersey, and of course visited only infrequently. When she did visit, however, we talked incessantly, though I cannot recall a thing we talked about. One of our real treats was going, with adults along, on bus rides down to Washington Square, which was a lovely place in those days. We never thought of each other as boy friend and girl friend. In fact, all my get-togethers with Shirley over the years, even in our later teens, could have been filmed and the movies shown in Sunday school.

I like to believe that I behaved like a gentleman because of my values, but cynics might say that it was because I remembered her punch.

． ． ．

The cloud of uncertainty which hung over me all summer as to what kind of class "5B-6A op" might turn out to be was quickly dissipated in September. We had moved across a school boundary line in the meantime, so that I was no longer attending P.S. 194 but was transferred back to P.S. 5—which had no such class. At P.S. 5, I was assigned to 6A2. Now that I was away from the old gang at P.S. 194, I was maturing enough to want to do good work. Unfortunately, I was also out from under the protection of a gang, and was bullied more than I had been for some time.

Academically, however, I began to do well. The teacher encouraged me a great deal and privately told me he would have asked to have me transferred to 6A1, except that his class was scheduled for many museum trips and other cultural excursions that he wanted me to be exposed to. It was the first time in a long while that any teacher had expressed confidence in my ability. The museum trips were not only an experience in themselves, they gave me a look around the city—little of which I knew outside of a few square blocks near where I lived and went to school.

During this school term, we were given a number of tests, including an IQ test, and I scored well on all of them. My class work was also good enough for me to be promoted to 6B1. Whether I knew it or not at the time, I had turned another corner.

● ● ●

The big news of 1941 in our family was that Birdie was pregnant. It was like a bolt out of the blue to me.

"Bert?" I said. "You mean Bert?" (Within the family, only Lacy called her Birdie regularly).

I knew that married people had babies, but Birdie and Lacy had already been married seven years without doing so, or even talking about doing so. Once I was over the initial surprise, however, I was not nearly as excited about it as everyone else seemed to be.

Lacy expressed concern that this all be explained to me in the proper way and Mom was concerned to have me understand that I could no longer expect to be Birdie's favorite, once she had her own baby. However, I was already at an age when the attentions of adults were no longer always welcome, much less a major preoccupation.

As the big day approached, Birdie and Mom were hard at work one evening, trying out different arrangements for a little place for the baby to sleep. Unfortunately, they were doing this just as I was trying to get to sleep myself, so finally I said: "Oh, just throw him down in there!" When Birdie started to cry, I felt terrible and said so, and she forgave me.

After Birdie went into the hospital, the first word to reach us was that she had a "big" baby—eight pounds and ten ounces. I, of course, had no idea how big that was. Moreover, I had never seen a newborn baby, so my imagination conjured up the kinds of babies I had seen— crawling around, playing with blocks, and the like. When we went to get Birdie and the baby from the hospital, it came as a great shock to me to see such a tiny, still little fellow. I felt so *sorry* for him and thought it was just whistling in the dark to call him "big." My heart went out to him immediately and, by the time I finally realized that this was how newborn babies were, I had already formed an attachment to him which I never lost.

The little boy was named for his father, whose first name was James. I am not sure whether I knew that Lacy's first name was James before this. In any case, the little boy's nickname became Jimmy. He was a happy, feisty little fellow. When he was lying on his back, he would draw up his legs and then, when I tossed a little blue pillow on them, he would kick it back to me and laugh. I knew that he and I would have a great time playing together as he grew up—and we did, often to the annoyance of the neighbors.

• • •

In February 1942, I entered 6B1. Initially, both the teacher and the students openly regarded me as someone who was on some sort of informal probation. I was an outsider. The other students in 6B1 had typically been together in 6A1 before and in other "one" classes earlier, whereas I had a checkered past in classes as low as "four." The teacher was willing to be convinced, but she was also going to have to be convinced.

It turned out to be an academically very successful term. I was consistently at the head of the class, often nosing out another boy who had previously been the undisputed top student in the class. Eventually, his frustration got to be too much, and he beat me up after school. But in general, as in 5B1 the year before, conduct problems and fighting were nowhere near the levels they were in the other classes. This year, my own conduct was also better.

As junior high school loomed on the horizon, I was concerned about two problems—one practical and the other symbolic. The symbolic problem was that Eddie Mapp was always being held up to me as a model, which I was falling short of matching. He was already in junior high school and was in a special "R" class for "Rapid Advancement" students. I asked my 6B1 teacher if she would promote me into an "R" class. She agreed to do so, while pointing out that the school to which I was being assigned—Junior High School 139—had no such class. For symbolic purposes, that didn't matter. Later, whenever Ruth asked me, "Why aren't you more like Eddie Mapp?" I could reply: "Why isn't Eddie Mapp more like me?"

The much more serious practical problem was that J.H.S. 139 was located in a rougher part of Harlem and had a reputation, even then, as a place where disruption and fighting made teaching and learning very difficult. Fortunately, I had learned through Eddie that you did not necessarily have to go to the school where you were first assigned. We had moved again, and were now close enough to the boundary of a better junior high school that we could make a case for a transfer. I prevailed upon Mom to go to the school, which she hated to do, and sign for me to get a transfer. We waited for hours for the bureaucratic processes to move but, in the end, I had my transfer. Without it, the last door might have slammed shut on me.

The rest of the family saw a very different symbolism in my going on to junior high school. They informed me, very gravely, that none of them had ever reached the seventh grade.

"You are going on further than any of us," I was told.

* * *

As I neared the end of my last term at P.S. 5, I was selected (as a second choice) as the student from my school to be offered two weeks free at a summer camp, courtesy of some anonymous white donor. When I went downtown to talk with the people in charge of the program, I was surprised to find that all the other kids were white. When I asked if there were going to be any other black kids going to this camp, they assured me that there would be—but they were lying. This was in fact an experiment to put the first black kid into that camp. It was also my first encounter with the notion that people who think they are doing something noble don't have to tell the truth.

The camp itself was a mixed experience. The people—children and staff—ranged from over-solicitous to obnoxious. Many seemed to feel that they had to have some definite "policy" toward me. However, I also made some friends. While I had dealt with white people before, it was usually in some structured role—teachers or grocers, for example—so this was my first large-scale encounter with them in more or less unstructured situations. I quickly learned that they varied all over the lot, a useful thing to learn in a setting where not much was at stake, especially since the junior high school to which I was transferring was predominantly white.

Apparently some of those at camp were forced to re-think some of their ideas about Negroes. One episode stuck out particularly in my mind. During a midday rest period, I was sitting alone under a tree when I noticed one of the smaller kids making his way, slowly and furtively, around the others toward where I was sitting. He obviously had something on his mind, and had taken this opportunity to get it cleared up. He began in a quiet whisper:

"Tommy . . . ?"

"Yeah."

" . . . can you tell me something?"

"What?"

"How come . . . you don't act like the colored people I see in the movies?"

That stumped me for a moment, and then I said:

"Well, they get paid to act that way—and I don't."

That seemed to satisfy him and, with a sigh of relief, he went back to where he had been.

When my two weeks at camp were up, he was one of those who came around to say goodbye. And he cried.

● ● ●

In September 1942, I entered Junior High School 43, located on 129th Street and Amsterdam Avenue, which was not yet part of Harlem at that time. J.H.S. 43 was in a lower middle-class white neighborhood and the school contained some forty different ethnic groups—including Jews, Asians, Puerto Ricans, and a whole array of refugees from various parts of Europe. It was proud of its diversity and perhaps just a little too self-congratulatory about how nothing mattered at "43" except what sort of person you were.

The quiet and orderliness of the classrooms, the casual pleasantness of student-teacher relations, and the great efforts to make the work interesting were very welcome contrasts to what I had too often encountered in the Harlem schools. I made a couple of friends quickly and my outlook was hopeful.

The incessant preoccupation with fighting—or running—was now behind me. There was fighting now and then, but fighting was not a way of life. In this age of Joe Louis, I could not take most white kids my size seriously as physical threats. When one of them landed a good punch on me during a fight, I tended to disregard it as a fluke. This confidence was, of course, an asset in itself. Had I known how close I was to being clobbered sometimes, I undoubtedly would have lost more fights. As it was, I do not recall ever losing a fight to a white kid my own size at J.H.S. 43.

Because the Harlem junior high school to which I had originally been assigned did not have an "R" (Rapid Advancement) class, my promotion to 7AR had been changed to 7A1. Even though I was now in a school which did have an "R" class, I entered it with the changed assignment to 7A1, and was content to remain there. My whole point had been to put a stop to invidious comparisons with Eddie Mapp. However, a couple of weeks after the term began, someone in the school office dug out the names of all entering students with IQs of 120 and up who were not already assigned to the "R" class. Mine was among them, so I was one of four students in 7A1 who were offered an opportunity to transfer to 7AR. The other three immediately accepted, but I was happy where I was, and saw no need to change. After attempts to persuade me failed, I was simply re-assigned to 7AR.

The "R" class was more challenging, but my self-confidence was at its height. If there were any latent tendencies among the white kids toward taking a patronizing attitude toward me or the other three black kids (in a class of about thirty), they were squelched early on, though by accident. One day, when our math teacher was getting ready to hand back to us an exam we had taken, he said:

"This didn't seem to be such a difficult exam for a class like this, and yet only one student made a hundred percent on it. His name was . . ."

Here he began to fumble through the stack of exams to find the right one.

"His name was . . ." he repeated.

"Thomas Sowell?" I ventured helpfully.

"Yes! That's the name," he said.

I had just been kidding around, but to my classmates it looked as if I had called my shot.

. . .

Within a short time, I was part of a little group that had gotten together—first two boys, Rosen and Valdez, and then two girls, Lilly
and Hannah. Rosen and I were intellectually very similar, not only in
over-all academic ability, but also in our particular strengths and
weaknesses. We sat together in a number of classes through the seventh grade and often received identical scores in the 90s, making the
same mistakes, as well as solving the problems in the same manner.
This pattern was noticed by more than one teacher. Where there was
any indication of a developing suspicion on their part, it was apparent
that they thought I was copying from him. One teacher even separated us, and was obviously surprised when the same patterns continued on our exams after we were seated some distance from each
other.

My work was usually very good in the major subjects and in such
minor subjects as interested me, but I was never preoccupied with
over-all grade averages and could be quite casual about low grades in
courses I didn't care about. One of these throwaway courses, as far as
I was concerned, was a shop course in printing. Here too, Rosen and I
worked together, sharing a big box of type that was almost never in order. In fact, our printing box was the laughing stock of the class. You
could reach into almost any compartment and find letters that belonged in some other compartment.

The printing teacher was one of those dedicated craftsmen who
took his course very seriously. Our examinations consisted of actually
printing some material we had been given. With the box that I shared
with Rosen being in the mess that it was in, he and I could achieve
neither speed nor accuracy. One day, as the teacher was handing back
the class' examinations, he read off each student's name and numerical score, starting with the highest scores. Most of these scores were in
the 90s or 80s, until he reached the last two, when he flushed with indignation as he said:

"Rosen——47 percent! Sowell——47 percent!"

He glared at us and demanded: "What do you have to say for your-
selves?"

"Well," I said, "at least in printing, nobody can claim that we copied off each other."

Rosen burst out laughing.

"For that smart remark," the printing teacher said, "You can stay after school today, Sowell. And for thinking it was funny, Rosen, you can stay with him!"

• • •

Although this school and class were much less concerned with fighting and much more concerned with education, the kids were by no means little tin angels. Mischief of one sort or another was almost always afoot, and I was involved in at least my share.

In one class, where boys and girls sat on different sides of the room, I sat in front of a boy named Francis Anaya. When he passed his exams forward to be collected, I would change the "i" in his name to "e," so that his name read "Frances Anaya," and his exam would be put among those distributed on the girls' side of the room. This always got a rise out of him, but he never discovered who had changed his name—otherwise, I might not be alive today.

One of the favorite lunchtime pranks which Valdez and I engaged in was staging a commando-style raid on Scarlotti, one of the larger boys in our class. Since Scarlotti could easily clobber either or both of us, our operation had to be executed just right. We had to see Scarlotti without his seeing us, then come up behind him, running silently but swiftly to build up momentum. I would then leap up onto his shoulders, while Valdez threw a flying block into his back. After Scarlotti fell forward heavily to the ground, we leaped to our feet immediately upon impact and ran for our lives.

If Scarlotti had caught us at that moment, he would have broken our necks (that was what made it exciting), but once we made our getaway—and sometimes we *just* made it—we were safe. Later, Scarlotti would probably give us a couple of angry words and maybe a punch on the shoulder, but he was too good-natured, after he had cooled down, to give us the kind of beating we deserved. Even so, we would say something like:

"Aw, Fred, I thought you were a sport."

. . .

The "R" class covered four terms' work in three terms. There was 7AR, 7BR, and then 8BR, as the whole class skipped the 8A term. "R" classes were expected to be not only intellectual, but also social, pace-setters. Traditionally, their students held most of the offices in student government, their classes brought to the weekly assembly the most daily conduct sheets free of any comments on misconduct, and "R" class students wrote most of the material for the school yearbook. The "R" class a year ahead of us carried on these traditions in deadly earnest, but our class took such things very lightly, and some—like me—openly scoffed at it all. Our teachers were flustered to find us frequently beaten out in the non-academic areas by the "one" class, and occasionally even by the "two" class, and they were more than a little disturbed by our lack of concern at being surpassed by these other classes.

Eventually, the teachers' concern about our attitudes affected their judgments of our intellectual ability. We began to hear increasingly that the "R" class was going "downhill"—perhaps a safe way to air publicly their fear that the school and the neighborhood were headed downhill, as the ghetto continued to expand in this direction. But, in point of fact, our class outdid the preceding "R" class intellectually by almost any index available.

The year the class ahead of us graduated, ten students took the entrance examination for elite Stuyvesant High School and only one passed. The only student from J.H.S. 43 to pass the even more difficult entrance examination for Brooklyn Tech that year was a member of *our* class who was leaving at the end of the eighth grade. The following year, everyone from our class passed every high school entrance exam we took, everywhere in the city—Stuyvesant, Bronx Science, Brooklyn Tech, Music and Art, etc. The teachers' gross misjudgments of our ability, compared to the ability of previous "R" classes, was a powerful example of what unspoken feelings can do.

. . .

By 8BR, our little gang had broken up and I became, and remained, pretty much a lone wolf throughout the remainder of my educational experience. The relatively color-blind atmosphere also began to change subtly, at least for some students, as we moved into adolescence and interest in the opposite sex. There were a few signs of resentment at my casual friendship with Hannah, a blond girl who had been in our little gang—especially when she complained to me about another boy in the class who had been bothering her. I told him that it would save me the trouble of punching him in the nose if he would leave her alone. I had done the same thing on another occasion, when the same kid was bullying a German refugee boy. But deeper meanings were read into the episode involving the girl.

● ● ●

There was little to indicate, at the beginning of 8BR, that it would be a disaster for me, a crisis for the school, and the end of the "R" classes. When the school year began in September 1943, things looked promising, for we had a very good home-room teacher. Miss Karoff was an attractive and pleasant young women who was both firm and adroit in handling the students. This was in fact demonstrated on the first day of class.

I arrived a few minutes late and wanted to hurry to my seat before the teacher came in. However, Miss Karoff was already there and was taking attendance, but she had dyed her hair over the summer, so that from the rear she looked just like our classmate Hannah, who also took attendance sometimes. Thinking that she was Hannah, I gently put my hands on her waist and tried to move her aside, so that I could get by to my seat. As I touched her waist, Miss Karoff turned slowly around and looked straight at me with a completely bland expression.

"Oh!" I gasped. "Miss Karoff! . . . uh . . . good morning."

"Good morning."

" . . . uh, your hair looks very nice."

"Thank you."

Miss Karoff was always imperturbable. Once, when she discovered a prank in the classroom, she said simply:

"Oh, if I ever find out who did this, Sowell . . ."

Although I usually behaved myself in Miss Karoff's class, my miscellaneous misdemeanors in other classes often led to her assuming responsibility, as my home-room teacher, for keeping me after school. One day, we found ourselves in a familiar situation, with me staying on after school as punishment and Miss Karoff sitting at her desk, working over some papers.

"Well, here we are again, Sowell," she said sarcastically, "just the two of us."

"Good grief, Miss Karoff," I said, "if we keep on staying in after school together like this all the time, people will begin to talk!"

Without even looking up from her papers, she said:

"We will just have to learn to live with the scandal."

• • •

At the opposite pole from Miss Karoff was a new math teacher, Mr. Leonard. He began by stapling cards on the walls all around the classroom. There were rules of conduct on each card. In no time at all, it became clear that he was a very petty and insecure man.

One day Rosen finished his math exam early as usual, and pulled out a paperback novel to read during the rest of the hour. Mr. Leonard grew red with anger and stormed down the aisle to where Rosen was sitting. He pointed agitatedly at one of the rules which Rosen was violating and angrily snatched the book from him. Since I had finished my exam early too, and had time on my hands, I said:

"You have no right to confiscate his property."

Mr. Leonard was startled at this and snapped:

"Do you know that *you* are violating one of the rules too?" He began looking around on the wall, trying to find the rule I had violated.

"I take your word for it," I said. "There are so many of them."

By this time, the rest of the class started joining in, and things rapidly began getting out of hand. Mr. Leonard announced that the whole class would be kept in that afternoon. For reasons which are not clear, he kept us in himself, though in Miss Karoff's room.

There was a Board of Education rule on how late a class could be kept in, and when that time arrived, I informed Mr. Leonard of the rule as I stood up and began packing my books. But he refused to let any of us go until he got ready, and backed his considerable bulk against the door to block anyone's leaving. One of the bigger boys, Seward, walked over to Mr. Leonard, pointedly told him that he had a job to go to, in order to earn some money to help his family—and that he had *better* get out of his way. Mr. Leonard relented just for Seward, probably the wisest decision he made that day. Half an hour later, the rest of us were still there, though with protests, arguments and counter-arguments, and finally a scuffle, in which Mr. Leonard shoved me and I hit him across the face.

While others tried to reason with the teacher, and some of the girls began to cry, I took a chair to the back of the room and placed it against the clothes closet.

"What are you doing?" he demanded.

In a voice dripping with sweet reasonableness, I explained to him in detail what I was doing. There was a ledge above the clothes closet, which I could reach by standing on the chair. From the ledge, I could open a large transom that opened out into the hall. Once out in the hall, I would go home. The only way he could stop me, I pointed out, was by leaving his post at the door—which would mean that the rest of the class would go streaming out into the hall.

He was livid. As I proceeded to carry out the plan I had just outlined to him, he said:

"I'm going to send a letter to your home tonight!"

"That's 504 West 145th Street," I said, "New York *thirty-one*, New York." Postal zone numbers were new then and I wanted to be sure he used them.

"I'll bring charges against you!" he shouted.

"I doubt it," I said, "—not after what you've done."

He of course did not dare bring charges, in view of his own violations of rules. But he did deduct enough points from my math grade, for bad conduct, so that I had a failing grade by "R" class standards, though still passing by general school standards. This meant that I had to be transferred out of the class for failure in a major subject. Seward was also transferred out.

The whole episode, as told by Mr. Leonard, alarmed the other teachers and confirmed their suspicion that this class and the school were going downhill. "R" classes were discontinued. When 8BR was promoted, it became 9A1. When 8B1 was promoted, it became 9A2, the "two" class became a "three," and so on down the line. I was as-signed to 9A2.

. . .

Since the ninth grade was the last year of junior high school, our schedule now included a class in guidance counseling, conducted by the civics teacher, Mrs. Sennett. Because we would not all be going on automatically to a neighborhood high school, guidance counseling was designed to help us choose among the various options open, in-cluding an array of selective public high schools, scattered around the city, for which entrance exams were necessary.

Mrs. Sennett began the first day of the guidance class by explain-ing at length that *everybody* could not go on to Bronx Science, Stuyvesant, Brooklyn Tech, and the like, that we should plan our fu-tures realistically, in view of our abilities and performances. To help us with that, she had gotten all our folders from the record files in the school office and had them on her desk. She mentioned also that J.H.S. 43 itself was going to screen us before allowing us to go take the tests for selective high schools, because it did not want a repetition of last year's embarrassingly low percentage of acceptances, which was a reflection on the school.

After pouring cold water on our plans for some time, Mrs. Sennett announced that she was now going to go around the class in order, asking each student in turn where he or she wanted to apply to high school. I was sitting in the first seat in the first row, slumped down a little and busy sketching away on a drawing pad, as I frequently did when bored. When Mrs. Sennett started with me and asked where I intended to apply to high school, I looked up briefly and said "Stuyvesant High School," then went back to my sketching.

Mrs. Sennett threw up her hands in exasperation and said:

"Have you been listening to anything I said? What makes you think that *you* can go to Stuyvesant High School?"

"I have a friend who goes there," I said, "and he has never seemed to be a better student than I am." I was of course thinking of Eddie Mapp.

"Oh, really?" Mrs. Sennett said sarcastically. "Let me just look at your I.Q." She began digging into the folders with great energy, as if eager to discredit me. When she got to my I.Q. records, her sneering expression turned to cold resentment. She went on to the next student.

Mrs. Sennett and I were to have many clashes, both in counseling and in civics. I was selected—over her protest—to take the examinations for Stuyvesant High School and Brooklyn Tech. Eight of us were allowed to take the examination for Stuyvesant, but only three of us were allowed to take the Brooklyn Tech exam—the other two being my old classmates Rosen and Valdez. We had a very enjoyable reunion. The exam itself consisted of only about five or six questions, for which we had something like two or three hours. Each question was clever, if not diabolical. However, all three of us were among the first to finish and we left well ahead of time.

On our way back to Manhattan, we compared answers—which were all the same on all the questions. The report of the results came to Mrs. Sennett, as our guidance counselor. She informed Rosen and Valdez that they had made 100 percent on the Brooklyn Tech exam and told me that I had passed. A couple of weeks later, one of the other teachers leaked to me that I had also made a perfect score.

● ● ●

Among the good teachers at J.H.S. 43 was our English teacher, Mrs. Collins. One of her pet projects was to get us used to speaking in public. We each had to get up in front of the class to present brief talks on whatever topic we chose.

On the day when my talk was due, I couldn't think of anything to talk about. I asked around among my classmates for suggestions, but most were too busy working on their own speeches, and even those who offered suggestions didn't come up with anything worthwhile.

When the dreaded moment for my presentation came, I went up to the front of the room and began:

"My topic for today is . . ." with no idea how that sentence would end. I paused, took a deep breath and turned away toward the side wall. There on the wall was a map of the world, and the first words on it that caught my eye were: "Mercator Projection."

" . . . is the Mercator Projection," I said. "There happens to be one over here on the wall," I added, pointing.

My classmates listened tensely, because everyone knew my predicament and they had no more idea what I was going to say next than I did. Fortunately, I had an interest in maps, so I was able to explain how a Mercator Projection differed from other kinds of maps and what the various types of maps were used for.

When my time was up and I was about to head back to my seat, Mrs. Collins told me to stay where I was. She came over, put her hand on my shoulder and said to the class:

"Now, that was a model of how a speech should be made."

They were as dumbfounded as I was.

"First of all," she said, "notice that he had studied his subject so thoroughly that he didn't even need notes."

My classmates were struggling to keep from cracking up.

"Notice, too," she continued, "how he paused after each statement to let it sink in, instead of rushing along helter-skelter."

Some of the kids took deep breaths.

"That was a very effective technique," Mrs. Collins said, "for I could see how he had the complete attention of the audience."

Somehow, none of us burst out laughing, so all was well that ended well.

• • •

The real bane of my existence in the ninth grade was Mrs. Bloom, our home-room teacher in 9A2 and our science teacher for the whole year. Mrs. Bloom was a stocky, middle-aged, and emotional woman, ranging from florid anger to tear-stained sentimentality. She was in one sense a dedicated teacher. She was determined that the students would get from the study of science not just certain facts, but also a sense of scientific reasoning. In this, she made a real contribution to my intellectual development. Her general view of people, however, was incredibly simplistic: You were either the "right" kind of person or the "wrong" kind of person with her. Early on, she made up her mind about me.

In the class a year ahead of me, the outstanding student was a black kid named Laurence. He was her special protege and they were devoted to each other. He was a smart enough kid, but I never detected the brilliance by which others claimed to be dazzled, and I resented the implied double standard in his receiving so much more attention than a white kid of the same ability would have received. Moreover, I considered him arrogant and preoccupied with tinsel glory. Mrs. Bloom apparently began the term with the belief that I was to be groomed by her to become another Laurence. My swift rebuffs to all her efforts in that direction soon convinced her otherwise. One day in class, she looked at me in puzzlement and resignation, and said:

"You know, Sowell, you're not at all like Laurence."

"Thank you, Mrs. Bloom," I replied. "That's the nicest thing you could have said to me."

After she turned against me, Mrs. Bloom began to apply harsher standards to my answers in class, my notebooks, and my exams, than the standards she applied to others. The other students quickly sensed this as well. For example, when I returned to class after having been out with illness for some time, she called on me on my first day back, asking me to describe the life of the bee, which the class had been studying in my absence. Murmurs of protest went up from some of the other students but she insisted that I answer, as she sat with her grading pencil poised over her notebook. Fortunately, I had sized her up by this point in the course, and had been studying an advanced textbook on entomology while I was out.

"Well, Mrs. Bloom," I said, "the common bee, or *apis mellifera* . . ."

Laughter from the class drowned me out as she sat stunned and frustrated. She had lost the battle but she continued the war throughout the remainder of my stay at J.H.S. 43.

As for Laurence himself, he apparently had heard of me somehow. My first personal encounter with him was in the public library directly across the street from where I lived. He had a job there after school. As I was sitting at a table reading one day, a hand suddenly reached down and snatched the book away from me. It was Laurence, who calmly riffled through the pages, losing my place, and then said, with a mock expression of being impressed:

"Well—no pictures. Maybe you do have something on the ball."

When he handed the book back to me and started to resume his chores, I said:

"You're lucky we are in a library."

"No," he said. "I think the good fortune is the other way around." And he sauntered on away.

Eventually, in school, we did get into a scuffle. Mrs. Bloom walked into the room in the middle of it, and pried me off him as my hands were clamping tighter on his windpipe. It confirmed all her worst suspicions of me.

On the last day of the fall term, there was some horseplay in our home room, one result of which was a magazine left lying on the floor between my desk and the desk of a girl in the next row. She was a very pleasant and mild-mannered girl, so Mrs. Bloom knew that she had not put it there and said as much. Turning to me, Mrs. Bloom then said:

"Sowell, pick that magazine up."

"I didn't put it there, either," I said.

"Don't argue with me! You do what I tell you."

"Not necessarily."

"Yes, you will!"

"No, as a matter of fact, I won't."

She reached across her desk and snatched my report card off the top of my desk. With her grading pen poised over my report card, she said:

"Now, either you bend down and pick up that magazine or I'll lower every grade on this report card by ten points."

The classroom was immediately very quiet.

"Mrs. Bloom," I said, "you may do whatever you wish with that piece of cardboard in front of you. But I doubt seriously if you are going down to the school office and change the *official records* there— which are the only records that count."

She threw the report card back onto my desk contemptuously and asked one of the "sensible" boys to "please" pick it up.

* * *

Our family situation was changing in a number of ways. Not long after I entered J.H.S. 43, we were able to get our own apartment—

Mom, Ruth, and me. Birdie and Lacy also got an apartment of their own, perhaps a mile away. Both the distance and changing circumstances caused me to see less of them than in the past, when Sunday visits to their place were the highlight of the week for me. After seven years of childless married life with two paychecks, Birdie and Lacy suddenly found themselves with only one paycheck and a growing family that reached three children in a few years. Moreover, one of these children was a "blue baby," his body unable to use oxygen effectively, so that he eventually died.

The new and heavy responsibilities of a family took a toll on them and Lacy, especially, began to change. Now working in a war plant, he put in much overtime and often arrived home too exhausted to give his own children the time and enthusiasm he once lavished on me. Decades later, his daughter would tell me how she grew up resenting hearing her father and me reminiscing about the good times that we once spent doing things together, for he spent no such times with her.

At one point during my teen years, Mom's son Herman made a visit to New York. As the only person available, I showed him around the city and we had a good time together. He never seemed to get over the fact that I was civilized and actually knew something.

Although Ruth had a room in the apartment, she was gone most of the time, because she remained a live-in maid. While I was never initiated into the mysteries of the family finances, it was pretty clear by this time that Ruth was our sole support, whether or not Birdie had been able to contribute much before she quit work to raise a family. Mom herself never had a full-time job during my lifetime, nor for some years before, because of her age and her infirmities, or presumed infirmities. She was one of those people who enjoyed poor health, and she was always threatening to die, though in fact she lived on into her nineties. With time on her hands, she could nurse her neuroses, build resentments of slights and imagined slights, brood over our growing estrangement, and make it worse with arbitrary assertions of her authority. She and I were increasingly living in different worlds.

Our budget seemed to become more pinched as the cost of living rose during the war. I found myself wearing more second-hand

clothes and we moved out of our nice little apartment with a refrigerator into a less attractive, though larger, apartment where we kept our
food in an old-fashioned ice box. As a housing shortage developed in
New York, we began taking in roomers. Ruth gave up the large front
room, which she was not really using, so that it could be rented out,
and I was moved out of my modest-sized room on the hall into a tiny
room at the back of the apartment, so that we could add another
roomer.

• • •

At school, my main preoccupation was with getting into a selective
high school, and particularly into Stuyvesant, which I had heard so
much about. School grades, as well as test scores, counted, so I became
much more conscious of grades now, especially my grades in math,
which was my best subject. Although Rosen and I were now in different classes, I knew that we were both competing to get into Stuyvesant,
and I had no way of knowing how tough the competition would be.

Usually each class period in math would begin with a few "quickie"
problems, conducted as a game to see who would finish first with the
correct answer. Since I was no longer in a class with kids of the same
ability level, I almost invariably finished first with the right answer.
One day our math teacher, Mr. Feinberg, said to me:

"You work out these problems pretty fast on paper, Sowell—but in
the 'one' class, Rosen can do them in his head."

I put the pencil and paper away and said:

"If Rosen can do them in his head, I can do them in my feet."

It was typical adolescent brashness, but Mr. Feinberg seemed
deeply distressed that I could say such a thing, as if something were
going wrong with the natural course of the universe.

At the end of the term, I received a 93 percent in math—and demanded a recount. Mr. Feinberg said that it was "selfish" of me to want
to take up his time quibbling over a few points, when other students
had to see him about passing or failing the course. But I knew that
Rosen had gotten a 98 and I wanted to get whatever I was entitled to.

"My quizzes and exams have been better than any 93 in this
course," I said.

"But all exams and quizzes are not *weighted* the same," Mr. Feinberg said. "I can't stop now and go through the whole process of how they are weighted with you."

"I didn't have a single grade under 95 on any exam or quiz all year," I said. "That can't come out to 93, no matter *how* you weight them."

"Well . . . there has to be a subjective judgment in there too," he said.

"In other words, you simply chose to knock off points that I had earned."

Mr. Feinberg changed the 93 to a 96, with the look of a long-suffering man who was being very much put upon.

• • •

Graduation ceremonies were held in the school auditorium, with parents in attendance. Birdie alone came to see me graduate.

One of the highlights of the graduation ceremony was inviting up on stage all the students who had gained admission to the various elite public high schools of the city. Students the previous year obviously relished this opportunity to receive the praise of the principal and the applause of the audience. But this year's class had some students who were different in this, as they had been in other ways. That was especially true of me. After what I had been put through, I was not about to go up on stage and let them parade me.

Some of my former classmates from "R" class days seemed ambivalent too, and when Dr. Davidman (the principal) called for the successful candidates for the elite schools to come up on stage, some of them looked at me. I shook my head to indicate that I wasn't going to budge, and some of them took the same position.

When only a few students straggled up on stage, Dr. Davidman looked very puzzled.

"I *know* that far more students than this were admitted to selective high schools," he said. Dr. Davidman was a decent sort, but he wasn't the issue.

Teachers, aware that many of us were just stonewalling, began to hiss at us in stage whispers to "get up on that stage." But nothing happened.

Birdie later told me that she could see my shoulders shaking and knew that I was chuckling about something.

* * *

I entered Stuyvesant High School in February 1945, with great hopes and eagerness. It was gratifying to be in with so many obviously bright and serious students, and not to feel that any attempt to use my own mind would be resented by slower classmates as "showing off." The teachers were also clearly a cut above what I had encountered before, both intellectually and as human beings. Rosen and Valdez were classmates of mine again in a special advanced class, and it seemed easy enough to make new friends as well.

The work was demanding. There were hours of tough homework every day, and I had one extra class period a day, because of being in the special advanced group. However, I was able to meet the demands, though they were such as to leave little or no margin for anything to go wrong.

One of the special burdens on me was simply the difficulty of getting to and from Stuyvesant every day. From west 145th street, where I lived, to east 15th street, where the school was located, was a long way. I had to leave an hour ahead of time on the subway and transfer twice, at two of the busiest subway stations—Times Square and Grand Central Station. Stuyvesant was on shifts, so I left in mid-morning and returned in late afternoon, at the height of the rush hour. The most packed subway I have ever seen was the one I took from Union Square to Grand Central. If someone were to pass out in that train, he probably could not fall to the floor.

I always arrived home exhausted, and often with a headache so bad that I could only flop down across the bed and sleep it off before doing anything—even eating supper. After I woke up and ate alone, it was time to begin the homework. Usually I finished it up the next morning, just in time to get under way again. It was like being on a treadmill around the clock. Soon I became a complete stranger to the rest of the family.

Many other neighborhood boys my age had part-time jobs, bringing home some much-needed money to help their families get by.

With my schedule, however, I could work only on Saturdays, when I was a grocery delivery boy in the middle-class Sugar Hill section of Harlem. The money I earned from this barely covered my subway fare and lunch money during the week. The boy in the apartment next door, who went to a regular high school much closer to home, was working every afternoon, bringing home much more money than I could. Invidious comparisons were inevitable—and frequent.

While everyone in the family understood—in the abstract—that Stuyvesant was a better high school, and they were proud that I was accepted there, its demands on my time were incomprehensible to them. Sometimes they even questioned whether I was telling them the truth, whether I was *really* at the public library as much as I said I was, or was off somewhere else getting into trouble. They simply did not know a living soul who spent that much time in a library.

Occasionally, I would say something about a patched piece of clothing that was an embarrassment to me at school, and that would set off another round of recriminations all around. In this tense atmosphere of mutual misunderstandings, almost anything could bring on a family crisis. One Sunday, I went over to East Orange, New Jersey, to take Shirley to a movie, without asking or telling anyone until I had done it. This flouting of authority provoked another angry family gathering.

As if all this were not enough, I became sick during my first term at Stuyvesant and was in bed for several weeks. When I finally returned to school, it was all too obvious that the pace at which the class moved made it impossible for me to make up the lost time. Seeing the futility of it all, I began staying out, even when I wasn't sick, and resigned myself to taking the term over again in the fall.

●　●　●

During the summers, my Saturday job at the grocery store became a daily job, though I could often get off for a couple of hours during the slow time in the afternoon and go play baseball.

Baseball was my new passion, whether for playing, watching, or listening to play-by-play descriptions on the radio. I had never been good in athletics at school, but here was something at which I excelled almost immediately. This was especially gratifying at a time when so much else was going wrong in my life. It was also a welcome change of pace from the wholly intellectual preoccupations of the previous few years. Finally, baseball put me in touch with the kids in the neighborhood for the first time, changing my companions from predominantly white to predominantly black almost overnight, though this racial change did not seem particularly momentous to me at the time.

Blacks, whites and Hispanics all played baseball on the two diamonds on the field. To all outward appearances, there were no racial tensions. However, most of the teams were all-black, all-white or all-Hispanic, though there were also racially mixed teams, especially when a game was put together on the spur of the moment and sides were chosen from the players who happened to be around. A special category of teams were those who were part of organized leagues. These teams often had official permits to use the fields at particular times, and their games took priority, even if an unofficial game among local neighborhood teams was already in progress. These organized teams were usually white.

Often the teams that had permits were teams of working men, playing in a league made up of other teams from the same industry. Usually there was no problem when they showed us their permit or told us that they had left it in the park director's office. Occasionally, they might even put one of our players on their team, if they were short-handed. Once, when I was filling in on an industrial team, even the opposing pitcher had to smile when he saw a skinny black teenager batting clean-up in a line-up full of beefy white men.

Overt racial remarks were very rare, not because everything was harmonious and color-blind, but because everyone knew that such remarks could turn a pleasant afternoon of baseball into a riot. When a black team was behind while playing an Hispanic team, someone might whisper to his buddies, "We're not going to let these spics beat us, are we?" What the players on the other team were saying to each other in Spanish, we had no idea.

One day, our team was on the field taking batting practice and, with the team captain being away, I was left in charge. While I was at the plate batting, a white team came in through the gate and simply began moving onto our diamond, saying nothing and offering no permit. They began throwing the ball around among themselves, laughing and talking, just as if we were invisible. Figuring that they were a league team, some of our players started to walk off the field, though sullenly, in view of the way things were being done.

"Don't go anywhere!" I said sharply and our players stopped where they were. If the other team was going to play baseball on the same diamond, just as if we didn't exist, then we would continue to play baseball there, just as if they didn't exist.

I held my hand out over the plate, to indicate to the pitcher where I wanted the ball. He put it right there and I hit a line drive straight at the white shortstop, who seemed to be the leader of his team. He wasn't even watching the plate, but was looking over at his first baseman, who was rolling a ball across the ground for him to field. The shortstop bent over to get the ground ball, just in time for my line drive to go whistling past his ear. He looked up, livid, and charged at me. A couple of his team mates grabbed him and held him, while he struggled to get loose.

"Turn him loose," I said. "He'll think somebody's scared of him." He was bigger than me but I had a bat in my hands.

"You wouldn't dare talk to me that way, back where I come from!" he shouted in a Southern accent.

"You're not back where you come from," I said. "And you may not get back."

Cooler heads prevailed when someone went to get the park director, who came on the field to assure us that the other team had a permit, which we could see in his office. We then quietly walked off the field, but with our heads up. I cannot recall any other team coming on the field like that one again.

●　●　●

When the fall term began at Stuyvesant High School, I was surprised to discover that I had been promoted, despite having missed most of the spring term's work. The special class that I had been part of had been promoted *en masse,* as an administrative convenience, on the assumption that none of the kids in it would need to be left back.

The school officials with whom I talked clearly thought that I should accept the promotion as a windfall gain. I told them that it was pointless for me to go on to the next grade, when I had not learned what I should have learned, and what I would need as a preparation for later work. They were very resistant to the idea of putting me back to my original grade level and letting me do the term's work over again. What was educationally obvious was apparently administratively or economically troublesome. My persistence finally wore them down, however, and the necessary papers were processed, though with much resentment on their part at the special attention I was demanding and the violation of precedent involved.

The term began well enough, but by now the atmosphere at home had degenerated into complete antagonism, with frequent, lengthy, and debilitating family arguments, making it impossible for me to do the kind of academic work that Stuyvesant demanded. I began taking off a day or two here and there, to give myself a breather, but finally I recognized the futility of what I was attempting to do, in the circumstances that existed, and stopped going to school altogether. This brought unanimous condemnation from Birdie, Lacy, Ruth, and Mom alike, as well as from other relatives. Among other things, they resented my throwing away an opportunity which they had never had. But they had no inkling that this opportunity had prerequisites which were being destroyed, day in and day out, by the incessant nagging and bickering at home.

Soon the truant officer entered the picture. He was a stern and crusty man, but a very decent fellow underneath. He tried to get me to transfer to an easier school, but I couldn't bring myself to do it. At Stuyvesant, the officials were quick to believe that the work was just "too hard" for me, and suggested that I take a special watered-down program, at least to keep me on the books in good standing until my sixteenth birthday, when I would be free to leave legally. I resented this for the insulting and meaningless thing that it was. At this time, I could not bring myself to discuss our internal family problems with these school officials, whom I neither trusted nor respected.

A few people in the neighborhood understood my situation, but there was little that they could do to help. One lady who tried to be helpful was a friend of Ruth's named Creole. She earned my undying gratitude by taking me to my first major league baseball game, at Yankee Stadium, and she also lent me some books. Mom immediately read sinister meanings into her interest in me, though Creole's husband viewed it all very positively.

Another couple who were very sympathetic were the building superintendent and his wife, who knew me not only as a tenant, but also as someone who did various odd jobs in the two buildings that the "super" ran. They actually approached Mom to ask her to let me come live with them, but she would not hear of it. She was not about to relinquish power, even though it was slipping away anyway.

My school attendance remained spotty and a sporadic source of problems until I was sixteen years old, when I was able to sign myself out of school. I took my first full-time, year-around job as a Western Union messenger, delivering telegrams down in the grim and sometimes dangerous Chelsea district in lower Manhattan. It was my first encounter with low-income and sometimes semi-literate white people. Some of the older people from immigrant backgrounds could not read English, so I had to read the telegrams to them, and sometimes interpret them as well. It was my first realization that life is tough all over.

Leaving school meant freedom from an enormous weight of conflicting pressures. This easing of pressures caused a temporary change for the better at home, especially now that I was contributing money regularly to the household. I also felt a certain pride in my new role as a self-supporting adult. But these positive feelings could only be temporary on all sides.

Delivering telegrams all day long and walking the streets along the New York waterfront in the winter were trying experiences—and experiences that led nowhere, except to a future of unending frustration and futility. Parts of the area where I worked were also sufficiently dangerous for me to begin to carry a push-button knife, which I had never found necessary to carry in my own neighborhood.

The fateful significance of my decision to leave school began slowly but inexorably to settle down upon me like some great new weight, and resentment at how I had been forced into it began to poison my relationships with everyone in the family, none of whom could see what strangers could see, that Mom's impossible behavior was destroying any hope of my getting an education or having a future.

• • •

One Sunday morning, Ruth came into my room and woke me up. Since I hated to be awakened, I muttered:

"The house had better be on fire."

"The house is not on fire," Ruth said. "But there's a pretty girl here to see you."

That seemed even less likely. However, I took a peek into the living room and, sure enough, there was a very pretty girl sitting there.

"I don't know her," I said. "But if she thinks she knows me, I am not going to argue." Soon I had myself washed up, dressed and was out in the living room.

"This is your cousin Mary Frances from Washington," Mom said. "She's passing through town and stopped by to see us."

Mary Frances was a personable and sincere young woman. She asked what I was doing and we exchanged pleasantries. After she left, I said to Ruth:

"You didn't tell me she was a relative."

"Would you have gotten dressed that fast if I had?" she asked.

This little episode made no real impression on me at the time, nor was there any reason to think that I would ever see Mary Frances again. It was months later before the truth finally came out: She was not my cousin Mary Frances from Washington. She was my *sister* Mary Frances from Washington. She had come to find me, but Mom had steadfastly refused to let her see me, unless she agreed to be introduced to me as my cousin.

• • •

Like a drowning man grasping at a straw, I decided to try to make some kind of future for myself by taking a commercial art course to become an illustrator. I had always been interested in drawing, and now hoped that developing my talents in that direction would offer me some way out of the grim present and the bleak future that loomed ahead.

I did the lessons after work and on the weekends, and met with my instructor at the art school downtown on Saturdays. But the same home atmosphere that had made it impossible for me to continue at Stuyvesant now made it impossible for me to complete the art course. Among other things, Mom began to complain whenever I left any of my art materials in the living room, and one day she simply threw some of them out. That was the last straw.

"People don't like losing their belongings," I said quietly to her, as I picked up her favorite vase and smashed it against a wall.

This of course brought on another family gathering, full of re-criminations all around. As relations continued to deteriorate, social workers and then the law were brought in, as Mom attempted to re-gain control of me. I told her that I was planning to leave home, but she threatened to have me put in a reform school if I did—and reform schools were cesspools, even in those days. That she would threaten me with such a thing destroyed whatever vestige of respect for her that I had left.

One day, when nothing in particular was going on, Mom some-how had the idea of calling in the police. I don't know what kind of story she told the policeman, but he entered the apartment looking grim and clenching his billy club as he came down the hall. But, as fate would have it, the policeman she got turned out to be the only police-man I knew—because I delivered his groceries. As he got close enough for us to recognize each other, he looked very surprised—al-most disoriented—and put away his billy club.

Mom, unaware that the policeman and I knew each other, could not resist over-playing her hand.

"He's the worst boy you've ever seen!" she said, not realizing that a policeman sees some pretty bad boys in his business.

"I'd like to talk with him alone," the policeman said to Mom, who was happy to withdraw and leave me in the hands of the law. When she was gone, the policeman asked:

"What's going on here?"

After I explained the situation to him, he went to Mom and said:

"This is not a police matter."

Mom was not through with trying to use the law to restore her power, however. One day I received a summons, ordering me to appear in court down on the lower east side of Manhattan, to answer charges of disorderly conduct. I could not imagine what story she had concocted to get this summons issued, but I did know that the burden of proof was on the prosecution.

To me, the court was a place where I might put an end to these farcical attempts at intimidation, and where I might find out whether Mom had any legal right to stop me from leaving. I was in a sufficiently upbeat mood to get into a long conversation with a receptionist at the court. When I was finally called into the magistrate's chambers, however, I found that Mom had completely won him over to her side, and that he saw his job as being to lean on me to bring me back into line.

"This is a very serious charge, young man," he said grimly.

"Yes, I know," I said, "and I'll be very interested to see how anybody can prove it."

From there on, it was downhill. The charge was simply changed to "wayward minor," which I suppose can mean anything. The magistrate also told me that my aunt—the truth about my adoption was out by now—had every right to refuse to let me leave and that the law would indeed back her up and send me to reform school if I left without her permission. The rights and wrongs of our disagreements did not interest him. He was laying down the law.

"All right," I said. "If that's the way this game is going to be played, we will *both* play it that way. Right and wrong don't matter? Fine. But if it is all just a matter of power, then I don't plan to do one thing that you don't have the power to make me do."

"Like what?" he asked.

"Like taking her back home," I said.

"How is your aunt going to get back home, then?" he asked, alarmed.

"I have no idea," I said, as I walked out the door.

It was now very clear to me that there was only one person in the world I could depend on—myself. It was equally clear that my only way out was to force Mom to agree to my leaving home legally. From that moment on, I refused to do anything whatsoever that was not legally required of me. I continued to live in the apartment but refused to contribute to it in any way, whether financially or even by carrying groceries home. I bought my own food, prepared it and ate alone. I laid in a large supply of canned goods, lest anyone doubt that I was prepared for a long siege. When I came and went, I refused to tell anybody where I was going or when I would be back.

As the weeks went by and then turned into months, Mom struck back with one of her favorite weapons—lies. She told Birdie, Lacy, and Ruth that she was willing for me to leave but that I insisted on staying on and being a parasite. Meanwhile, she insisted to the magistrate downtown that she could not possibly bring herself to "abandon my dead sister's child." I was in fact her dead sister's grandchild, but accuracy was less important to her than effect—and the magistrate bought it all.

Birdie, Lacy, and Ruth also bought Mom's opposite story to them, and grew bitter with me when I insisted that she was lying. There is probably no diplomatic way to tell people that their mother is a liar, or if there is, I am probably not the person to discover it. Only two people knew the truth, Mom and me, and it all came down to a test of wills.

"How long is this gonna go on, Thomas?" she asked one day.

"Until someone cracks," I said. "And it won't be me."

She tried being sanctimonious as I walked away, but I turned on her.

"You lying hypocrite!" I said, and launched into a tongue-lashing that left nothing to the imagination.

Wild with anger, she grabbed a hammer and drew it back to throw it. I was too far away to take it away from her, so I said:

"Throw it—but you had better not miss."

Trembling with anger, more so than fear, she put the hammer down. Afterwards, she seemed to understand at last the reality of our relationship, that we we re simply enemies living under the same roof.

When we went to another scheduled meeting with the magistrate in January 1948, he talked with Mom alone first, as before, and then called me in.

"Have you made any arrangements for a place to live?" he asked.

"No," I said. "I wasn't aware that my aunt had agreed for me to leave."

"She's just agreed," he said.

"Then I'm ready to go, right now."

"You're still under age," he warned. "Only seventeen. If you go, you will have to report in to me regularly until you are twenty-one. Since you have no place of your own, I can arrange for you to move into the Home for Homeless Boys in the Bronx."

"Fine," I said.

I felt as if I had been released from prison—and earlier than expected.

My first stop after leaving the court was East 23rd Street, where I had seen a cheap little cardboard suitcase in a store window. Small as it was, it was big enough for everything I owned.

My next stop was home. A lady who was rooming with us immediately sensed that something out of the ordinary was happening, when she saw me coming in alone and carrying a suitcase. But she was also clearly torn as to whether it was her place to say anything. After I packed my belongings and was headed back up the hall toward the door, she finally asked anxiously:

"What will I tell Mrs. Sowell?"

I smiled to reassure her, and said:

"Tell her I'm gone—if she doesn't notice it herself."

3

A Four-Leaf Clover

It was nightfall by the time I got off the elevated subway station at 149th Street in the Bronx. Neon store lights were blinking in the streets below, and somewhere I heard for the first time a catchy new song being played on a radio:

> I'm looking over
> A four-leaf clover
> That I overlooked before . . .

I liked the song. Its carefree jingle was a bittersweet note as I moved into a new and unknown phase of my life. Maybe it would be a sign of good luck. Little did I know how long that good luck would be in coming.

The Home for Homeless Boys was a small place on a side street in the Bronx. A couple of kindly old gentlemen were in charge and kept as much of a homey atmosphere as group living will permit. The other guys there were about my age. They seemed okay and were well-behaved here, whatever they may have been before they got here. Some of them played checkers, which I liked. Nevertheless, I maintained a certain wariness, which I had already developed from having been so much alone, even when I was living at home. When time came to go to bed, I casually pulled out my push-button knife, flicked it open, and put it under my pillow. In the language of a later era, that was "making a statement" about "sexual preferences." I also put my wallet alongside my knife, in case anyone had any thoughts about that.

. . .

Now that I had my freedom, I wanted it to be complete freedom. I could not see reporting to a magistrate for years to come. However, since he had been considerate enough to schedule our first meeting in the evening, because I was working during the day, I thought that I should be considerate enough to tell him that there was no point waiting needlessly for me to show up. I phoned him.

"I've decided not to come in for any meetings," I told the magistrate.

"It's not up to you!" he said angrily. "The law *requires* you to come in."

"I'm not coming in."

"We can go get you."

"You can't find me."

"We know where you live!"

"I've moved."

"We know where you work!"

"I've quit."

"We can *still* find you! You're in violation of the law!"

"There are eight million people in New York," I said. "You'll never find me."

There was a long pause on the other end of the line. When the magistrate came back on again, he had a wholly different tone and a quieter voice.

"You've really burned your bridges behind you, haven't you?"

"Yes."

"Good luck to you, son."

"Thank you."

. . .

My new home was a small room which I rented a few days after entering the Home for Homeless Boys. It was in a little house in upper

Manhattan, near 163rd Street and Amsterdam Avenue, still a somewhat middle class and racially mixed area at that time. There was a
very good public library at the corner that provided me with many
books to fill my solitary hours.

My room was probably not as large as a 9 X 12 rug. It contained a
small bed, a chest, a chair, and a gas heater. It had no closet, just a nail
on the back of the door, but that was sufficient for my wardrobe at the
time. I bought myself a hot plate, so that I could cook some of the
canned goods and potatoes I bought at a nearby supermarket. I bought
the same things at the store most weeks, and it came to $13.75. Room
rent was $5.75 a week, and subway fare to work (at a nickel each way)
came to 50 cents a week. That added up to $20, out of a take-home pay
of $22.50 from my weekly wages of $25. I worked as a general helper
and delivery boy at a clothing factory in the garment district. Occasionally I had opportunities to work overtime, and always seized those
opportunities.

My break with the past was almost complete. I wrote to Shirley,
perhaps just so that she would not believe whatever lies she might be
told.

There was one other piece of unfinished business. I had to go back
to 145th Street to pick up a couple of things I had forgotten to take
with me. As I entered the apartment, the only person who was in was
an elderly lady who roomed there and who was on welfare.

"Thank you for leaving me your canned tomatoes, Tommy," she
said.

"You're welcome, ma'am," I said, "but I left you *all* my canned
goods—the pineapples, the soup, the peas . . ."

"Mrs. Sowell told me you left me the tomatoes," she said. "That's
what she gave me."

When I walked out the door of the apartment, I was more convinced than ever that I never wanted to see this place again.

●　●　●

The peace and freedom of my new life were a welcome change, but the
future was still an unresolved concern. The boring and low-paying
work I did, which took me out in all kinds of weather, was something

I very much wanted to escape, though I was not sure how, much less when.

One possibility was to resume studying to become an illustrator, but this was not something I really wanted to invest more money in, with my budget so tight. Another area in which I thought I had some talent was writing. Over a period of weeks, I slowly saved up enough money to buy an old second-hand typewriter, and began to write fiction to submit to various magazines.

The mail was very fast in those days, so I could drop a manuscript into the mailbox on Monday morning on my way to work and find it waiting for me when I returned home Tuesday night. Apparently the editors did not waste much time deciding whether to accept or reject it. I was not even a good enough writer to realize how bad I was, until the accumulation of rejections slips made their message unmistakable.

One short story, which I regarded as my best, did elicit a letter from a literary agent, who said that he detected some undeveloped talent. However, there would be a fee for his help in developing it. The mere mention of money was enough to kill the idea. There was a momentary exhilaration when four lines of verse that I had written were accepted for publication in one of the most inconsequential of the little literary magazines. I don't know whether it ever actually appeared in print, because the magazine folded.

The third and last of my hopes for instant success was baseball. I had a try-out with the Dodgers. It was held in a semi-pro ball park in the Williamsburgh section of Brooklyn. There was an old abandoned building behind the right field fence, and I could just envision hitting a few home-run balls through its window when my turn came to bat. Unfortunately, the Dodgers allowed you to bat only after you had passed fielding tests—and I booted a couple of ground balls at first base. As I took the subway back home from Brooklyn, I knew that I was going to have to try to get ahead the hard, slow way, by returning to school and going at night.

In September 1948, I went to an office of the Board of Education, to get the papers necessary for enrolling in night school. It so happened that my old truant officer was now the official in charge of such things. He recognized me and sadly shook his head that it had taken me so long to realize the importance of education, which he had tried to tell me about, two years earlier. Even now, I couldn't bring myself to explain the futility of my home situation back then. Instead, I said cheerfully:

"Well, at least I am going back now and starting over, right where I left off."

He handed me the papers I needed, saying however:

"But it's too late now. Your opportunity has *already* passed you by."

He was not a cruel man, but that hurt me more than anything else he could have said, and it came back to haunt me again and again, probably because it echoed what I already felt in my heart.

●   ●   ●

At the end of 1948, the owners of the little company I worked for in the garment district called the employees together to announce lay-offs, and to say that they hoped to be able to call some of us back before too long. I was out of work—and had very little saved to fall back on. I remember wondering what the future held, as I looked out the factory window, down into the canyons of midtown Manhattan, where the Christmas decorations were still out and the snow was softly falling.

That snowfall would eventually turn into the biggest snow storm since the blizzard of 1888, and the new year—1949—would turn out to be one of the worst years of my life. It was a recession year, and I was plagued with recurrent unemployment. I walked the streets looking for work, seemingly forever, though in fact I was never without a job longer than two weeks at a time. If nothing else, I learned how to look for a job—relentlessly. Each day, I would decide which was the most promising job to go for, and would arrive early enough to be the first in line. When that interview was over, it was off to the next job on the list, and so on all day long, until I finally returned home, tired and dispirited, at the end of a long day of being turned down or told that they would get back to me. Then it was more of the same the next day, and the next, until I finally found something.

During one of these periods of unemployment, I fell behind in the rent and began to skimp on food. It finally occurred to me that I could get some money by pawning my one suit. I took it down to the lower east side of Manhattan, where there were many pawnshops, and got some money for it. Immediately, I went to a little fast food place near the corner of Third Avenue and 14th Street, where I ordered a knish and an orange soda. It was delicious. No meal that I have ever had since then, anywhere in the world, has ever topped it.

With recurrent spells of unemployment, eventually I was literally down to my last dollar when I finally got a part-time job, working at night in a machine shop on the lower east side. I knew where to buy day-old bread for 5 cents a loaf and a jar of jelly for 10 cents. That and water constituted my meals. There was not enough money left for me to take the subway both ways, so I walked to work from Harlem all the way down to just below the Brooklyn Bridge—about eight miles.

When I was paid, I discovered that it was company policy to hold back a few days' pay. Since I was working only part-time, that left precious little money in my first pay envelope. I had to ask the foreman—Ed Gally was his name—if I could borrow five dollars from him. That was a lot to ask for in those days, but he lent it to me from his own pocket, so I was able to eat the next week—and ride to work.

This job was special to me. Although it was only a part-time job, it paid more per hour than any other job I had held thus far. Moreover, I was acquiring a little bit of skill and experience working in a machine shop. My many job interviews had made it painfully clear how important skills and experience were. In addition, Ed Gally took a fatherly interest in me, at a time when there was nobody else to offer me any guidance. He even tried to warn me against becoming involved with a pretty young woman who worked in the shop, though unsuccessfully in this case.

Working at night brought my night-school education to a halt temporarily, but it left me free to look for other jobs during the day. Eventually, I found a full-time job working as a Western Union messenger again. Working 40 hours a week at Western Union and 20 hours a week in the machine shop, I was able to make enough money to pay off the back rent that I owed and to put aside a little money for another rainy day. That day came much sooner than I expected.

One afternoon, near quitting time, a great number of telegrams suddenly came into the Western Union office, and the manager told me that I would have to work overtime to deliver them. When I told him that I couldn't do it, because I was due at my night job right after I finished this one, he told me that I would have to choose which job I wanted. This was a very tough choice, in a situation with very little margin for error.

Western Union was paying me $26 for 40 hours, while the machine shop was paying me $18 for 20 hours. Financially, Western Union was obviously more important, but it offered no future, while the machine shop seemed to offer at least a hope of a step up in skills. I quit Western Union.

This painful decision made my finances precarious once again. But, shortly afterward, Ed Gally offered me a full-time, daytime job in the machine shop. While my new job was full-time, it was not permanent, because the number of employees varied with the orders that came in, and the regular unionized workers had seniority. Still, I was very happy that things had turned out as well as they did.

Now that I was back to working days, I resumed going to school at night. The night school classes I attended were held in Washington Irving High School, located near Union Square on the lower east side. Although I could now afford to take the subway, I often decided to save the nickel by walking there from work, a distance of about two miles. Sometimes the young woman from work would walk with me, and we would sit in Union Square talking until time for me to go to class. She called me "schoolboy."

* * *

Even aside from going to night school, my intellectual development was proceeding. I had moved up from reading about sports in the tabloids to more serious reading in the *New York Times,* which I went through for hours on Sundays. My interest in political analysis was especially piqued by reading *Actions and Passions,* a collection of essays by columnist Max Lerner. One day, I found an old second-hand set of encyclopedias for $1.17 and bought it. It was ten or twenty years out of date but many entries were about things which did not depend on timeliness. One of the entries was about Karl Marx, to whose ideas I was to be attracted for the next decade. These ideas seemed to explain so much, and they explained it in a way to which my grim experience made me very receptive.

More grim experience was in store for me when the orders ran out at the machine shop and I was among those laid off. Ed Gally told me that he would call me back when there were more orders for the kind of work I did, but he didn't know when that would be. It was back to the relentless search for a job, but this time I could at least claim some experience in a machine shop, and this enabled me to get two or three other jobs in machine shops. These jobs too lasted only until orders ran out, but they all paid more than I had been making a year earlier—and it was enough for me to save to tide me over periods of unemployment.

Somehow, I heard about civil service jobs and looked through listings until I found one that I could qualify for—an entry-level government clerk. A white-collar job with security seemed like more than I dared to hope for. Unfortunately, I discovered this job in a civil service newspaper a day before the deadline for applying to take the exam. There was only half an hour between quitting time on my job and closing time at the civil service office, but I decided to try to make it. I took the subway and then ran through the streets of downtown Manhattan, breathing heavily and wondering if it would ever be worth all this. I barely got in the door before it was closed, and filed to take the clerk's exam.

Some weeks later, when I took the test, I did well on it but was told that there were no openings, and that there was no way to know when there would be any.

* * *

One evening, I went to a stationery store near 155th Street and Broadway. As I turned to go in, I barely noticed a young boy who was coming out, until we suddenly met face to face at the entrance.

"Tommy!"

"Jimmy!"

Despite my problems with other members of the family, I still felt the same about Jimmy. We stood silently looking at each other for what seemed like a long time. Finally, he said in a soft voice:

"Come home with me."

The words cut into me, but I said, "I can't do that, Jimmy."

We shook hands and went our separate ways.

*   *   *

As 1949 neared its end, I began working in yet another machine shop. It was a highly organized assembly operation, geared to each man's doing 60 units per hour in his part of the process and then passing the product on for the next step. Try as I might, I could not seem to meet that quota, and the foreman told me that he could give me only one more week to get up to the required output.

More effort was not the answer, because I was already doing everything that I was physically capable of. I would have to wrack my brain to think of some alternative method of working. With the shadow of unemployment looming over me once again, my waking hours became dominated by the need to come up with this alternative way of working that would speed up my output and save my job.

Eventually, an idea came to me—and when I tried it out on the job, it worked. Soon I was doing so many units per hour that I exceeded the quota, and boxes of my output began piling up at the work station of the next worker in the sequence. It was like a deliverance.

Now I had time to relax and chit-chat with the other guys in the shop, and even to take part in some of the pranks we played on each other. As the new year 1950 dawned, life was noticeably better. One week, working much overtime, I earned the unheard-of pay of $64 a week, much more than I had received for working two jobs just a year earlier. I felt that the worst was now behind me—and it was. What still remained unclear was how I was to move on further, to some way of life with which I could be content in the long run. I was still going to school at night, and doing well, but part-time school meant that my education was advancing at a snail's pace.

The year 1950 saw a number of things happen whose importance for my future was not at all obvious at the time. One of these things was that the young lady from Ed Gally's shop lent me her camera and I took pictures for the first time. I was very pleased with the results, which revived my interest in pictures from the days when I had thought of being an artist. Photography became a lasting interest, and one that would later play a major role in my evolution. Another event that was to have lasting consequences in my life was that a war broke out in Korea.

The summer of 1950 found me working in yet another machine shop. By now, the periods between jobs were shorter and I had enough saved to see me through the transitions. However, I still did not want to spend my life in machine shops. I was especially anxious to move on to something else after an accident in which the index finger of my left hand was smashed under a power press, tearing loose the fingernail and making the end of the finger look like hamburger. The machine was so swift and powerful that I barely felt any pain, but the sight of my smashed finger was sickening.

Frank, the foreman, leaped to my aid and then led me out through the streets to a doctor's office. As we passed a number of doctors' offices, I asked him why we were not stopping there.

"They will amputate your finger, in order to get paid by workmen's compensation," he said. "The doctor I'm taking you to will try to save your finger, if he can."

While the doctor was examining me, I could see spots before my eyes, and felt that I was going to sleep. But the doctor suddenly grabbed my head and forced it down, causing the blood to rush to my brain, bringing me out of it. He said he thought he could save my finger, but that I should never expect to see a fingernail there again.

• • •

Near the end of the summer, I heard from the Civil Service Commission about the job I had applied for a year earlier. They now had an opening for a clerk—in Washington. By this time, with my finger still heavily wrapped in bandages, I was more than ready to give up working in machine shops.

As I prepared to move to Washington, I realized that I was not going to take my heavy old typewriter with me. Before I left, I put a brief note in the mail to Birdie, telling her that she could have my typewriter if she wanted it, and including the address where I had been living. It was the first time that I told anyone in the family where I was—or rather, where I had been.

In Washington, I made contact with my other family—Mary Frances and my brothers William and Charles. I spent my first two weeks in Washington staying with Mary Frances and her husband, who had a house. My sister was a year older than me and William was a year older than she was. Charles was the oldest and was in his early thirties. It was good to have a family again, and especially to discover many similarities in personality and interests with people whom I had never known before. By this time, the physical resemblance between Mary Frances and me was so striking that people commented on it wherever we appeared together.

Although I resumed a rather solitary life after I moved into my own rooms—two, for the first time—I did see William with some regularity. He was a student at Howard University, going to school on the G.I. Bill and earning money with various odd jobs to support himself and his car. Charles was a mailman and Mary was a housewife. William and I had the most interests in common and discovered that we had even memorized some of the same verses. It was not uncommon for William to say to me, out of the blue:

"It was many and many a year ago . . ."

To which I responded: " . . . in a kingdom by the sea."

"That there lived a girl whom you may know . . ."

" . . . by the name of Annabelle Lee."

He and I were also devotees of Edward R. Murrow. William would shush anyone when time came to hear that classic phrase at the beginning of Morrow's program: "This—is the news," recalling Murrow's wartime broadcasts that began, "This—is London."

Charles also took a keen interest in current events. His other interests included electronics, classical music and jazz. Although he had only a high school education, he had taught himself enough electronics to build his own amateur radio transmitter, with which he could sometimes reach as far as Australia. He also built himself a high-fidelity sound system, inside an old-fashioned console. However, there were few outlets for this kind of talent among black people in the Washington of this era.

Washington was almost a typical Southern town, with a few exceptions like not having racially segregated buses and streetcars, and having one high-quality movie theater without the racial bans common in other downtown theaters. The school system was still racially segregated, though some were beginning to question that. In November 1950, I wrote a long letter to the *Washington Star,* urging the desegregation of the city's public schools. It was the first thing I had written that I know was published.

The government job was all right and the steady income—about $47 a week before taxes—was good. The city of Washington, however, increasingly got on my nerves. When I went downtown taking pictures, I found it a pain that I could not simply walk into a restaurant and get something to eat when I was hungry. At a number of fast food places downtown, whites could sit down and eat, but blacks could only eat standing up at the counter. I went hungry rather than subject myself to that.

. . .

Not all my relatives in Washington were a pleasure to deal with. An especially overbearing woman was Aunt Adrue, who had raised William and Mary Frances after our mother died. Aunt Adrue seemed to think that she was going to take me over, like a wholly-owned subsidiary. She tried to draw me into her church and wanted to save me from falling into the clutches of the wrong kind of women. I did not consider it nearly so urgent to avoid falling into such clutches, and thought it was none of her business anyway.

"Aunt Adrue is our father's sister," William told me, trying to smooth things over, "and they were always very close. That is why she feels a responsibility."

"I wouldn't care if they were Siamese twins," I said. "She's not going to run my life."

Mary Frances must have sensed from the outset that Aunt Adrue and I were not going to get along. When I first arrived in Washington, Aunt Adrue came over to meet me, and Mary Frances paused on her way to answer the doorbell to say to me:

"Now, be nice."

. . .

Around Christmas of 1950, I received something of an unexpected present. I was still having to change bandages on my injured left index finger, even though it was now six months after the accident. As I unwrapped the bandage one day, I noticed a sort of "U" forming on the smashed end of the finger. In the weeks to come, a fingernail began to grow back again.

• • •

The war in Korea was becoming more intense on the battlefront and in the nation's consciousness, and was now a cloud on my personal horizon, as a young man of draft age. From the moment the war began, I took a keen interest in its history and its unfolding. What I discovered was that, while the Soviets had set up a puppet government in North Korea, the United States had also set up a puppet government under Syngman Rhee in South Korea. I was appalled at this discrepancy between the ideal and the actual, which is how I judged, as a young radical—not according to what the limited alternatives might have been.

My initial opposition to the war was solely ideological. It appeared at first that it would not be a long war, so there seemed to be little likelihood that I would become personally involved. However, the entry of the Chinese Communist army turned this war into something whose end was nowhere in sight. Suddenly, it was personal. I wrote a little verse, which I recited to William, who was much more favorably disposed toward American involvement:

> When we fight with our backs against the sea,
> Die for MacArthur and Syngman Rhee.

William thought I was too radical on a lot of things, including my great bitterness about racial segregation in Washington. He thought that the racial situation was going to change, that some of it was already changing, that blacks were making "giant strides."

"If I hear 'giant strides' one more time in this town, I am going berserk," I said.

William was very good at rhetoric, but whenever he scored some point and looked pleased with himself, my response was:

"Great, William. Why don't we go drink to that—at a bar down-town?"

*   *   *

As the war in Korea raged on, and the Selective Service Board was tak-ing more and more of an interest in me, I decided that I wanted to re-turn to New York, to spend whatever days I had left as a civilian. In the Spring of 1951, I wrote to Ed Gally to ask if there was a job available for me. He said that there was, so I headed back.

I roomed in various places until I found a very nice place on a quiet street, where I rented two rooms—one a bedroom and the other a sort of living room-den. It was on the ground floor of a building on the corner of 152nd Street and Riverside Drive, at a time when it was still rare to find blacks living on Riverside Drive.

I made contact again with the family in New York. Nothing could restore things to where they had once been, but we achieved civility and I had the pleasure of taking Jimmy down to Central Park, to teach him how to ride a bicycle—something I had just learned myself only a few months earlier. One of my favorite pictures shows the two of us standing with our rented bicycles, Jimmy looking very proud.

By now, I was getting more and more interested in photography and could develop my own film. I was also buying more sophisticated cameras. The borrowed camera with which I first started taking pic-tures was a simple box camera. In Washington, I bought a folding camera called a Kodak Vigilant, second-hand and already obsolete, but with adjustable lens openings. For months, I admired another camera in a pawn shop window. It was an Ansco Speedex, which had not only adjustable lens openings but also adjustable focus and adjustable shut-ter speeds. It seemed like perfection, but it cost $25, and that was more than half my weekly take-home pay. Finally, during a George Wash-ington's Birthday sale—a big event in Washington—it was marked down to $17.50 and I bought it. As my interest in photography con-tinued to grow in New York, I eventually traded in the Speedex on a still better camera called a Voigtländer Bessa, my first brand-new cam-era. I wanted to take the best pictures I could of New York while I was still there as a civilian on borrowed time.

With my nephew Jimmy in 1951. I was 21 years old and he was ten.

I went back to night school, more for social life than from any expectation that the draft board would let me finish out the term. My expectations proved to be correct on both counts. When the inevitable notice arrived, ordering me to report to Selective Service for induction into the armed forces, a girl I had met at night school said that she would wait for me to return. I discouraged the whole idea.

"For one thing," I said, "I may not be coming back."

There were large numbers of people being killed in Korea. That was something I would have to face alone. But I had faced an awful lot alone by this time. It did seem a shame, though, that just as I had gotten my life together a little bit, it was all going to change in unforeseeable ways.

4

Halls of Montezuma

On October 30, 1951, I reported to the Selective Service Board in downtown Manhattan for induction into the armed forces. After various bureaucratic preliminaries, we draftees found ourselves in a large room where an Army sergeant was in charge. He had a professional military bearing, but also an ironic sense of humor.

"Gentlemen," he said to us, "this morning every fourth set of papers has been stamped 'USMC.' Now, let me explain what that means."

What it meant was that (1) one-fourth of those present would be drafted into the Marine Corps instead of the Army, that (2) instead of being assigned to nearby Fort Dix in New Jersey, they would be sent away down South to Parris Island, South Carolina, and that (3) instead of having weekend passes during basic training, they would spend two solid months in Marine Corps boot camp, without a let-up. This news seemed to put a damper on some of the more light-hearted chatter among the young draftees in the room.

The induction process got under way with the sergeant calling out names and handing out papers to each man as he came forward. The stream of inductees was starting to move pretty quickly when the sergeant paused with one man, put his hand on his shoulder and announced:

"Gentlemen, this is the first one this morning—USMC."

The fellow turned pale and seemed a little sick. Some of us found this hilarious, and burst out laughing. Then the process resumed, as more names were called and the lines started to move briskly. Eventually, the sergeant called out:

"Sowell."

I stood up and strode forward in a determined way, swinging my little canvas bag. It accidentally struck an empty folding chair and sent it clattering across the floor. The sergeant smiled.

"Oh, you're just the kind of man they are looking for," he said as he handed me the papers, "——USMC."

Those of us who were destined to be Marines were led off to another building some blocks away, where the Marine Corps recruiting office was located. After a few preliminaries, we were told that the officer in charge would come out and say a few words to us. After a while, a Marine Corps captain appeared, looked over the motley group of young civilians in front of him and said:

"You men will hate every minute on Parris Island—but you'll come out Marines."

Then he turned on his heel and walked away. There was a silence like I had never heard before.

• • •

After a long, tiring train ride down to South Carolina, followed by a bus ride after we got there, we finally arrived at the Parris Island Marine base in the middle of the night. We were told the rules of boot camp in no uncertain terms and at a high decibel level. Among these rules were that we were not to walk anywhere; we were to run if alone and march when in formation.

After these and other arbitrary edicts were barked out to us, we were sent scurrying off to get our cots, blankets, and other gear, with Drill Instructors yelling and cursing at us. We quickly picked up the unspoken lesson as well: Everything we did was wrong, and we should expect to be chewed out for it. Drill Instructors and officers alike were very frank about the purpose of Parris Island. It was not only to turn us into trained combat troops; it was also to see if we would crack under incessant pressure.

"If you are going to crack up, we want you to do it at Parris Island, not in combat," we were told more than once. In combat, you could get others killed.

Never in my life did race mean less than during those two months at Parris Island. The Drill Instructors saw their job as making everybody miserable, and they did so without regard to race, color, creed, or national origin. In terms of their objectives, their methods were a complete success. One of the guys in our platoon had once been in the Army, but he said the Army was never like this.

Some people say that the Marine Corps builds men. In reality, you had better be a man before you go in. Fortunately, I was in the best physical shape of my life when I went to Parris Island—and I needed all of it. Even so, there were times when I wondered if I would eventually join those who suddenly went berserk, or who just quietly crumpled to the ground while standing in formation. I have never seen so many grown men pass out in my life. I was told that the psychiatric ward at a nearby hospital was filled with Marine Corps recruits who cracked up at Parris Island.

There was no single thing that did it. Physical exhaustion, inadequate sleep, the pressure to learn innumerable new things from an abusive Drill Instructor all contributed. So did the uncertainty that prevailed from day to day and from moment to moment. There were schedules but we were not told what they were. We might be in our tents when a voice would suddenly bark: "548 outside!" and we knew that everyone in Platoon 548 was to come piling out of the tents as fast as humanly possible—which was still never fast enough to suit the Drill Instructor.

Once outside, we would fall into a formation, the D.I. (called that only out of earshot) would yell "Ten-HUT!" then "Right FACE!" and "Forward MARCH!" And we would be off—not knowing where, what, or why, or when we might be back. It might be a ten-minute march to a class on how to disassemble a rifle, or out to the parade grounds for a couple of hours of drilling under the hot sun, or perhaps a trek way out into the boondocks for the day.

What most got to me was inadequate sleep. Fortunately, I could fall asleep immediately whenever the opportunity presented itself—

such as in chapel, where we were marched right after bayonet practice. However, opportunities to sleep were few and far between, unless you made your own. No one was allowed to lie down on a cot during the day, not even when you had a respite in the tents. But I figured out how to deliberately tie the tent flaps incorrectly, so that a Drill Instructor who tried to enter would get momentarily ensnared. By putting an empty bucket by the entrance, I virtually guaranteed that he would kick it while trying to untangle himself, thereby making a loud noise to wake me up, so that I could be on my feet at attention when he finally got through. It was the beginning of a long battle of wits between me and the Marine Corps.

As an individual, I was never subjected to as harsh punishment or abuse as some others. Our platoon as a whole was also not quite as unmercifully driven as some other platoons. Many a night, for example, as I crawled into the sack exhausted, I could hear some of the other platoons still drilling out on the parade ground. Perhaps it was the luck of the draw on Drill Instructors, but it was probably also due to the fact that most of us in Platoon 548 were draftees from New York. The guys in Southern platoons were overwhelmingly volunteers and therefore, like fraternity initiates, more likely to take more abuse before complaining to higher authorities or writing to their Congressmen.

Still, we were not treated gently, by any means. One night, after lights out, the Drill Instructor heard some talking. He immediately yelled: "548 outside!" We came rushing out of the tents in our underwear into the cold December night, standing in formation in our bare feet. The Drill Instructor, warmly clad, walked back and forth slowly calling the roll. There were about 70 men in our platoon.

When he called "Sowell," I immediately shouted "Here, sir!" but he was not about to be hurried along.

"My, you answer quickly, Sowell," he said. "You're not usually that cooperative." And he proceeded to philosophize on this point while the wintry winds swirled around us.

When the Drill Instructor finally sent us back into the tents, there was the quietest quiet I had heard since that day in the Marine Corps recruiting office back in New York—which now seemed so long ago and far away.

• • •

One of the many uncertainties hanging over our heads was Elliot's Beach. We heard vaguely ominous things about it but had no real idea what it was all about.

One Sunday, when we had a little time to rest, someone started singing the Marine Hymn, "From the halls of Montezuma . . ." Suddenly the Drill Instructor was in our midst, livid.

"You haven't earned the right to sing that!" he yelled. "After we get to Elliot's Beach, you can sing it."

Weeks passed. Then one day we were told to pack a full field pack. We were moving out to Elliot's Beach.

By this time, my glasses had gotten broken, so I had to stop by the infirmary on the way to pick up a replacement pair. As I walked into the infirmary, I saw a young Marine recruit on crutches, a cast on his leg and bloody bandages on his head, hobbling down the hall. Two doctors walked by and one asked the other:

"What happened to him?"

"He just got back from Elliot's Beach."

"Oh, well then."

On that cheerful note, I rejoined my platoon heading for Elliot's Beach.

Actually, Elliot's Beach was not so bad, if you could do all the things they expected you to. It was a strenuous series of activities but I was in good shape and could have done more. On one run, carrying a full field pack, I deliberately moved up toward the front, until I was on the heels of the Drill Instructor, matching him step for step. The other D.I.s were hard, but this one was nasty, so I just wanted to show him that he wasn't really quite as tough as he thought he was. Jumping over ravines while weighted down with equipment was not all that hard but, if you didn't make it, I could see how you might end up looking like the fellow back at the infirmary.

One of the more interesting exercises at Elliot's Beach was the gas attack drill. We were all issued gas masks and told how to use them. Then we were told *not* to use them during the drill. We were herded into a huge Quonset hut, which was then sealed up and tear gas was released in our midst. Our orders were to march around inside the hut, singing the Marine Hymn through completely three times—without putting on our gas masks. We did it, with tears rolling down our cheeks and some coughing here and there, but we did it. Nobody in our platoon put on his gas mask. When the doors were finally opened and we poured out into the fresh air, you never saw a prouder bunch of guys.

. . .

One of our Drill Instructors, named Sergeant Lennon, had come back from the battlefields of Korea. He had been a Browning Automatic Rifle man and many B.A.R. men did not come back alive, because silencing automatic weapons on the battlefield was a big priority of the enemy. Sergeant Lennon was a quiet, decent, soft-spoken man. Not very large, he had an agility and a wiry strength that may be why he beat the odds and came back alive. On one rare occasion when he felt like talking about it, he mentioned how, in battle, he would fire his B.A.R. from behind some cover and then grab the weapon and scamper off to throw himself behind another rock or tree somewhere else. From his new position, he would often see an enemy mortar shell come in and blast the spot where he had just been. They were always trying to zero in on him, in a deadly game of cat and mouse.

Never talkative but sometimes good-humored, Sergeant Lennon would at other times sit alone in the mess hall staring off into the distance, his mind clearly far way from anything happening round him.

. . .

Somewhere along the way, we all took mental tests. When the results came back, one of the testers asked:

"Where are you guys from? New York or Pennsylvania?"

"New York," someone said.

"I thought so. You don't get this many high scores from Southern platoons."

Weeks went by before we understood the full significance of those tests. Our next assignment after Parris Island would depend on the results. Whether we would be sent off to various electronics, photographic or other schools, or into the combat still raging in Korea, would depend on our test scores. Somehow I learned that the Marine Corps was short of photographers, which made me glad that I had listed photography as my hobby on one of the forms. A buddy in the platoon, also from Harlem, was a camera bug too. He had an old pre-war film-pack camera with a Voigtländer lens (I never forget a lens). He had neglected to mention photography among his hobbies and I urged him to go back and add that. He was always "going to do it"— but he never did.

As our training period at Parris Island finally drew to an end, the orders came in for our next assignments. Sergeant Lennon gathered us around and began reading our destinations to us. To my great surprise, a majority of the men in our platoon were sent off to a wide variety of schools, scattered all around the country. Sergeant Lennon was astonished too.

"Who's going to fight the war?" he asked.

My orders were to report to the Navy's photography school at the Pensacola Naval Air Station in Florida. Among the few members of our platoon to be assigned infantry duty was my friend with the Voigtländer lens. He was sent to Korea—and came back with a steel plate in his head.

• • •

After a brief leave in New York and a few weeks' stay in a "casual company" of Marines in transit at Camp Lejeune, North Carolina, I joined a group of about 15 or 20 other Marines assigned to go on to Pensacola for the photography class to begin in February 1952. This group included three blacks.

In charge was a white Marine from New York named Como, a Private First Class like the rest of us, but authorized by a letter from a general to be in charge of taking us to Pensacola. For the first leg of the journey, we had our own railroad car to ourselves but, in Atlanta, we had to change trains and join the general passengers the rest of the way.

By the time we arrived in Atlanta, we were getting hungry, so Como decided that he would march us into a restaurant in the train station. This was the era of racial segregation in the South and I wondered if Como was aware of that.

"Are you sure you know what you're doing, Como?" I asked.

"I'm in charge here, Sowell," he said.

"Aye, aye, Como."

Turning to the other Marines, he said, "Follow me!" and proceeded to lead us into the restaurant. Customers already seated in the restaurant began popping up from their tables like toast popping out of a toaster. They looked like they didn't know what the devil was going on. Meanwhile, we just stood quietly in line. In a few moments, a contingent of police arrived.

An elderly policeman in charge of the detail said, "I'm sorry but I'm going to have to take you out of here," as he took hold of my arm. Como immediately grabbed my other arm and started pulling the other way.

"Let's not settle it that way," I said. They turned me loose.

"My orders are to keep all the troops together," Como told the policeman and began fishing around in his pocket for a copy of his orders.

"Please don't bring out that letter from the general," I told Como. This whole situation was farcical enough already.

Como brought out the letter anyway and tried to read it, but the policeman in charge remained adamant. However, the policeman was also clearly embarrassed at his task and offered to find an eating place for the three black Marines, though none of us had any stomach for food at this point. We were all too disgusted and angry.

Como had apparently learned nothing from all this, however. When time came to board the train for Pensacola, I suggested that he give me the three tickets for the black Marines, since we would have to ride in a separate car. Como would not hear of it. Putting himself at the front of the line, he again said "Follow me!" and went up the steps into the train. As I started up the same steps, a conductor stepped in front of me.

"You can't go in there," he said.

"Well, the man with my ticket is already on the train," I said, "so I don't know what I am supposed to do."

"Go on into the other car," he said, "and I will take care of the tickets."

We did so and the train proceeded on to Pensacola.

• • •

The Marine barracks at the Pensacola Naval Air Station was an impressive structure. The men permanently stationed there were guards at the gate, at the brig, and at other security posts. They had one wing of the barracks and the photography students had the other. We were the first of a large contingent of Marines from around the country to go through the photography course. Eventually, there were about two hundred Marines at the school at the same time, in various stages of the course, which lasted about three months. However, we were still substantially outnumbered by the sailors taking the same course.

A real camaraderie developed among the students in the Marine Barracks. We were all about the same age, mostly draftees fresh out of boot camp, and virtually all had the same rank—Private First Class. But what we most had in common was a love of photography. Our wing of the barracks was always abuzz with talk of cameras, lenses, films, and developers.

Sometimes someone would find the constant talk on one subject too much and cry out: "Can't you guys talk about anything but photography?" But, usually within the hour, he was talking about photography himself.

My three months at the naval air station were my happiest times in the service. It had a wonderful subtropical climate, palm trees and an attractive lay-out, including a lovely beach. The photography school and its grounds were like an idyllic college campus. There was something almost unreal about it, especially in the context of the times. One brief glimpse of the reality outside came home one day when I noticed a Marine I hadn't seen before—not a photography student—hobbling down a corridor in the Marine barracks, with various signs of multiple injuries.

"What happened to him?" I asked another Marine.

"The war, Sowell—the war in Korea."

I was in photography school at the Pensacola Naval
Air Station when this picture was taken.

• • •

Although I did not choose to be in the military—and certainly not the
Marine Corps—and was in fact looking forward to my discharge day
as a day of deliverance, nevertheless my previous struggles to make a
living in civilian life made me assess the military in terms of what benefits I could take with me from it back into the civilian world. Veterans' benefits, such as the G.I. Bill for college, were obvious examples.
But now that I was in photography school, I saw photography as a skill
that could help me earn a better living in civilian life. With this and
other things throughout my stay in the Marine Corps, any conflict between short-run military duties and longer-run civilian concerns were
resolved in favor of my future as a civilian. For example, when a
muster was called out while I had film to process or print, my usual
practice was to stay in the darkroom and let myself be marked absent

at roll call. I did not realize how often this had happened until one day, when I was present in the ranks as the sergeant in charge was calling the roll:

"Sowell."

"Here!"

"Where?"

I raised my hand.

"So nice to have you with us," he said acidly.

Not all my problems with military rules were due to my putting civilian concerns ahead of them. In general, I tended to take the rules much more casually than the Marine Corps did. It was a tradition at the photography school that sailors received demerits but that Marines never did anything to get them. Other Marines maintained that tradition. If there were 200 Marines in the photography school, 199 of them had no demerits. I had ten.

• • •

While most of my frictions and skirmishes with "the system" were minor, one serious episode taught me some lessons of lasting value about human beings. Among the sergeants stationed permanently at the Marine barracks, the two we came in contact with most represented opposite ends of a spectrum. Sergeant Gordon was a genial, wise-cracking guy who took a somewhat relaxed view of life. On the other hand, Sergeant Pachucki was a disciplinarian who spoke in a cutting and ominously quiet way. Pachucki wore a blond crew-cut, had an athletic build, a military carriage, and wore uniforms that were always impeccable and sharply creased. He was the very picture of a Marine sergeant, as he might appear on a recruiting poster. Not very tall, Pachucki was referred to—always out of earshot—as "little Caesar." It was said that the colonel in charge of the Marine barracks respected and relied on Pachucki, and that was easy to believe, but those of us attending the photography school all preferred Sergeant Gordon, hands down.

One day I received a notice that a package had arrived for me at the Railway Express Agency in the city of Pensacola. It was a second-hand camera I had ordered by mail. Since I was at school during the hours when the Railway Express Agency was open, I had no choice but to seek permission to go into town. At school, I approached the Chief Petty Officer in charge of such things. He was completely uninterested in my explanation of the situation and said:

"Don't bother me, Sowell. Here's the sign-out sheet if you want to go somewhere."

"But Chief, where it asks for my destination, do I put down Pensacola or the Marine barracks?"

"Well, which one are you going to?"

"Both. I'm going to the Marine barracks first, to change from my dungarees into a dress uniform, so that I can go into town."

"So you're going to the Marine barracks from here?"

"Right."

"Then put down Marine barracks."

I signed out as instructed, changed clothes at the Marine barracks, and went into Pensacola to get my camera. Later that afternoon at the school, roll call was read and I was marked absent. Someone checked the sign-out sheet, saw that I was supposed to be at the Marine barracks, and phoned over there—only to be told that I wasn't there either. When I returned, I found that I was being charged with being A.W.O.L. (absent without leave) and that a summary court-martial was being scheduled for me. This would be a court-martial with the commanding officer serving as the court.

I went back to the Chief Petty Officer with whom I had signed out, but he said that he could remember no such conversation as I described, and that the court-martial would go forward as scheduled. When I could find no one else who was in the room who could remember anything either, I began to suspect that this might not all be an honest mistake, even if it started out that way. To say that I was not universally popular with the non-commissioned officers would be to understate the situation considerably. I was precisely the kind of wiseguy draftee they didn't like—and the wrong color on top of that. Someone may have decided that this was the time to make an example of me.

The way the court-martial was set up reinforced my suspicions. Ordinarily, a summary court-martial would have been held at the photography school, with the officer in charge of the school conducting the proceedings. That was not done. Commander Simonsen, who was the commanding officer at the school, was a kindly old gentleman who took a sort of indulgent father's attitude toward his young students. The charges against me were taken instead to the colonel in charge of the Marine barracks, a much tougher customer.

I decided that my best bet was to turn to Sergeant Gordon. He was in the room when I explained what I was doing to the Chief. Surely he must have heard me say *something*. When I took him aside to explain the situation and ask if he couldn't remember anything that I had said, Sergeant Gordon did not flatly deny having heard anything, but instead said:

"You're just going to have to take your punishment like a man."

I was thunderstruck by his response. In other words, Sergeant Gordon was not going to stick his neck out by crossing the Chief Petty Officer. Pensacola was a pretty nice place to be stationed while other Marines were being slaughtered on the frozen battlefields of Korea, and he wasn't about to jeopardize that. This taught me something painful but valuable, not only about Sergeant Gordon, but also about other people who are everybody's friend—which usually means that they are nobody's friend.

The denouement was as unexpected as it was improbable. It so happened that Sergeant Pachucki, back at the Marine barracks, was engaged in a telephone conversation with someone in that room at the photography school at the time when I was explaining to the Chief Petty Officer why I wanted to sign out. Unasked, Pachucki came forward. When the time for my court-martial arrived, Sergeant Pachucki went in to see the colonel, leaving me outside in the anteroom. A few minutes later, he came back out and said to me:

"Go on back to your duties, Sowell."

There was no court-martial.

Later, Pachucki put in an appearance at the photography school— at the very room where the disputed conversation took place. Looking coldly around the room, he said:

"I could hear what Sowell said over the telephone. It's strange that no one in this room could hear him."

After a moment of silence, he turned on his heel and walked away.

* * *

As we neared our graduation time, those of us in my class began to speculate as to where we were likely to be sent next. The sailors were traditionally given their choices of the available posts, in the order of their class standing at graduation, but the Marines had no such tradition. However, this year at the eleventh hour the Marine Corps authorities decided that they would use that system as well.

Although there were about two hundred Marines at the photography school, they were spread out over different phases of the program, and only about twenty of us were graduating at the same time. When we gathered to select our future assignments, we discovered that only four of the possibilities were clearly within the United States—all at Camp Lejeune, North Carolina. Most of the other assignments were in Korea, and three were mysteriously labeled "Marines Pacific." This meant that the commanding officer of the Marines in the Pacific area would assign these Marines wherever he needed photographers at the moment. We all had visions of being stationed up in the Aleutian islands or in some other equally God-forsaken place.

The four slots at Camp Lejeune seemed like the most desirable of a bad lot—and I was fifth in my class. However, the top man in the class volunteered for Korea. The next four of us, all draftees, took Camp Lejeune. The bottom three guys in the class were left with "Marines Pacific." This assignment turned out to be living in a hotel in San Francisco.

* * *

The four of us who reported for duty at the Camp Lejeune photo lab were the first wave of the graduates from the Pensacola photography school to reach that facility. The other photographers there had acquired their knowledge in various ways, including tutelage from Captain Galvin, the commanding officer in charge. The captain himself had a very uneven knowledge of photography, with both gaps and misinformation alternating with sound knowledge, so he may have been self-taught as well.

While other photographers might debate the relative merits of incident-light exposure meters versus reflected-light exposure meters, Captain Galvin swore by a third variety, called an extinction-type meter. That kind of meter was so unreliable that it was itself already on the road to extinction. Yet some of the younger fellows in the lab were shocked when some of us from Pensacola told them that they would be better off guessing at the exposure than they would be using an extinction-type meter. They really looked up to the captain, and it is hard to believe that he did not begin to sense an erosion of some of that respect after the smart new kids arrived from Pensacola.

By and large, we were better photographers than the others in the lab, though much worse as Marines. Irreverent young draftees, for whom this was just an unwelcome interlude in our lives, we made no great effort to fit in, hung out after hours with one another, and became known—not always affectionately—as "the Pensacola gang." One of the expressions we had picked up at Pensacola was "Don't sweat it, ace." We used it so much that we ran it into the ground, driving others up the wall.

Our assignments varied across a wide range. We took pictures of officers pinning medals on Marines, human interest pictures for the camp newspapers, pictures of troops on maneuver, and pictures associated with investigations by the Criminal Investigation Division, including photos of auto accidents and of the resulting corpses in the morgue.

We took turns being Duty Photographer, which involved staying overnight in the lab, to handle any emergency photographic work that might come up. If it was more than the Duty Photographer could handle by himself, he could get the rest of us roused out of our beds in the barracks to come over to the lab and help him. One night, around midnight, I was roused from a sound sleep to go over to the lab to print fifteen 8 X 10 enlargements of each corpse from an auto accident which had just been photographed by the Duty Photographer.

There were literally hundreds of auto accidents as young Marines went far away from this God-forsaken part of North Carolina on weekend passes and sped back to try to avoid being late and marked A.W.O.L. Remarkably, however, no one ever died in an auto accident that I photographed. One car was upside-down at the bottom of a hill, with all the paint burned off the body and all the tires burned off the wheels, but none of the people packed into it was killed. I thought my good-luck streak was going to end when I heard that we were going to an accident where a convertible had flipped upside down at high speed. But, when we arrived, the lone occupant was walking around at the scene, with nothing more than a scratch to show for it. Apparently he had been going so fast that the car flipped completely over in the air, landing right side up. Covering these auto accidents did, however, have the effect of renewing my interest in flying, leading me to bum rides on military aircraft heading north when I went on leave.

The Duty Photographer, whatever his rank, was officially in charge of the photo lab after hours, which could include a whole weekend. One weekend, when I was on duty there, some of the fellows came over to hang out and shoot the breeze. One of these guys was a certain Sergeant Grover, who sat around smoking and flicking his cigarette ashes on the floor.

"Stop dropping cigarette ashes on the floor, Grover," I said. "I'm going to have to sweep this place out."

When Grover ignored me and continued to drop cigarette ashes on the floor, I finally said, "That's it, Grover. Out!"

"What are you talking about?" he said.

"Get out of the lab, Sergeant Grover—and that's an order."

"You damn fool," he said. "You may be Duty Photographer today but tomorrow you'll be plain old Pfc. Sowell."

"Out!" I said—and he left.

Some people were surprised that I dared to give Sergeant Grover a hard time, on this and other occasions, especially since he was a nasty character to deal with. Unfortunately for him, I knew that he was going to give me as hard a time as he could, regardless of what I did. That meant that it didn't really cost me anything to give him as hard a time as I could. Though I didn't realize it at the time, I was already thinking like an economist. Giving Sergeant Grover a hard time was, in effect, a free good and at a zero price my demand for it was considerable.

One day Sergeant Grover told me to mix up a fresh batch of developer for our film, to which I responded with the inevitable, "Don't sweat it, ace." But I had still not gotten to it that afternoon, when I started packing up my gear to go off and take a picture of a colonel.

"Where's that developer I told you to make?" Sergeant Grover asked.

"Haven't gotten to it," I said. "I've been tied up with other things."

"Well, get to it right now," he said.

"Can't do it," I said. "I've got to go take a picture of the colonel at 4:30."

"I think you have time enough to do both," Grover said.

"It's good to know what public opinion is," I said. "But unless you are prepared to give me a direct order, I am going over to take pictures of the colonel. Now, if you do give me a direct order and I arrive late, and the colonel wants to know why I kept him waiting, naturally I will have to tell him that I had a direct order from Sergeant Grover to mix some developer first."

Grover did not give me a direct order.

Little episodes like this did nothing to add to my popularity or to the popularity of the Pensacola gang. However, one day as I was sacked out in the darkroom, someone woke me up to tell me to report to Captain Galvin. With a wry smile, the captain told me that some official papers had just come through, saying that I was now promoted to corporal. Although I received this promotion in the minimum time possible, it was to be my last promotion.

No one who knew me in the Marine Corps ever questioned why I never made sergeant. But quite a few expressed amazement that I was not busted back to private.

• • •

One of my on-going assignments was to follow a group of Marine reservists taking their summer training at Camp Lejeune. I accompanied a sergeant from the public information office who was writing up the story of their summer exercises. This assignment stretched out over several days, beginning when they first arrived at their encampment, carrying their duffle bags. We followed them out into the field where they fired their weapons and engaged in maneuvers. Some of my best pictures came out of this assignment, so I was anxious to find out when and where they would be publshed.

"None of them are being published," the public information office sergeant said, in response to my question.

"Why?" I asked. "They are some of my best pictures."

"They are good pictures," he said. "But they do not convey the image that the public information office wants conveyed."

"What's wrong with them?" I asked.

"Well, take that picture of the reservists walking across the little wooden bridge carrying their duffle bags."

"Yeah. What's wrong with it?"

"The men in that picture are perspiring. You can see the damp spots on their uniforms."

"Well, if you carry a duffle bag on a 90-degree day, you are going to sweat."

"Marines do not sweat in public information office photographs."

"Okay, what was wrong with the picture of the reservists picking up shell casings after they had finished firing? That was one of my favorites."

"Marines do not perform menial chores like that, in our public relations image."

"But all these photos showed a very true picture of the reservists' summer here."

"We're not here to tell the truth, Sowell," he said impatiently. "We are here to perpetuate the big lie. Now, the sooner you understand that, the better it will be for all of us."

• • •

When the guard company fell seriously below strength, a call went out for other units to contribute men to bring the guard company up to strength. The photo lab was no exception and one of the men they contributed was me.

Although the guard company was part of the base personnel—as distinguished from the fighting unit stationed at the base, the Second Marine division—its discipline was more like that of a fighting unit, rather than having the laxity commonly found among the units whose tasks and skills were remote from combat. Moreover, as a corporal in the photo lab, my duties were no different from what they were as a Pfc., but in the guard company I was sometimes assigned responsibilities for others as corporal of the guard. It was not a job I relished but it was a job I did. Apparently I did it well enough to be less than universally popular. One day, someone said to me:

"All corporals of the guard wear a .45, Sowell, but you're the only one who really needs it."

As elsewhere throughout my life, I made enough enemies to get me in trouble and enough friends to get me out. Luck at crucial times also helped.

* * *

With experience, I was developing a sense of when you "go by the book" and when you don't. One day, when I was corporal of the guard, I received a phone call at the office from a guard on duty out in the boondocks. He had just discovered that two of the bullets he was supposed to have were missing.

This was serious business because the Marine Corps wants to know when and why people have been shooting, so there was likely to be a big stink whenever a guard could not account for all the ammunition he was issued. Unfortunately, the guard who discovered the shortage might not be the one who did the shooting, but he could end up being the one who had to do the explaining, if he didn't report the ammunition missing when he took over the post at the changing of the guard. The poor guy who was calling was already into his tour of duty when he discovered two rounds of ammunition missing. Chances are it was one of the guards on earlier shifts who did the unauthorized firing. Southern boys all by themselves out in the boondocks sometimes could not resist taking a shot at a racoon or a 'possum.

Theoretically, I was supposed to write up the incident in the official records, which would have led to an official investigation and God knows what else. Instead, I told the guard to leave it to me, and that I would be out there to see him. Then I called the truck driver who took guards out to their duty stations.

"We are going to take one of those trips that never happened," I told him.

"Gotcha," he said.

We drove several miles out to where the guard was on duty. He was still agitated when we arrived.

"What am I going to do, Sowell?" he asked. "What am I going to do?"

"You're going to take these bullets and put them into your ammunition pouch—and shut the hell up," I said, handing him two rounds of ammunition. It was a deal he was more than ready to accept.

With that, I got back on the truck and returned to the guard shack, from which I had pilfered the bullets. No doubt the shortage would turn up at the annual inventory, but there would be no one who could be held responsible, given how many corporals and sergeants of the guard had been in charge there since the last inventory.

A more serious instance of going against the book occurred when I was myself on guard duty out at the ammunition dump, well out in the boondocks. It was around midnight when I heard the soft but unmistakable sound of someone trying to sneak up on me from behind a building. No one had any legitimate business out there and the next nearest guard was at least a mile away, so whatever was going to happen would already have happened by the time he could get there.

There are all sorts of rules about performing guard duty—and especially about the use of firearms. I had a carbine but it had to be carried unloaded, with the safety locked, and the ammunition clip not in the weapon. There were a set of stages you were supposed to go through before you were ready to fire. Certain things would justify putting the clip into the carbine, but then you were supposed to wait for certain other things before successively unlocking the safety, putting a bullet into the chamber and, finally, putting your finger on the trigger. Here too, whatever was going to happen would already have happened before I could go through all this rigmarole.

I remained very quiet and still, so that whoever was sneaking up behind that building would have no clue as to where I was. But I quickly put the clip into the carbine, unlocked the safety, put a bullet in the chamber and put my finger on the trigger. I steadied the butt of the carbine under one arm while I held my flashlight in the other, though the flashlight was not on.

As a shadowy figure turned the corner of the building, I flicked on the flashlight, shining it right in his eyes, and yelled:

"Halt!"

He threw his hands up in front of his face to shield his eyes from the flashlight.

"It's only me, Sowell!" he cried. "It's only me!"

It was the sergeant of the guard. He obviously had been trying to sneak up on me to catch me asleep on my post—which would have been a court-martial offense.

* * *

From time to time we had little impromptu boxing matches of a few rounds on the grass outside the barracks. Although we had no ring, we did have one of the guys serve as a referee.

The first time I took part in one of these bouts, I quickly discovered that I was in with a much classier boxer. In order to neutralize his skill, I suddenly threw a wild right hand at his jaw. Surprised, he sprang back, tripped and fell heavily to the ground. He lay there with the wind knocked out of him while the referee counted him out.

"Wait a minute," I said. "I didn't touch him"—but nobody believed me. It happened so fast that it was like those punches in the movies that barely miss, but look so real. The guy himself thought I had hit him, though I might have grazed him at most. All he knew was that he suddenly saw a punch coming, and the next thing he knew he was lying on the ground, looking up at the sky, while the referee counted ten.

After this quick "knockout," some of the guys in the barracks called me "One-punch Sowell." It was a label that was to come back to haunt me the next time I boxed.

My next opponent was a buddy of mine named Douglas, but we exchanged such heavy punches in the first round that the referee asked us between rounds if this was a grudge match. However, the first round was the only round in which I was really in it. The next couple of rounds—it was only a three-round fight—were all Douglas. At the end of the second round, the referee said he thought he should stop the fight but I argued him out of it. The beating I took in the third round only illustrated the old saying: "A referee should look at a fighter, not listen to him." In the excitement of the match, with the adrenalin flowing, I wasn't in nearly as much pain as I was for the next few hours after the fight.

Although it was clear that Douglas won the fight, the referee also congratulated me.

"I have never seen anybody take the kind of punishment you just took and still stay on his feet."

I decided that I could do without compliments like that—and never put on boxing gloves again.

Douglas said afterwards that the reason he dared not let up on me was fear of that "one punch" that could turn the fight around at any time. Sometimes it doesn't pay to have too big a reputation.

• • •

When time came for me to have a new identification photo taken, of course I had to go back to the photo lab where I had worked. As I walked in the door, the first thing that struck me was a big, framed picture dominating the foyer. It was a picture that I had taken. Seeing it there was a very bittersweet experience—but more bitter than sweet.

This was only one of the things driving me to seek a way of getting transferred out of the guard company. I missed the photography and the camaraderie of the old Pensacola gang, though more and more photographers from Pensacola were being transferred to the guard company. Captain Galvin had made some noises about how he would try to get us back when he could, but it strained my imagination to think of the captain knocking himself out to get me back. This was going to have to be a self-help operation.

Part of the folklore of the guard company was that nobody could get himself transferred out. Maybe now and then the guard company might decide that they didn't need you and get rid of you, but there was no such thing as your seeking and getting a transfer. Because the discipline and the work of the guard company were both so much more demanding than the duties of the clerks, photographers, and others who made up the base personnel, obviously no one from these softer jobs would stay in the guard company if they could get themselves transferred out.

Even in the best of times, guard duty was exhausting. If you had a given shift on a given day—say, 12 to 4—that meant that you stood that duty twice that day, from noon to 4 PM and from midnight to 4 AM. Trying to get some sleep in between, in a barracks full of young Marines, was often a challenge. To minimize the damage, there was a day off in between standing guard duty. The company was divided into two sections, called port and starboard. Port might stand duty on Monday, Wednesday, and Friday, while starboard stood duty on Tuesday, Thursday, and Saturday. Ordinarily, there was a chance to recuperate—and you needed to.

My one talking point for a transfer was that I was highly trained, at considerable taxpayer expense, in a skill which I was not practicing. This would cut no ice at all in the guard company, where a formal application for transfer should start, but it might carry some weight with someone higher up, if it ever got there. I knew that there was such a thing as going through channels, but I also knew that there was such a thing as getting results. It would be hopeless to expect the people who ran the guard company even to give me straight answers as to how to go about it. I had to find some other source of information who would tell me how to set things up, so that my application did not gather dust on someone's desk.

One day I decided to go over to the base headquarters to see if anyone there could give me any clues as to how I should proceed. As I was explaining the situation to a secretary, her boss overheard me and asked me to come into his office. It turned out that he was a lieutenant colonel on the staff of the commanding general. Already, though inadvertently, I had committed the military sin of jumping the chain of command and going way over the head of my commanding officer at the guard company, a second lieutenant. I knew that this would not play well back home, but the die was already cast.

The colonel agreed that it made no sense for the taxpayers to have paid so much to train me in a skill that I was no longer using. Moreover, he knew that the Marine Corps Supply Depot on the base was in need of someone who knew photography, to work in its photographic supply unit. It sounded great to me and he said he would have the orders issued to transfer me there.

This episode not only did not play well back at the guard company. It had all sorts of people up in arms, including Captain Galvin, who summoned me to his office at the photo lab. When I walked in, I could see that he was livid.

"I have been working quietly behind the scenes to try to get the photographers back from the guard company," he said, "and now this just throws a monkey wrench into everything! You've completely violated the military chain of command by going over your commanding officer's head, and over my head. You keep this up, Sowell, and one of these days *you are going to end up getting court-martialed!*"

By this time, however, I regarded a court-martial as one of the normal hazards of the business. Moreover, I knew that he wouldn't be threatening me with it if he could actually do it.

The old hands, however, were not without their bag of tricks to get in their retaliation. Although the orders were issued as taking effect immediately upon being presented to me, so as to speed up the transfer, the people at the guard company took this to mean that I could not transfer until they chose to hand the orders to me—and they didn't even tell me when they arrived.

Labor Day weekend was coming up. In order to let some of the guards have a three-day weekend, the usual schedule alternating between port and starboard section was changed. The port section would get the entire weekend off and starboard would have guard duty for three consecutive days (and the corresponding night shifts). In order to enable them to withstand the extra fatigue, guards received booster shots from the medics. The plan then called for the port section, after it returned from the holidays, to be on guard duty for three consecutive days (and corresponding night shifts), so that starboard could catch up on its rest and recuperate.

I was on port, which was scheduled to have the Labor Day weekend off. But the guard company transferred me to starboard. Then, when port came back from leave and was preparing to go on its three-day guard duty, I was transferred back to port. In other words, I was scheduled for six consecutive days and nights of guard duty.

When I went to see the First Sergeant to protest, there were other people ahead of me, to see him about other things. As I waited, a young Pfc. in the office picked up some papers lying on a shelf and walked over to me with them.

"Are these yours, Sowell?" he asked innocently.

"Yes, they are," I said.

They were my orders—and having them in my hands was like being touched by a magic wand. The guard company's plans for me, including the additional three days on duty, were now null and void.

By this time, the First Sergeant was free.

"What do *you* want, Sowell?" he asked belligerently.

"Nothing at all, Sergeant," I said genially. "I have to go pack."

The young Pfc. who pretended to make a mistake when he asked me about my orders was nevertheless taking a chance. Later, he told me that I had once helped him with his photography when he came to the photo lab some time after I did. I had forgotten all about it, but fortunately he had not.

●　●　●

The Marine Corps Supply Depot was my kind of place—lax discipline and regular hours. The photographic supply unit was especially lax. When I arrived, there was only one man there, a good-natured sergeant named Joe Voiselle. He did not even pretend to know anything about photography and welcomed me as someone who would make his job easier.

Shortly after I arrived, we were joined by a young Pfc. named Albert Greuner, recently graduated from the photography school at Pensacola. His orders out of Pensacola were to report to the base photo lab at Camp Lejeune. But when he arrived at Lejeune, he discovered that his orders had been changed. Captain Galvin had apparently had him transferred, sight unseen. By now, the captain had cleaned out all the remaining photographers from Pensacola and could hardly be expected to welcome another one.

The photographic supply unit was located in a fenced-off back corner of a huge warehouse. Because of all the costly equipment stored there—cameras, enlargers, lenses, and the like—we had to be kept isolated to prevent theft. This in turn gave us a certain amount of privacy. I could bring magazines and books to read and we even re-arranged the crates stored there so that we could play stickball.

This was the central supply point for all the photographic labora-tories on the base. These included not only the base photo lab, where I had been, but also the photo lab for the Second Marine Division and, I believe, another smaller lab elsewhere on the base. In addition to storing photographic hardware, we stored great quantities of film and enlarging paper—in a huge refrigerator, large enough to walk around in—as well as chemicals for processing film and prints. When orders for equipment and supplies came to us from the photo labs, via the front office, our job was to gather the stuff together physically and—more important—to handle the paperwork that this entailed. When we had it ready, the people from the labs would come over in their own trucks, which we would help them load.

My arrival on the scene made all this go faster and more accurately than before, simply because I was already familiar with photographic equipment and supplies, and did not have to try to figure out what everything was from catalog numbers and descriptions in manuals. There were little words of appreciation for my work from the front office and, when efficiency ratings came out, I was given an unusually high one for someone of such low rank. This rating, however, caused consternation among the guys in the rest of the warehouse, who knew that those of us in the photographic supply unit were not working ourselves to death, least of all me. One fellow said:

"What's he efficient at? I've never seen him doing anything."

What the people in the front office saw was only the bottom line—the work going faster and with fewer mistakes and headaches than in the past—and that was ultimately what mattered.

. . .

While I had been the only black in the photo lab, and was probably the only black in the warehouse, there were enough black Marines in the barracks for me to have regular games of bid whist, a card game once widely popular in times past, but by then played almost exclusively by working-class blacks.

We had an interesting little group of card players, the most colorful of whom was an older man whom we called "Sergeant Major," though in fact he was a buck private. Sergeant Major had once actually held that rank, but he was a man who marched to his own drummer, so much so that he had been put in the brig, as well as having been busted to private. Like a number of people among the base personnel, he had a specialized skill—something to do with producing or maintaining artillery pieces—and was the only person of such low rank doing such work. However, he never seemed bitter about having fallen from grace, nor particularly interested in regaining his old rank. Sergeant Major was just waiting to finish this tour of duty in the Marine Corps, so that he could leave and go join the 82nd Airborne Division. He mentioned that his commanding officer had commented on his good work and hinted that a promotion might be in store.

"Oh, that's all right, sir," Sergeant Major told him.

Sergeant Major even spoke cheerfully, indeed nostalgically, of the time he had spent in the brig. He also had his own wild way of playing bid whist—which quite a few times astonished the rest of us when it worked. While he liked to clown around, he was not just a clown, however.

One evening as we were playing cards, the Officer of the Day came through the barracks and was not at all happy at the noise he heard. The Duty N.C.O. was with him, obviously uncomfortable at the officer's displeasure, and said:

"These are the men who were making the noise."

"That's a lie," I said.

The Duty N.C.O. spun around and looked at us.

"Who called me a liar?" he demanded.

Sergeant Major was instantly on his feet, yelling loud enough to drown me out:

"I say you're a God-damned liar!"

"That's enough of that!" the Officer of the Day said, and led the Duty N.C.O. away.

"What was all that about, Sergeant Major?" one of the other card players asked when they were gone.

"Sowell's got two stripes to lose," he said matter-of-factly, as he picked up his cards. "I don't have anything to lose."

• • •

Every Marine, regardless of his occupation, is required to go to a rifle range every year to shoot and have his score recorded. This was taken seriously enough to set aside two weeks away from regular duties. The first week was to be spent engaging in various "dry run" exercises with an unloaded rifle, to get your body in shape for properly assuming the various prescribed positions for firing. These were called "snapping in" exercises and they ranged from boring to painful, depending on what kind of condition you were in. These exercises were held at the Supply Depot and the following week the shooters were sent off to the Rifle Range Detachment, located about 30 miles away by road, where the second week was spent shooting in the mornings and continuing the exercises in the afternoon.

I liked target shooting and the thought of a week's change of scene was all right, but I hated to think of all those dreary hours of rifle exercises. By this time, however, I had developed a sense of how the Marine Corps operated—and especially what the weaknesses in those operations were. I was handed my liberty card in my warehouse unit and told to report to a sergeant from another unit who would be in charge of all of the enlisted men from the Supply Depot who were going to be shooting in the next couple of weeks. My orders were to turn my liberty card over to him, which would give him control of our comings and goings over the next two weeks.

The logical thing for the Marine Corps to do would be to give the sergeant a list of all the men who were to report to him, but somehow I didn't think that they would do it that way. My hunch was that he would learn who was under his command only when we came to him to turn in our liberty cards. Obviously, if I never went to him to turn in my liberty card, I would never be on his list. Not being on the list, I would never be absent when roll call was taken. The one drawback to this theory was that illegal possession of your own liberty card was a court-martial offense. On the other hand, one cannot be faint-hearted.

The entire week when the other shooters were out doing their rifle exercises, I was off reading a new novel—*From Here to Eternity*—about military life. There was also time to spend in other parts of the base, photographing the scenery, or in the library, improving my mind. The second week, we moved out to the rifle range area and stayed in the barracks there.

After shooting in the morning, we would go to chow in the mess hall. I was always among the last to enter the mess hall and lingered over my dessert while the others went back to the barracks to prepare to go off to do their afternoon exercises. By the time I returned to the barracks, they were empty. That was when I changed into a dress uniform and caught a bus, which was conveniently scheduled so that it arrived just about the time when I finished dressing.

Usually I spent the afternoons in the main part of the base, 30 miles away, though I could have gone into town with my liberty card. Usually I caught another bus back, to arrive in time for evening chow.

As for the shooting, I was doing as well as those who were going through hours of daily rifle exercises—and better than I had done the previous year at Parris Island, when I had to go through those exercises myself. On the last day, when our scores were recorded on our permanent records, I had my best score. One reason was a special incentive used that day.

As we moved back from one distance to another on the rifle range—from the 200-yard line to the 300-yard line, for example, each rifle coach's lowest shooter had to carry the box of ammunition to the next position. In the event of a tie, the shooter with the lowest rank carried the ammunition box. I happen to have been paired with a master sergeant, which meant that I had to outshoot him at each distance to avoid lugging the ammunition box. As in other cases, incentives worked wonders.

I did my best shooting ever, good enough to win a sharpshooter's medal, missing "expert" by one point. It was a fitting climax to a successful two weeks.

• • •

Back at the Marine Corps Supply Depot, one feature of our half-military and half-civilian existence was the weekly rifle inspection, which was conducted by having us leave our rifles on our bunks when we headed off to work, so that the Officer of the Day could inspect them while we were away. This of course is not how it was done in a real combat unit, where rifle inspections are conducted with the troops in military formation and the officer in charge directly facing each man being inspected. However, the standards of the rifle inspection, even in our absence, were high—which is to say that a speck of dust in the barrel could get you marked down and punished for a "dirty" rifle.

It usually took me about two hours to clean a rifle to Marine Corps standards. The rifle had to be disassembled and all the parts cleaned with the right chemicals, which then had to be removed and the barrel polished by drawing special patches of cloth through them. It was a real pain.

One day I estimated what the probabilities were that a given rifle would be looked at during a given inspection, since the Officer of the Day did not have time to inspect every rifle in every barracks. Then there was the probability that an inspected rifle would be found unacceptable, even if it had been cleaned conscientiously. Finally, one had to weigh the punishment—an hour of mowing the lawn around the barracks. Putting it all together, my conclusion was that it did not make any sense to try to clean the rifle at all. Moreover, I announced this conclusion to my colleagues in the barracks.

Most of the guys were appalled at this reasoning, either for its attitude or its impracticality. However, I insisted that it was practical, and that I would demonstrate it by practicing it. From then on, when the other Marines were busy working on their rifles the night before inspection, I would be reading quietly on my bunk or else would go out to take in a movie. The next morning, I would leave my rifle on the bunk, without even a pretense of having cleaned it.

Week after week went by without any official comment on my rifle, which obviously had not been among those inspected. The guys who had been reprimanded or punished because their rifles were not clean enough were especially resentful.

"Oh, you're really going to get it one of these days, Sowell," they kept saying.

But that had a more and more hollow ring as the weeks turned into months. After a very long run of luck, however, I found a note on my bunk from the Officer of the Day. I read it to the guys in the barracks:

> Your rifle failed inspection, but I noticed that it still had grease from the rifle range on it, so obviously you must have gotten back here just before inspection. You'll get a warning this time.

• • •

One of the front office people we dealt with at the photographic supply unit was a soft-spoken and gentlemanly master sergeant named Strong. Under stress, Sergeant Strong tended to become very nervous and I learned from others that he was one of the survivors of the infamous Bataan "death march" in World War II. I made it a point not to give him any trouble, and occasionally I could help him with trouble that grew out of his unfamiliarity with photographic equipment and supplies.

A very different master sergeant was a Sergeant Wilson, who regularly came over from the Second Marine Division's photo lab to pick up equipment and supplies. Sergeant Wilson was an officious and perennially suspicious character, always convinced that someone was trying to cheat him out of something he had ordered—and always vociferous that he wasn't going to take any crap, that he would make Trouble. Whenever he got back to his photo lab with a shipment and thought that there was something wrong with it, he would be on the phone, complaining to Sergeant Strong in our front office. These complaints were almost always unfounded, but Wilson was one of those people who are often wrong but never in doubt.

One day I was called to the front office by Sergeant Strong, who was very nervous because Sergeant Wilson was on the phone demanding a replacement for a film pack adapter missing from a Speed Graphic camera outfit that he had just received from us.

"Do we have an extra film pack adapter we can give him, Sowell?" Sergeant Strong asked. "Can we order one from someplace?"

"May I speak with him, Sergeant Strong?" I asked.

"Sure," he said, handing me the phone.

"Sergeant Wilson," I said, "have you looked in the back of the Speed Graphic?"

"The back of the Speed Graphic?"

"Yes, the back of the Speed Graphic."

"No."

"I'll wait while you look."

A moment later he came back on the phone.

"That's where it was!" Sergeant Wilson said, pleasantly surprised but utterly unapologetic.

"That's where I thought it would be," I said, as I turned the phone back to Sergeant Strong, who breathed an audible sigh of relief.

It was not just Sergeant Strong whom Wilson would pick on. One day, during a visit to pick up a shipment, he told us that he had run out of flash bulbs too quickly after his previous shipment.

"I didn't count 'em," he said, "but I am sure some of those flash bulbs were missing. Now, you can't fool me. I know what goes on! "

"Sergeant Wilson," I said, "no one here took your flash bulbs. For one thing, they are a kind of flash bulb that no one else would have any use for." But a defense against his accusations only made him more hostile.

"Don't give me that!" he said. "I've been around—and let me tell you something. From now on, I'm going to count every flash bulb I get. You can't fool me! "

Once he put it like that, I took it as a challenge. The next time Sergeant Wilson was due over to pick up a shipment, it included 4,500 flash bulbs. The bulbs came packed 600 to a crate and, so long as the crates were unopened, I knew he wasn't going to question those. Any problems would be with the uncrated 300 flashbulbs needed to fill his order after we had given him seven crates containing 4,200 bulbs. I asked Greuner if he would count those 300 bulbs very carefully and he in fact counted them twice, to be sure.

Just as I suspected, Sergeant Wilson counted the 300 uncrated bulbs before leaving, while we loaded the crates on the truck. Satisfied, he said as he got into the truck:

"We'll get along all right, as long as you guys play it straight with me."

After he drove off, we had a good laugh. Although I counted out the seven crates to him, we loaded only six onto the truck. The crate we short-changed him out of sat unopened on the warehouse floor. As I had told him, no one was interested in those bulbs.

• • •

My various peccadillos in the Marine Corps often involved skating on thin ice. I skated on the thinnest ice one Saturday, when we were scheduled to have Commanding General's inspection.

Usually, everyone from the lowliest private to the most senior colonel is so scared of doing something wrong at a Commanding General's inspection that he has no time to think about other people. At the previous Commanding General's inspection, no one took roll call, on the assumption that no one would dare to be absent. However, I was not one to go along with assumptions. I decided to take the day off to go visit friends on the other side of the base, spend some hours in the library, and take in a movie.

Monday morning, I was summoned to the First Sergeant's office. He looked grim as death.

"I don't recall seeing you out there for Commanding General's inspection last Saturday," he said.

I said nothing.

"Well," he asked, "what do you have to say for yourself?"

"I have nothing to say for myself."

"And why is that?"

"Because I am not responsible for the memories of First Sergeants."

Since I was never one of his favorite people, I knew that if he had any hard evidence, he would have started proceedings for a court-martial, instead of trying to trap me into some damaging admission. When he realized that I was not going for his bait, he dropped the questioning. But he had more to say.

"Let me tell you something, Sowell," the First Sergeant said. "From time to time, we get requests for lists of people to be sent over to fight in Korea. Your name would have been on that list before now, but the Marine Corps has a policy of not sending anyone overseas who has less than a year left to serve, and you have only eleven months left. But that policy is going to change—and when it does, I am personally going to see to it that you will be one of those on the list to be sent to Korea."

"Is that all, Sergeant?" I asked.

"That's all."

Several months passed. Another Commanding General's inspection was scheduled. On the Friday before it was to take place, I was again summoned to the First Sergeant's office.

"Tomorrow is Commanding General's inspection, Sowell," he announced, as if anyone within a radius of ten miles did not already know that.

I said nothing.

"Over the past month," he said, "I have seen to it that you served as Duty N.C.O., that you were on the emergency standby, that you were Barracks Orderly—in short, that you have already fulfilled all duties that might possibly interfere with your falling out tomorrow for Commanding General's Inspection."

I still said nothing.

"Moreover," he continued, "I have called over to the camp infirmary, to ask that, if anyone from this unit appears there tomorrow morning, they be put at the front of the line so that—after they are examined and found to have nothing wrong with them—they will have time enough to get back here and fall out for Commanding General's inspection."

I remained silent.

"So," he concluded, "I *will* see you out there tomorrow at Commanding General's inspection, won't I, Sowell?"

"Oh, Sergeant," I said, with great humility, "who am I to predict the future?"

I thought the S.O.B. had me, but I wasn't about to give him the satisfaction of saying so. However, luck came through when all else failed.

On Monday morning, I was once again summoned to the First Sergeant's office.

"*We took roll call last Saturday,*" he began pointedly, "and you were not there for Commanding General's inspection."

"That is correct," I said.

But rather than volunteer an explanation, I decided to let him work for it.

"Where were you?" he asked.

"I was in Barracks 1209."

"Doing what?"

"I was Duty N.C.O."

"Oh, no!" he cried, like a cat pouncing on a mouse. "You were *already* Duty N.C.O. this month. Corporal McIntyre was on the schedule to be Duty N.C.O. last Saturday."

"That is correct," I said.

"Then why were you Duty N.C.O.?"

"Because Master Sergeant Anderson decided to make me Duty N.C.O. instead."

"I'm going to check that out," the First Sergeant said. "But why would he do a thing like that?"

"Corporal McIntyre had never been Duty N.C.O. before, and Sergeant Anderson thought that a Commanding General's inspection was not the place to be Duty N.C.O. for the first time."

The First Sergeant seemed stunned and deflated by this turn of events.

"Because you had already made me Duty N.C.O. just recently," I continued, "Sergeant Anderson remembered that I could handle the job and appointed me to replace Corporal McIntyre."

As the First Sergeant had predicted, the Marine Corps did change their policy on how much time had to be remaining before someone would be sent overseas. Now, only six months needed to be left—but by then, I had only five months left. However, the First Sergeant was sent to Korea.

• • •

My first job at the rifle range was pulling a heavy ammunition wagon. Fortunately, I was reassigned to be a rifle coach after a week or so. My glasses must have been broken about this time because I had trouble seeing distant targets, making it hard for me to advise the shooters. I was transferred again, this time to the pistol range, where I remained for the rest of my stay in the Marine Corps.

Although part of the Rifle Range Detachment, the pistol range was better duty than the rifle range itself. There was less preparation each morning before pistol shooting began, so lights were turned on in the pistol coaches' part of the barracks about half an hour later than in the part of the barracks where the rifle coaches slept. Our day was usually not as long, nor the number of shooters nearly as great. Everyone in the Marine Corps had to shoot a rifle but only officers and people in certain occupational specialties, such as photographers, had to fire a .45 for the official record.

Safety is much more of a problem on a pistol range than on a rifle range, simply because it is so much easier to accidentally point a loaded pistol at someone. While we stressed safety to everyone, we learned from experience that there were great differences in the extent to which safety rules were observed. Combat veterans were the safest shooters. They needed no reminder that firearms were dangerous. Next in safety were Marines from units trained for combat, like the Second Marine Division. When you got to people who had civilian-like jobs, things got lax and dangerous if you didn't stay on top of them. Then when you had shooters who were in fact civilians—reservists—things got really dicey, as you would find them casually pointing the pistol in all directions, gesturing with it, and in general being a menace. More than once, I had to take a loaded .45 from some reservist's hands—a somewhat delicate operation—because he was paying no attention at all to where he was pointing it.

One morning, as the pistol coaches were gathering in our little room for coffee and donuts and a little chatter, our commanding officer came in, looking grim and shaken.

"Men," he said, in a somewhat wavery voice, "our shooters today are———women———Marine———reservists."

Never have I heard a roomful of chatter so instantly replaced by aching silence. You could just conjure up a vision of a bunch of secretaries in civilian life now standing around in Marine Corps uniforms, all holding loaded .45s in their hands for the first time in their lives.

Our commanding officer proceeded to describe the most extraordinary safety precautions—to a very attentive audience. Ordinarily, a coach might have two or three shooters at a time, but today each coach was to have only one shooter at a time and was to give her his undivided attention. Moreover, this one shooter was to have her pistol loaded by the coach, one bullet at a time. However, neither these nor other safety precautions really impressed me very much. With only a month remaining before I was scheduled to get out of the Marine Corps, there was no way I was going to go out to that pistol range and let one of those women shoot me. Better to take a chance on getting court-martialed for disobeying orders.

As the commanding officer led the coaches out the door to the pistol range, I went over to a table, poured myself another cup of coffee, picked up another donut, as well as a magazine to read, and bent down to get under the table, where I would spend the next couple of hours.

"Don't crowd, Sowell," I heard a voice say from under the table. "There's room enough here for all of us."

• • •

Always a voracious reader, I began to read more and more things in preparation for my return to civilian life, and my bunk was often overflowing with reading matter. One morning, as time was approaching for the pistol coaches to get over to the range, I was busy trying to get things put away when a staff sergeant from the pistol range passed by.

"You're going to be late, fooling with all this junk," he said.

"No, I won't."

"Yes, you will."

"I'll get it done a lot faster if you will leave me alone, sergeant."

"SHUT UP, SOWELL!" he yelled.

Suddenly the barracks got very quiet.

"You don't have rank enough to tell me to shut up, sergeant," I said, as I very deliberately took off my glasses and dropped them on the bunk, "—and you're not man enough to shut me up."

After a moment's pause, he said, in a vaguely threatening tone, "You just keep on talking, Sowell."

"I intend to, sergeant," I said as I picked up my glasses and put them back on. "I intend to."

He was a little bigger than me but I was younger than he was, so it would probably have all evened out. However, the situation was completely asymmetrical otherwise. As I realized later, he was a career Marine with a family depending on his paycheck. If we had both gotten busted for fighting, it would have meant nothing to me as a draftee about to leave. Still, it always looks bad for the bigger man to back down, especially after having come on so belligerently. I knew the Marine Corps well enough to know that my humiliating him like that in front of his men was sure to bring retaliation. Even with only a short time remaining in the Corps, I went over to the company office to ask for a transfer.

"Why transfer," the office clerk asked, "when you can get out?"

"I'm not due to get out until the 29th of this month," I said.

"Yeah, but the Marine Corps has a new thing they are experimenting with," he said. "They think they can save money by mustering out everybody on the same date in each month."

"What date?" I asked.

"The fifth," he said.

"The fifth! That's less than a week from now."

"Now, this is all voluntary," he said. "You don't have to be part of the experiment if you don't want to."

"I'll take it."

"You can wait until your regular discharge date on the 29th."

"I'll take it."

Although I was drafted for two years of military service, I thus ended up spending one year, eleven months and five days in the Marine Corps. But who's counting?

5

Halls of Ivy

New York was my first destination after getting out of the Marine Corps, but I was not to resume either the life or the relationships I had left two years earlier.

Family relationships in New York were severed once again, this time with a sense of finality, because war bonds I had been forced to sign up for at Parris Island, and to send home, were not returned to me when I wrote for them. I made no fuss about the money, but decided that they could not have both my money and my trust—and that they had already made their choice.

I worked very briefly again in the machine shop where Ed Gally was foreman, but moved on to a job in the stockroom of Willoughby's camera store. Meanwhile, I resumed going to high school at night, even though I had passed tests in the Marine Corps which would enable me to get a high school equivalency diploma, if I wished. I still needed to sort out just how I would go about going to college, and I had no reliable source of guidance.

One interesting source of encouragement was the elevator man at Willoughby's. He was an elderly man of British background who was impressed that I was going to school at night. One night, however, as I was leaving the store, I mentioned that I was too tired to go to school that evening. He became distressed, almost alarmed, and urged me to go to school anyway.

With surprising emotion, he told me how he had thrown away opportunities when he was young and regretted it ever afterwards. When he was a veteran returning home from war, he had a rare opportunity to go to Australia and make something of himself—and had passed it up. As he lamented his mistake, with painful frankness and as vividly as if it were yesterday, it slowly dawned on me that what he was talking about had happened right after *the First World War.*

● ● ●

For some reason, I needed information on my old job in the government for some official documents. When I wrote back to Washington, I learned that I was still eligible, as a military veteran, to return to that job—now with permanent civil service status and with all the raises for which I would have been eligible during the time when I was in the Marine Corps. This was an offer I could not refuse, so I was off to Washington once more.

By now, many of the old racial segregation patterns had been gotten rid of in Washington, even though there were not yet any laws or court decisions behind this trend. It was a more livable place for me than before. I had been struck by the difference, even when passing through D.C. in 1952, while on leave in the Marine Corps. Mary Frances met me at Union Station, and when I asked where we could find a convenient place to eat in this town, she said: "Right here—in the station."

● ● ●

As a fan of Sherlock Holmes, I knew that the great detective was often reluctant to reveal his methods, for fear that people would then say that they were "obvious"—even though they themselves would never have thought of them in a million years. I had an example of this on my first day at my new job in Washington, when I was introduced to my immediate supervisor in a clerical section of the General Accounting Office.

"It's good to meet you, Mr. Davis," I said. "It's always a special pleasure to meet a fellow photographer, especially one who does as much photography as you do, and who works alone in the darkroom, as I do."

He looked thunderstruck. Our work had nothing to do with photography and there were no cameras or other photographic gear around his desk to give a clue as to what he did after work. Yet, after I explained to him how I figured it out, he said:

"Of course."

When I shook hands with Mr. Davis, I noticed that he had dark brown stains on the fingernails of one hand and no stains at all on the fingernails of the other hand. That told me all I needed to know. I recognized the stains as developer stains, and how dark they were told me that he developed a lot of film or prints. Because the stains were on only one hand, that told me that he put only one hand in the developer, even though it is easier to handle film or prints when you use both hands. The only reason for using one hand is that you are working alone and therefore use a different hand when working in the developer than the one you use in the acid solution, so as to avoid contaminating the two chemicals. When you work with someone else, each person uses both hands, but in a different solution, so that one will end up with developer stains on both fingernails and the other with no stains on either.

Sherlock Holmes would undoubtedly have called it "elementary."

• • •

I rented a couple of furnished rooms within walking distance of Howard University, where I planned to attend college at night, while working for the government during the day. Although I had still not obtained a high school equivalency diploma, my results on a battery of armed services tests were enough to get me a chance to take Howard's entrance examination, which I passed easily.

Given cost and convenience, Howard University was the logical place for me to go. Unfortunately, they had no evening school *program;* just some courses held at night. The first course in a sequence might be held in the evening and the second course in the same sequence held in the morning. This made it very unlikely that a coherent program could be put together to get a degree through night classes. However, my immediate concern as an entering freshman was to get a number of introductory courses out of the way. At some later point, I would want to be in a financial condition to go to college during the day.

It was an interesting experience going to a black college, reputedly the best of the black colleges, but my main concern was to get an education. The readjustment to academic work, after so many years away, was difficult at first, especially when I started out taking 15 semester hours at night, while working full-time during the day. The next semester, I cut back to 12 semester hours and, in my third semester, I finally did the sensible thing and cut back again to 9 semester hours.

Now that I was receiving money from the G.I. Bill, in addition to my salary, I could afford a few amenities. With the rooms which I rented, on the second floor of a family house, there was a kitchen. After a while, I bought an enlarger and my kitchen then doubled as a darkroom. I also bought a nice record-player, ambitiously listed as "high fidelity." With it, the salesman threw in a long-playing record— "Scheherazade." I was not used to classical music but, since I did not have enough money left to buy many records right away, I ended up listening to "Scheherazade" enough times to become familiar with it, to like it, and finally to become open to the world of classical music in general. It added a whole new dimension to my life. The Grieg piano concerto moved me more deeply than any other music I had ever heard.

This was my studio apartment in Washington, where I lived after getting out of the Marine Corps and before going off to Harvard.

. . .

If racial policies in Washington had changed substantially in some respects, in other respects things remained as before—in practice, even if not always with legal sanction. I worked in an almost totally black section of the General Accounting Office, ruled—that is the only word for it—by a white woman from Georgia. Under her were her loyal black supervisors and section heads. We were subjected to harsher rules than other sections—that is, the white sections. For example, lateness for work usually meant signing a "T" for tardy on the official record in other sections. In our section, it meant losing an hour's annual leave—which is to say, the value of an hour's pay.

This and other abuses depended on the fact that many of the people in our section either did not know their legal rights or were afraid to exercise them. However, I was not planning to have a career in the government, so I could afford to make waves. I was already counting on cashing in my annual leave for some much-needed money when I would go to college full time, and was not about to lose any of it because of arbitrary rules. I refused to sign for an hour's pay when I was late, and told the officials in charge that if they took the hour anyway, I would protest it up through the personnel department and all the way to the Civil Service Commission, if necessary.

The response was in the classic tradition of administrative expediency: Thereafter they never attempted to dock *me* an hour's leave for being late, but continued to dock everyone else. This allowed the system to continue as before, and deprived me of any legal standing to challenge it.

This arrangement was by no means secret. Sometimes, when the trolley was late in the morning, a number of us would arrive together and report in at the same desk. All the people in line ahead of me would be asked to sign for an hour's annual leave, I would be asked to sign in tardy, and all those behind me would be asked to sign for a hour's annual leave. Far from being emboldened by my refusal to sign away my annual leave, the people around me seemed determined to believe that I had some special "in" with somebody in high places.

"You're not *sleeping* with that cracker woman, are you?" I was asked. Some of my co-workers noticed that I was called to her office a lot, and that I seemed to be very relaxed and amused in there. Apparently they did not notice that *she* was neither relaxed nor amused.

• • •

One evening, our sociology professor came to class visibly emotional about something.

"The most amazing and momentous thing has happened today," he said, "and I want us all to talk about it, instead of the regular assignment for tonight." He told us that the U.S. Supreme Court had just over-ruled the "separate but equal" doctrine and decreed the end of racial segregation. He asked each student in class to express an opinion or a reaction. All of us were, of course, in favor of it, but many of my classmates seemed to have the most Utopian expectations that this was going to lead to some magic solution to problems of race and poverty. When my turn came, I said:

"It's been more than fifty years since *Plessy v. Ferguson*—and we still don't have 'separate but equal.' What makes you think this is going to go any faster?"

The question only cast me in the role of party-pooper. My classmates seemed to think that racial integration was going to do it all. They were not alone.

• • •

In September 1954 I moved into my own apartment for the first time. Only someone who has been a roomer for years in other people's homes can fully appreciate what that means. It was a landmark in my life.

The apartment itself was only an "efficiency" or studio apartment—one large room with a stand-up kitchenette and a bathroom. However, next to the bathroom was a walk-in closet, which immediately became my new darkroom. But the financial strain of the move, including the buying of furniture for the first time, forced me to sell a camera I loved, a 4 X 5 Busch Pressman, and to be without any camera at all for several months. But my backlog of negatives was enough to keep me busy in the darkroom whenever I could find the time, with all the conflicting demands of work and school. I also had my own telephone for the first time and Mary Frances gave me an old television set of hers, so I was in some ways fixed quite nicely.

• • •

At Howard, I took a course in writing from Sterling Brown, a man whose name meant nothing to me initially, and whom I came to appreciate and respect for his own qualities, long before I ever came across any of his writings or learned of the reputation he had made.

Mr. Brown's first assignment was to bring in a sample of our best writing. This was an easy choice for me. For six years I had saved my favorite short story—the one that caused a literary agent to tell me that I had promise. Although I had stopped writing, I was still very proud of this particular manuscript.

When Mr. Brown returned our assignments, I found that his criticisms of my manuscript were longer than the manuscript itself. Worse yet, all these criticisms were obviously and devastatingly true. This short story, which I had cherished all these years, was rubbish. He didn't say so, but he didn't have to.

Once I realized how little I knew about writing, I could start to learn. By the end of the term, I knew enough about fiction writing to realize how much more I needed to know, so I gave up any thought of writing short stories or the great American novel, or even an adequate novel. The term's work was not wasted, however. I did acquire an appreciation of the beauty and power of plain writing, which helped me the rest of my life when writing non-fiction. I also learned a lot about life from Mr. Brown's careful and sharp analysis of some of the fiction we read.

Unfortunately, most of the professors at Howard were not like Mr. Brown and most of the students were not like those attracted to his small class.

The values of Howard University first struck me one winter evening as I headed home and passed a student in flowing robes, standing alone out in the snow, reciting from a large book that he had open in front of him. This was part of his fraternity initiation. To someone from my background, it seemed like a hell of a way to waste your time in college. It was just one symptom of a broader problem at Howard: Most students—and faculty members—were just not *serious* about intellectual work. They might sometimes be somber about it, or unctuous about it, or even pompous about it, but they were not *serious* about it.

Faculty and students alike seemed content to *be* at a university, rather than being preoccupied with what they were supposed to accomplish there. At Howard, everyone from the most naive freshman to the most cynical dean seemed to be playing a role. Sometimes it reminded me of *Green Pastures*. When I mentioned this to Sterling Brown, he smiled in an easy-going, fatherly way and said:

"You don't understand, Mr. Sowell. You see, *we're not as far off the plantation as you might think.*"

All too typical of what was wrong with Howard was a professor in the social sciences who can be called William Dean. He began his 5:30 PM class consistently at 5:40, took attendance religiously for about five minutes and left promptly at 6:25, five minutes ahead of time. In this way, he reduced his teaching time by twenty minutes out of every hour. Dr. Dean dealt in hollow generalities and big words, sometimes used correctly and sometimes not.

If he was bad, the students were pathetic. They knew so little about the Nazis and what they stood for that they took at face value a speech by Hitler that we read—and concluded that the *Führer* believed in disarmament and was distressed at discrimination against Negroes in America!

In Dr. Dean's class, a student's failure to read assignments or to understand them was dealt with very leniently. Challenging the instructor's views was not. Few students had either the desire or the knowledge to do so, in any case. When I raised some serious questions in class, that brought only resentment from the other students and umbrage from Dr. Dean. This made the course very uninteresting for me, so I began to miss classes, though I was present for all the examinations and made A's on all of them. Nevertheless I received a B for the course—because of attendance. I wrote a six-page, single-spaced letter to the dean of the college, criticizing this and other aspects of life at Howard University. He did nothing—except read the letter to a faculty meeting.

Although the dean did not read my name at the faculty meeting, at least one faculty member figured out who it was and told another, and word must have gotten around. When I went to one of the administrative offices and signed my name on some document, the lady at the desk looked up at me and said:

"So *you're* Thomas Sowell?"

This local notoriety was only one of a growing number of reasons why I found the thought of continuing at Howard University to be very painful. It was, however, by far the cheapest college education available in Washington. To go anywhere else would mean giving up my little apartment and all that it meant to me, to return to rooming and a cramped existence.

*   *   *

Although I was earning about as much as I could reasonably expect at the time, working at the General Accounting Office, I was nevertheless very interested in getting a job in photography. I scanned the civil service newspaper for openings but each time I arrived for an interview, I was told that the job had just been filled. While I suspected racial discrimination, I knew that I could never nail it down until I eliminated the other possibilities. To do this, I took a day off and was at an all-night news stand early in the morning on the day that the new civil service newspaper came out. Spotting a job for a darkroom worker at the National Security Agency, I was off to a government employment office and was the first in line, bringing along with me some photographs I had taken and printed.

There was no opportunity for me to show those photographs to anyone, however. The lady who interviewed me said that there were no jobs in photography at the National Security Agency. When I showed her the civil service newspaper, she said that it must have been a mistake on the paper's part, because the National Security Agency had *no photographic facilities.*

I went home and wrote my Congressman. A few weeks later, I was contacted directly by the National Security Agency and invited out to their headquarters. There, one of the big pooh-bahs greeted me warmly and gave me a guided tour of their large photographic facilities—treatment that probably very few applicants for entry level jobs in photography ever received. When we finished, I attempted to show him the photographs I had brought with me.

"No need for that," he said. "The job is yours."

"No, thank you," I said. "I don't want it that way."

● ● ●

These were grim times. Many things were going wrong—at work, at Howard, and in my personal life. Where I lived now was much farther away from Howard, and when I made the long walk home on bitterly cold winter nights, I often wondered *What the hell am I doing—and will it ever be worth it?*

William was going through some bad times in his life as well. One day we sat around commiserating with each other in my little apartment. Suddenly, he looked at me and said:

"Do you know, if our mother were alive, she would think that we had succeeded beyond her wildest dreams!"

● ● ●

Howard University had just enough good people to keep me hoping to be able to continue there and complete my education, without destroying my whole painfully achieved way of life and going back to a cramped existence in a more expensive college. One of these good people was Dr. Marie Gadsden, a gem of a human being, as well as someone with both an intellect and a sense of humor. She too was alienated from the university administration and unhappy with the general atmosphere there. "Mrs. G," as I came to call her, invited me to her home and she and her husband visited me in my little apartment. She became a confidante with whom I kept in touch the rest of my life.

Ironically, many Howard students were more impressed by phonies like Dr. Dean than by the first-rate people like Sterling Brown and Mrs. G. While the phonies liked to drop names, especially *white* names, Sterling Brown did not talk about the public figures he knew or the prestigious institutions where he had taught as a visiting professor—and which had asked him to stay on as a permanent faculty member. He returned to Howard, where he was needed, though never fully appreciated, and was at odds with the administration. He often illustrated points in class with anecdotes about "a friend of mine down at Seventh and T Streets"—a notorious corner in the ghetto. One girl who was awed by the phonies said that she didn't know what to make of Mr. Brown.

"All his friends seem to be on Seventh and T Streets," she said.

Eventually I found myself forced to recognize that I simply could not stay at Howard University, however painful the sacrifices required to go elsewhere. There was just no way for my mind to develop in the stultifying atmosphere there. This had brutal implications financially.

In those days, for many colleges, financial aid was out of the question for transfer students during their first year after arriving. This meant that I would have to find a way somehow to finance my first year in a new college myself, hoping to make a good enough academic record to receive scholarships in the following years. The only way this could be done would be to take every cent I could get hold of— savings, retirement money from the government, proceeds from selling my furniture, etc.—to pay for that first year at a new college, betting everything on the outcome of that year.

Not only did I need to make this gamble, I also had to find a good college that would gamble on me—a 24-year-old high school dropout with mediocre grades in a mediocre institution. True, I had made those grades while carrying an excessive load in night school and working full-time during the day. But, whatever the excuse for mediocre work, the only proof that you can do top quality work is to do top quality work—and I had done that in only some of my courses. My over-all grade average was about a B minus. Nevertheless, my sights were aimed high: Harvard, Yale, Wisconsin, and Columbia. (Wisconsin was where Mrs. G had earned her Ph.D.)

The responses of these institutions to my inquiries were cautious rather than encouraging. Harvard warned me not to do anything rash, like quitting my job or withdrawing from college where I was. They would *consider* my application, but that was all. Columbia rejected my application outright, a week *before* I took the College Board exams.

My test scores saved me. They were well above the national average and the college acceptances began coming in—though only Harvard offered any financial aid for the first year, in the form of a loan. They were candid enough to say that they were not convinced that they were doing me any favor by offering me admission and the small amount of aid that they did, for it would be very hard on me, both academically and financially. I liked their frankness and decided to go to Harvard.

Mrs. G and Sterling Brown, both of whom had written strong letters of recommendation for me, also helped me in making the transition. Mrs. G put me in touch with a lady who lived in Cambridge and who would rent me a room. Later, Mrs. G sent me the name of a girl she knew who was a student at Radcliffe. Sterling Brown gave me much good advice before I left. Although a bitterly eloquent critic of racism in his writings, he also understood the pitfalls of a victim mentality.

"Don't come back here and tell me you didn't make it 'cause white folks were mean," he said.

Nor should I let myself become overly impressed with Harvard or with my achievements there. In his best Southern accent, Sterling Brown said:

"Harvard has ruined more niggers than bad liquor."

• • •

After only a few weeks of rooming about a mile away from Harvard and commuting on foot or by bus, I realized that I needed to be on campus if I wanted to make good use of my time, as well as the libraries, and to be in the general stream of things. I was put in with two other transfer students living in Apley Court, an old building located about half a block from Harvard Yard and affiliated with Kirkland House, where we ate our meals. My roommates were named Norton and Ralph. Nort had transferred in from Cal Tech and Ralph from M.I.T. Both were outstanding students, even by Harvard standards, and this proved to be very fortunate for me, for their study habits were to provide a very valuable model.

Being at Harvard represented a great opportunity, but I had no idea at first just how precarious my situation was. My verbal test scores were a little higher than those of the average Harvard student but my math test scores were not as high, though still well above the national average. This was ironic because math had always been my best subject. The problem was that I had been away from math for a whole decade, while I had continued to read voraciously all that time. It had also been a whole decade since I last successfully completed a semester's work as a full-time student in an academic institution; that was in the ninth grade at J.H.S. 43. My work at Howard was a further handicap, for that experience gave me no inkling of the kind of time and effort required at Harvard, and in fact lulled me into a false sense of security. I thought I was being a conscientious student, so I was shocked one day when Nort suddenly said to me:

"Tom, when are you going to stop goofing off and get some work done?"

Goofing off! I didn't know what he was talking about. But I learned the hard way when the mid-term grades came out. Four courses was the standard load at Harvard and my four grades were two D's and two F's. I was summoned down to Kirkland House for a meeting with the Housemaster. He was sympathetic, friendly, and adroit, but the bottom line was that I was going to have to shape up or ship out. Shipping out was hardly a viable option, if only because I had no place to ship out to. Every dollar I owned had gone into financing this year, and part of my future income was already mortgaged by a loan.

Desperate, I began taking stay-awake pills, so that I could study on into the night. Soon, however, my system became immune to the pills and sleep would overtake me anyway. I then shifted strategies and began going to sleep immediately after returning from dinner, waking up later in the middle of the night, refreshed, to study for as long as necessary into the wee hours of the morning. It worked—but I was still so far behind that I had a lot of catching up to do.

During the Christmas holidays, I stayed at the apartment of an old girl friend in New York. While she was at work during the day, I stayed in bed surrounded by the books I was studying, getting up only to go to the kitchen or the bathroom. More than once, she returned home to find me still in my pajamas and asked:

"Don't you ever get out of bed?"

I memorized German words by the hour, worked out math problems, taught myself to use a slide rule, and went through the chemistry textbook, solving every problem in it from cover to cover. As this relentless work went on, day after day, things began to fall into place and material that had once seemed impenetrable to me now turned out to be quite manageable. I returned to Harvard at the beginning of 1956 much better prepared, and with more confidence, to face the last month of the semester and its final exams.

Chemistry was my worst subject. By this time, I had gotten two F's and a D on the three exams in the subject. When I went to get my course grade at the end of the term, the teaching assistant was amazed when he looked it up:

"You got a C!" he said. "You must have made 100 percent on the final exam, or very close to it."

It turned out that I received a C in each of my courses that first semester. It was a moral victory after a bad start. In the spring semester, I received all B's and began to feel that I was heading upward. One day, while reading through the college catalogue, I said to my room-mate Ralph:

"Do you realize that I could still graduate *magna cum laude* from this place?"

Ralph burst out laughing.

I graduated *magna cum laude*.

Economics and Karl Marx had a lot to do with it. Although I did well in most of my courses, economics was the only subject in which I received A's—and I received A's in most of my economics courses. It was not hard to decide what I should major in. By this time, I had been reading the writings of Karl Marx for years, so it was also not hard to decide what I would write about for my senior honors thesis. In those days, you needed a certain grade-point average to be eligible for honors, but the degree of honors depended on the quality of your honors thesis. By this time, after years of reading Karl Marx on my own, I knew Marxism backward and forward, so my thesis gained me higher honors than those received by some students with higher grade-point averages than mine.

My thesis advisor was Professor Arthur Smithies, a noted authority on fiscal policy who also taught the history of economic thought, but who had done little work on Marx. He said to me:

"I don't think I can be of much help to you, frankly, because my own knowledge of Marxian economics is so limited."

"That's all right," I said. "I plan to do it all by myself anyway."

"I know," he said, "but usually the student needs some guidance and suggestions about organizing the work, as well as some helpful readings on the subject."

"My plan is to ignore all interpreters of Marx, read right through the three volumes of *Capital,* and make up my own mind," I said.

"Well, it so happens that Paul Sweezy, the leading authority on Marxian economics, is right here in Cambridge, and I could introduce you to him."

"That won't be necessary," I said.

He looked baffled for a moment, and then there was a slowly spreading smile of understanding.

"All right," he said. "Go to it."

I wasn't about to have anything I did attributed to ideas picked up from Paul Sweezy or anyone else. The thesis I wrote was good enough that parts of it were published in scholarly journals in later years.

• • •

While the transition from one intellectual level to another had been agonizing, the new level was no harder than the old, once the transition was made. In fact, I found the work easier and more enjoyable than I had at Howard, and my grades were better. With the desperate efforts of the first year now behind me, I simply kept up with my assignments as they came along, became more systematic in my studying, and seldom had to cram for an exam. I often went out to a movie on the night before a final, so that I would be relaxed and well-rested for the exam the next day.

Social adjustments were not as successful as academic adjustments, but they worked out somehow. I coped with the social situation rather than feeling at home in it. I was, after all, seven years older than most of the students around me and came from a very different background. It was not just a question of race, for most of the other black students there were much more part of the social scene than I was, and one of them was selected as class marshal.

Any attempt by my white classmates to be intellectually patronizing seldom lasted beyond one or two exchanges. Occasionally, I would encounter one of those thoroughly smug people who prompted the saying, "You can always tell a Harvard man—but you can't tell him much." Here my strategy was to ask innocent-sounding leading questions, until he had gotten himself way out on a limb—and then begin sawing off the limb. After one particularly brutal session of this sort, my room-mate Ralph said:

"Did you *have* to make a complete fool of him in front of everybody?"

"Don't give me too much credit," I said. "I had good raw material to work on."

· · ·

Summers were times to earn money to help with college bills. Although I received scholarships, they did not cover the full costs, not even with the G.I. Bill money thrown in. During the summers of 1956 and 1957, my standard of living was cut back to a bare-bones level, in order to save as much as possible for the coming academic year. I lived more poorly than I had when I was a delivery boy in the garment district.

I worked for the government in Washington and roomed with a family friend named Mrs. Nash who had a house where she lived with her brother Sam, who was a friend of mine, and her teen-age daughter Sandra. I didn't even have a radio but Charles put together some electronic tubes and devices for me, with no cabinet, and this served the purpose.

One of the things I did have with me was an iron, so that I could wash and iron my own shirts to save on laundry bills. One day Mrs. Nash called up to me from downstairs:

"Tommy, Sandra would like to borrow your iron———"

"Sure."

"She just wants to use it to———"

"*Never mind* what I want to use it for," Sandra hissed at her mother.

"Oh, child," Mrs. Nash said, "Tommy's seen plenty of brassieres in his time. I don't know why you bought that old thing, in the first place. You don't have no *use* for it."

• • •

Although I had entered college with no thought of pursuing education beyond college—I am not even sure that I knew you could—by the time my senior year came around, I knew that I wanted to continue on to graduate school. I applied to Columbia, Yale, Berkeley, and the University of Chicago in economics, and to Brandeis for study in the history of ideas. I also applied to Harvard for graduate study in economics, but it was strictly a fall-back possibility. By this time, I was fed up with Harvard.

Perhaps any place with such an awesome reputation was bound to be something of a disappointment. What I most disliked about Harvard was that smug assumptions were too often treated as substitutes for evidence or logic. The idea seemed to be that if we bright and good fellows all believed something, it must be true. Unquestionably, Harvard made a major contribution to both my intellectual and social development. But when time came to leave, I felt that it was not a moment too soon. I did not wait for Commencement day. I left a forwarding address to which they could mail the diploma. When I walked out of Kirkland House for the last time and settled into the back seat of a taxi that would take me to the railroad station, I felt that a great weight had been lifted off my shoulders.

• • •

I spent the summer of 1958 in the medical students' dormitories at the N.Y.U.-Bellevue Medical Center in downtown Manhattan, along the East River. I was taking some summer school courses at N.Y.U. with a generous grant from the Jessie Smith Noyes Foundation. My last truly poverty-stricken days were now behind me. Perhaps the turning point came when I went to Macy's department store to buy a new supply of underwear to replace the ragged underwear I had on. At Harvard, I had saved up ten dollars to buy new underwear, but then came across a copy of the third volume of Marx's *Capital* at a second-hand book store—on sale for ten dollars. The book was invaluable for writing my honors thesis, so I had to wear ragged underwear a little longer.

I also bought a bicycle, which I rode around Manhattan, from as far south as The Battery to as far north as Harlem. It was a great feeling to get acquainted with New York again, to go to evening concerts in Central Park, and to take pictures of the Brooklyn Bridge and the midtown skyline.

One day, riding in an elevator, I heard a little boy say proudly:

"My father is working on that baseball player."

It only slowly dawned on me that his father was a doctor at the medical center, and that "that baseball player" was the great Roy Campanella, who had just been crippled in an automobile accident.

* * *

If the summer was something of a happy interlude, Columbia University was something of a rude shock. I had applied to Columbia specifically and explicitly to study the history of economic thought under Professor George J. Stigler and had turned down a larger fellowship from the University of Chicago in order to do so. Now, when I arrived at Columbia in the fall of 1958, I learned for the first time that Stigler had gone to the University of Chicago.

Despite my having said in my application why I wanted to study at Columbia, no one told me that Stigler was leaving. Nor did they tell me that the tuition was going up, so that my fellowship was not enough to cover the full cost of attending Columbia. It was my first lesson in academic ethics. There would be more.

To add insult to injury, when I applied for additional money to cover the larger tuition, I was told by one of the Columbia bureaucrats that I should "wait and see" how things worked out financially. I replied that I did not have to wait and see whether the rules of arithmetic would be vindicated in the course of time. The Jessie Smith Noyes Foundation, however, came through with some additional money, so that problem was surmounted.

A problem not so easily surmounted was a stomach ailment that plagued me for months. The medication for it made me drowsy and unable to master my academic assignments. Fortunately, Columbia allowed three courses a year to be taken as audits, rather than for credit. I took all three audits in the fall semester. Even so, I made only a B and a C in my other two courses. This was hardly the kind of record likely to get my fellowship renewed at Columbia, much less get me a fellowship at Chicago, where I wanted to go to study under Stigler next year.

Fortunately, the one thing I had going for me was that I was writing a Master's thesis on Marx's business cycle theory under Professor Arthur F. Burns, the biggest name at Columbia in economics. When Chicago sent me three recommendation forms to submit in support of my application, I threw two of them away, because I was convinced that if Arthur Burns said I was good, I was in, and if he said I wasn't, I was out. Sure enough, when the official letter arrived from the University of Chicago in the spring of 1959, it began: "Due to the strong recommendation of Professor Arthur F. Burns. . . ." The fellowship they offered certainly could not have been due to my fall semester grades.

I got off my stomach medication, cold turkey, in March 1959, when I also stopped going to classes for the entire month, in order to ease the pressures behind the stomach problems. I bicycled around the city, went to movies, and otherwise got away from it all. My stomach problems went away and I never took the medicine again. I resumed studying before I resumed going to class. At least one professor thought that I had dropped out of school. My grades went up just enough for me to receive my Master's degree in the minimum time— nine months.

My master's thesis at Columbia derived from my undergraduate honors thesis at Harvard. So did an article which I wrote for the *American Economic Review* while at Columbia, though it came out a year later, when I was student at the University of Chicago. I was so resentful of the way I had been treated at Columbia that I listed my institutional affiliation as the University of Chicago, even though I had never set foot in Chicago when the final draft of the manuscript went to the *American Economic Review* in the summer of 1959 for publication in their March 1960 issue. It was my first publication.

• • •

In the summer of 1959, as in the summer of 1957, I worked as a clerk-typist at the headquarters of the U.S. Public Health Service in Washington. The people I worked for were very nice and I grew to like them.

One day, a man had a heart attack at around 5 PM, on the sidewalk outside the Public Health Service. He was taken inside to the nurse's room, where he was asked if he were a government employee. If he were, he would have been eligible to be taken to the medical facility there. Unfortunately, he was not, so a phone call was made to a local hospital to send an ambulance. By the time this ambulance made its way through miles of downtown Washington rush-hour traffic, the man was dead.

He died waiting for a doctor, in a building full of doctors.

Nothing so dramatized for me the nature of a bureaucracy and its emphasis on procedures, rather than results.

• • •

Classes at the University of Chicago did not start until early October, so I was able to work a little longer than usual at my summer job and earn some more much-needed money. But I was eagerly looking forward to my new academic home.

I was as well aware that the University of Chicago economics department had a reputation for conservatism as they were that I was a Marxist. What made this not matter was that we were both devoted to intellectual standards and intellectual argumentation, quite unlike the question-begging smugness too common at Harvard. I developed much more respect for the University of Chicago than I ever had for Harvard.

As fate would have it, Milton Friedman was my advisor and I also took his course in price theory. It was considered a very tough course and Professor Friedman had a no-nonsense attitude toward students. For example, he did not permit students to distract attention from his lecture by entering class late. If you arrived late, you had to turn around and go on back. I had this experience once—and I made it my business to be on time thereafter. I did not realize how tough his course was until I was sitting outside his office one day, when another student passed by and looked surprised when he saw my exam paper.

"You got a B?" he said.

"Yes," I replied. "Is that bad?"

"There were only two B's in the entire class!" he said.

"How many A's?" I asked.

"There were *no* A's."

One of the reasons why grading was so much harder at Chicago than at most other graduate schools was that grades at Chicago were meant primarily to inform the student of how well he was doing. Technically, it was not necessary to pass any course to qualify for a Ph.D. in economics at the University of Chicago. There were comprehensive exams to take, in order to advance to candidacy for the doctorate, and it was these exams that would determine whether or not you could go on.

My biggest complaint about the economics department was not the toughness of the grading nor our ideological differences. What bothered me was the extremely abstract way that the courses were taught. In one course in monetary economics, for example, the whole presentation was in terms of equations and graphs, including three-dimensional graphs. I liked theory as well as the next fellow, but a steady diet of nothing but abstractions became a little much.

When time came to do a term paper in Professor Friedman's course, I decided to make it, among other things, a parody of the abstract theoretical approach. I illustrated the simplest notions with equations loaded with subscripts and superscripts, and I drew two three-dimensional graphs on separate sheets of paper. The two sheets of paper had to be held up to the light together and the graphs lined up, in order to determine the solution. Friedman gave me a good grade on it, but added:

"I got your heavy-handed humor."

• • •

Some of the most important things I learned at the University of Chicago did not seem at all important at first. One of these things whose relevance I did not see immediately was an essay by Friedrich Hayek entitled "The Use of Knowledge in Society." It was assigned in Milton Friedman's course and it showed the role of a market economy in utilizing the fragmented knowledge scattered among vast numbers of people. It would be nearly twenty years later before I would realize the full implications of this plain and apparently simple essay—and then be inspired write a book called *Knowledge and Decisions*. Students are often in no position to judge "relevance" until long after the fact.

Another thing whose importance was lost on me at first was the distinction between an equation and an identity. It seemed like a mathematical fine point at the time, and I grew tired of hearing the question, "Is this an equation or an identity?" Often I thought to myself: "Let's just flip a coin."

In reality, it was a question of enormous importance, far beyond the boundaries of mathematics or of economics. An equation is true only under certain conditions, while a mathematical identity is true simply because of the way you define the terms. Many people do not understand that what they are saying may be true just because of the way they use words—and those people may be deceived into believing that they are saying something true about the real world. Many political beliefs depend on such circular reasoning.

In one of those crucial pieces of good fortune that have come along from time to time in my life, I happened to become interested in the philosophy of William James at about this time, and this in turn led me to read Charles Sanders Peirce, who inspired James' philosophy. In this unlikely way, I came to understand why it was so important to avoid having your own definitions trap you in beliefs that would not stand up under scrutiny. Peirce wrote that it was "terrible to see how a single unclear idea, a single formula without meaning, lurking in a young man's head" could block his thinking and commit him to things he would never believe if he fully understood what he was saying. According to Peirce:

> Many a man has cherished for years as his hobby some vague shadow of an idea, too meaningless to be positively false. . . .

Years later, when I became a teacher, I often put that quotation on the first page of the syllabus of my courses. I hope my students understood its significance more quickly than I did when I was a student.

• • •

One day I wrote a blistering letter to the student newspaper, denouncing the university's use of government "Urban Renewal" programs to dispossess poor and black people from nearby areas where the university wanted to expand. I was surprised when Milton Friedman said that he had read my letter—and that he agreed with me.

Down South at this time, much more serious problems and much more serious protests were going on. There were sit-ins at lunch counters and other public places to protest racial segregation. To a friend at Tuskeegee who sent me some clippings, I wrote in March 1960:

> Received the clippings you sent. Found them very interesting and was very proud of the way our people have sprung to life and the good judgement with which things have been handled.

Only in later years, when desegregation went from being a principle to being regarded as a panacea, did I begin to question the preoccupation with this issue to the neglect of other concerns that seemed to me much more important for racial progress.

• • •

In the winter quarter, I finally took a course from the man who was the reason for my coming to study at the University of Chicago: George J. Stigler. Although I had first been struck by his intellect from an article of his that I read in Professor Smithies' course at Harvard on the history of economic thought, the first course I took from Stigler was in industrial organization. In the spring quarter, I was finally able to enrol in his course on the history of economic thought. It was an outstanding course, as expected, though by this time I had done enough research myself to be emboldened to question his conclusions on some things. Stigler took it in stride, but his sharp wit made crossing swords with him a hazardous undertaking.

Although things were going along well academically, the university administration was going through one of those economy drives which sporadically occur in academia. One of the non-essential expenditures eliminated in this particular economy drive was my fellowship! By now, I had learned to roll with a lot of punches, so I simply checked out the job market and took some civil service exams. But my work as a graduate student continued as before.

One day, as I came up to the front of the room after class, to question some conclusions about Ricardian economics, Professor Stigler, dead-pan, reached into his jacket pocket and pulled out an envelope.

"You might want to take a look at this sometime," he said drily.

It was an offer of a fellowship—from the Earhart Foundation, which I had never heard of, and of course had never applied to. Stigler had arranged it all. It was a larger fellowship than I had had before, or had ever heard of before.

●   ●   ●

The summer of 1960 was special for a number of reasons. I had my first job on a professional level, as a summer intern in economics at the U.S. Department of Labor in Washington. The work and the money were both very welcome.

My social life also picked up. At first this caused some difficulty because one young lady I met was rooming in the same house where I was rooming. The landlady became concerned when we began to talk to each other, and was visibly distressed when I took her out to a movie. She knew the girl's mother and felt responsible for anything that might happen. To make everybody comfortable, I moved out and rented a basement apartment some distance away. This apartment was furnished in such bad taste that it was invaluable as a conversation piece. Being a basement apartment, it was also cool during the hot Washington summer—no small consideration in an era before air conditioning became widespread.

One event marred this otherwise very happy summer. One day I received a phone call from Mary Frances:

"I have just heard from the family in New York," she said. "Jimmy is dead."

"Oh my God!" I said. "Jimmy!"

I sent flowers. Many years later, I learned that those were the only flowers at his funeral. As of 1960, I had no idea that they had fallen on such hard times.

. . .

My work at the Labor Department made a lasting difference in the way I thought. After being immersed in theory at the University of Chicago, this was my first experience with the application of economics to public policy issues.

My work involved studying the sugar industry of Puerto Rico, where the Labor Department ran a program setting minimum wages on an industry-by-industry basis. At that point, I was a supporter of the idea of minimum wages, as a way of helping low-paid workers to earn a decent living. In the course of going through the history and statistics of the Puerto Rican sugar industry, however, I was confronted by the fact that employment was going down as the minimum wage rates were being pushed up. Some economists, including Stigler, had warned that minimum wages caused unemployment and now that warning was hard to ignore.

Union representatives and employer representatives on the boards that set minimum wages had very different explanations as to why employment was going down in the Puerto Rican sugar industry. Employers said that the minimum wage level made it too expensive to produce as much sugar as before, given the natural difficulties of producing sugar in Puerto Rico and the relatively low productivity of the labor there. The union officials said that sugar production was down, and employment with it, because a series of hurricanes had passed through Puerto Rico in each of the past several years, destroying part of the crop.

There was no obvious way to determine which of these two theories was correct. However, we had been taught at Chicago that if there are two different theories, there should be some empirical fact that would be different if one theory were correct, rather than the other. I spent much of the summer trying in vain to come up with something that would tell us which theory was right. As for the permanent Labor

Department people, they were reluctant to believe that the minimum wage program was costing workers their jobs. And they left it at that.

Toward the end of the summer, I came in one morning and announced that I had a way of determining which theory was correct.

"What we need," I said, "are statistics on the amount of sugar cane standing in the field *before* the hurricanes came through Puerto Rico."

There was a stunned silence, as if they were afraid I had stumbled onto something that could turn out to be embarrassing for the Labor Department.

"Well, it's not that easy," one of the Labor Department economists said. "We don't have those statistics."

"I'll bet the Department of Agriculture has them," I said.

"That's still not the same as if we had them in the Department of Labor," I was told.

"Why can't we get them from the Department of Agriculture?" I asked.

"That's easier said than done. First of all, we would have to make a request, going all the way up through channels to the Secretary of Labor. Then he would have to seek approval from the Secretary of Agriculture, who would then have to forward the request down the chain of command in the Department of Agriculture, to see if the data are available and can be released."

"Well," I said, "John F. Kennedy says that a journey of a thousand miles must begin with a single step. Let me file the request."

That was 1960. I have yet to receive an official reply to my request.

This was more than an isolated incident. It forced me to realize that government agencies have their own self-interest to look after, regardless of the interests of those for whom a program has been set up. Administration of the minimum wage law was a major part of the Labor Department's budget and employed a significant fraction of all the people who worked there. Whether or not minimum wages benefitted workers may have been my overriding question, but it was clearly not theirs. They had reasons to want to believe that it did, but no real incentive to probe too deeply to find out.

This realization began to make me want to re-think the larger question of the role of government in general. It was the beginning of the erosion of my faith in government programs. The more other government programs I looked into, over the years, the harder I found it to believe that they were a net benefit to society. I had remained a Marxist, despite being at the University of Chicago, but now my experience in Washington began a process of changing my mind completely as to how to deal with social problems. Fortunately, it was a gradual process, so that I was spared the traumatic conversions which some other Marxists have suffered.

• • •

In the course of my research on the history of economic thought, I began to read the collected works of classical economist David Ricardo, including his correspondence. In one of his letters I found a passage which made such an impression on me that, decades later, I would often inscribe it in books that I gave to young people:

> I wish that I may never think the smiles of the great and powerful a sufficient inducement to turn aside from the straight path of honesty and the convictions of my own mind.

• • •

The academic year that began in the fall of 1960 was the last year required to fulfill the residence requirement for the Ph.D. Although I was still far from fulfilling the other requirements—comprehensive exams, foreign languages, and the dissertation—completion of the residence requirement meant that I could leave the university, take a job, and resume a normal life, leaving the other requirements to be completed in absentia. I was very anxious to leave the cramped life of a graduate student behind me, though I could undoubtedly have gotten another fellowship to finance another year in residence, and was in fact urged to do so. But I was burned out by now. I was thirty years old and had nothing, not even a little apartment such as I had lived in six years earlier.

Looking for a job, I went to the annual meetings of the American Economic Association, held in St. Louis that year. This was still the era of racial segregation in the South, so I was not at all anxious to go to St. Louis, a border state city with Southern practices. However, the American Economic Association had made special arrangements in advance, so that all its members were to have all the facilities of the convention hotel available to them. I stayed in the convention hotel and found the service both good and friendly. Outside the hotel, however, we were on our own.

One day, while out walking, I became hungry and simply walked into a restaurant in the neighborhood and sat down, without thinking. After a moment, I noticed a buzzing among a group of restaurant people gathered in the back. Then it dawned on me that this was a racial segregation problem—but I decided to let it be *their* problem and continued to sit there. A young waitress approached somewhat timidly and asked for my order.

"A glass of milk and a piece of apple pie," I said.

She seemed relieved and promptly went to get it.

At another restaurant—again, not in the convention hotel—the manager came over to the table to say politely and quietly that I could not be served there. I simply got up and left.

In earlier years, I am sure that there would have been none of the ambivalence about segregation implied by both these incidents and by the convention hotel's agreement to serve everyone alike. Racial segregation was still very much in effect, but the moral underpinnings of it were already starting to erode in people's minds. In Washington that erosion had gone much further than in St. Louis, and no doubt in the cities of the Deep South things had not even gone as far as they had in St. Louis—but nationally the process was underway.

My job interview at the American Economic Association ran the gamut from colleges to oil companies to government agencies and *Business Week* magazine. My strongest desire was to teach at a black college—*if* I could accomplish something there. My interview with the economics department chairman from Howard University did nothing to inspire confidence. When the convention was over, I returned to Chicago with no clear sense of the direction my career would take. I suspected that I would have to spend some time drifting along, until things sorted themselves out.

6

Drifting Along

I could hardly wait for my final year in residence to end. In fact, I didn't wait. I left a couple of weeks early and headed for Washington, where I had a job waiting as an economist in the Bureau of the Budget, predecessor of the Office of Management and Budget. None of the courses in which I was enrolled at Chicago when I left were for grade credit or required me to attend classes, so I was unlikely to be missed, much less penalized.

At this point, I was eligible to be hired as a GS-9, either under a job title of "management intern" or as an economist. Three federal agencies offered me jobs: The Bureau of the Budget, the Federal Reserve System, and the Labor Department. The Bureau of the Budget and the Federal Reserve System sought to hire me as an economist and the Labor Department offered to hire me under either title. For some reason, however, there was a bureaucratic hang-up in the Civil Service Commission as to my being hired at the GS-9 level as an economist, rather than at the usual GS-7 beginning level. This problem did not affect the Federal Reserve, which had its own job standards, nor did it limit the Labor Department, which could have me work as an economist under the "management intern" title.

Although I preferred the Bureau of the Budget as a place to work, I was in no financial condition to pass up higher-paying jobs elsewhere. The Bureau of the Budget assured me, however, that they would hire me as a GS-9, so I declined offers from the Federal Reserve and the Labor Department. But, when I arrived in Washington, the snag had still not been ironed out. I do not recall exactly how my hiring was handled officially when I came on board on a Monday morning, but I do know that I soon realized that I had been deceived. After only three days on the job, I resigned on Thursday—effective Friday.

That got a lot of people's attention, which is what I intended. I did not want whoever was responsible for this double-dealing to escape scrutiny. One of the people who became involved was a black secretary, who took me aside in the hall, to ask me to reconsider. She pointed out to me how recently blacks had begun to be hired in worthwhile positions in many government agencies.

"Do you realize that I am the first black secretary in the history of the Bureau of the Budget—and that you are the first black professional?" she said. "So you see, you *can't* leave."

"On the contrary," I said. "Now I will have the further distinction of being the first black professional to *resign* from the Bureau of the Budget."

• • •

At various times in the past, I had heard dire predictions that resigning on short notice would ruin your chances of being hired by the government again. However, within a couple of weeks I was at work in the U.S. Department of Labor, as a GS-9 management intern.

Management interns were a sort of specially anointed group who were being groomed for future leadership roles. This caused a certain amount of resentment among the old-line civil service people, who had slowly worked their way up the ladder over a period of decades. It also made us a group of people whom some others wanted to study to death. Someone had the bright idea of giving management interns an extensive battery of psychological questions to answer and turn in. It was the usual intrusive kind of thing, including questions about what kind of woman I wanted to marry. I paid no attention to it. In due course, one of the busy-bodies phoned me.

"We haven't gotten your questionnaire back," I was told.

"I know."

"When are you going to send it in?"

"I'm not going to send it in."

"Why not?"

"It asked questions that were nobody's business."

"Will you at least return the blank questionnaire? Those things cost a lot of money."

"I can't. I threw it out with the trash."

"Threw it out! What would happen if everybody had your attitude?"

"You would have to stop asking nosy questions."

• • •

When my GS-9 rating as an economist was finally straightened out at the Civil Service Commission, I withdrew from the management intern program. This did not affect my day-to-day work, which was that of an economist all along. I just stopped going to the management intern meetings, which were a little precious for my taste anyway.

After initially getting a very boring assignment, which my supervisor in the Bureau of Labor Statistics described as "a wonderful opportunity" to become acquainted with "the basic data," I got myself transferred to another unit which did special research assignments in the Wage and Hour Division of the Labor Department. My first assignment in my new job was to do research on the possibilities of applying the wages and hours law—the Fair Labor Standards Act—to agriculture, which was currently exempt. The Labor Department was particularly interested in the claim on which agriculture's exemption was based—namely, that many farm operations, especially at harvest time, required long hours of work, in excess of the 40-hour week in industry. Were there any elements of flexibility or any methods by which the harvest peaks could be smoothed out? This assignment kept a little group of four of us busy in the U.S. Department of Agriculture library for months.

Typically, we would report for work at the Labor Department at 8:15 AM and by 8:30 we were in a taxi headed for the Department of Agriculture. We might arrive back at our offices about 15 minutes before quitting time or, on some days when we were running late, we might go home directly from the Department of Agriculture. This long, unsupervised period was my happiest time working for the government. We were so out of touch with the rest of the people in our division that I was introduced at a staff meeting as a "new employee"—six months after I was hired.

• • •

The apartment in which I lived was an efficiency or studio apartment, very much like the one I had lived in before I went off to Harvard, six years earlier. It made progress look somewhat illusory.

Slowly I began to furnish the apartment with better things than I had before, including the first television set I bought. Then one evening, when I came home from work, something looked different about the apartment. Most things were exactly where they always were, but suddenly I noticed—the television set was gone! So was my typewriter. When I looked in the closet, my best suits were missing. I had been burglarized.

It was obviously a very quick, clean job, with no signs of ransacking. I then learned, too late, that other apartments in the building had been burglarized recently. Another was burglarized in the few weeks before I moved out.

Over a period of time, the stolen belongings were replaced. But the psychological after-effects hung on long after that.

• • •

At the Labor Department, I met a couple of other young black economists named Bernard and Jim, who were also beginning their professional careers, and who would remain friends of mine for decades to come. Jim told me how he happened to hear of me and to seek me out.

Jim began working at the Bureau of Labor Statistics shortly after I left. One day, he was complaining about the statistical methods used by B.L.S.

"You call yourself the Bureau of Labor Statistics?" he said. "This is the Bureau of Labor *Arithmetic!*"

"Oh, God!" someone said. "Another Tom Sowell!"

"Who's Tom Sowell?" Jim asked.

A secretary leaned over and whispered: "I'll tell you about it out in the hall during the coffee break. If we talk about it in here, it will just upset the whole office."

I had no idea that I had made such an impression at the Bureau of Labor Statistics.

• • •

Before leaving the University of Chicago, I had approached Professor George Stigler with the idea of writing a doctoral dissertation on the history of one of the old standby theories of economics called Say's Law. Stigler, however, did not think that enough could be said that was new on the subject, which was already a century and a half old, and which many others had written about during that time. Moreover, my interpretation of some of the early nineteenth-century economists involved in the controversies over Say's Law were interpretations that Stigler did not agree with, and which he in fact considered to be fundamentally erroneous. Unfortunately, that was exactly my view of his interpretation. Our lengthy discussions at Chicago were followed by exchanges of lengthy letters after I went to Washington. The best I could get from him was a statement that he was willing to step aside as my thesis advisor in favor of someone else, since "we seldom see eye to eye."

This was fine in itself, though somewhat ironic in view of my going to Chicago specifically to study under Stigler. In any event, it remained a moot point for the time being, because there were the dreaded comprehensive exams to take. The economics department allowed a student three chances to pass these exams, after which you were dropped from the doctoral program, so one could hardly afford to risk taking them without being prepared. The failure rate was about 50 percent at each testing. Much of my spare time after work went into preparing for those exams. Fortunately, I passed them all on the first try.

Almost immediately, letters began arriving from colleges, asking if I were interested in teaching.

One of the institutions that interviewed me was Douglass College in New Jersey. Only after arriving there did I discover that it was a women's college, almost all white women. As a black, unmarried male, I really did not expect to get hired, but there was no point simply turning around and going home, so I went through with the interview. One of those interviewing me was a white-maned professor who was about to retire, creating the vacancy for which I was being considered. He was concerned over the fact that I had written on Marx and might be a radical influence on the students.

By this time, there was not a snow ball's chance in hell that I would be a radical influence, but rather than reassure him on that, I let him know that I thought the question itself was out of line.

"My political philosophy is irrelevant," I said, "because I plan to teach economics and not my political philosophy."

"But I think it's relevant in the over-all picture," the old fellow said.

"Why?" I asked. "I don't plan to draw demand curves sloping upward rather than downward, regardless of my politics."

"Well, that's not the point."

"Are people brought here to teach economics or to indoctrinate students in their political philosophy?" I asked.

"To teach economics, of course . . ."

After a few exchanges of this sort, I really wrote off the whole thing as a wasted day. But, a week later, they made me an offer and I accepted.

• • •

It would be several months before time for me to leave the Labor Department to go teach at Douglass College, and I saw no useful purpose being served by giving the Labor Department that much advance notice.

After our long stint working in the Department of Agriculture, our little group of four economists returned to the Labor Department and did most of our work there. At one point, I was given the assignment of preparing some material for Secretary of Labor Arthur Goldberg to include in a presentation to Congress. As a lower-level staffer, I of course never came in contact with the Secretary of Labor, but other pooh-bahs informed me of what the Department's position would be and supplied me with four sets of unpublished statistics, obtained from the Census Bureau, to be used in writing up my report.

Two of these sets of data seemed to support the Labor Department's position, but the other two tended in the opposite direction. When I wrote up my report, I pointed out how and why each set of data tended to support the conclusion that it did—and how the four sets put together were inconclusive. The powers that be were both surprised and disappointed at my report, with perhaps some additional annoyance that I had missed their little hints as to what conclusions were desired. This forced them to spend time drastically editing what I had said before passing it on to the Secretary of Labor, who presented it, in his usual confident way, to Congress.

● ● ●

My initial positive response to efforts to desegregate the South began to be mixed with some doubts, especially when those efforts went beyond trying to end Jim Crow laws, and the methods used also raised questions. I wrote to a friend in August 1962:

> The more I follow the integration struggles in the South, the more I am inclined to be skeptical as to the actual fruits of it all. It is awkward to stand on the sidelines and criticize people who are suffering for their ideals, and yet the question must be asked, "What is this going to *do?*" There seem to be so many other things with greater priority than equality-of-public-accommodations that the blind preoccupation with this one thing seems almost pathological. When one considers the apathy in the Negro community toward such things as the hopeless incompetence and irresponsibility of their own colleges and other institutions, the fervor generated in the fight for "integration" in all things and at all costs seems more an emotional release than a sensible movement toward something that promises a worthwhile benefit.

It struck me as a classic problem in economics. Black people did not—and do not—have unlimited time, unlimited resources, or unlimited goodwill in the larger society. Given all the urgent needs for more and better education, for example, and for all the things that can be obtained with the fruits of work skills and business experience, how much time and effort could be spared for endless campaigns to get into every hamburger stand operated by a redneck?

In Washington, there happened to be some fifth-rate college—I am not even sure whether it was accredited—that would not admit blacks. I thought the local civil rights groups did the right thing when they denounced this racial policy, but I was appalled that they actually invested further efforts in trying to get the policy changed. Not only did this seem like an investment that ought to be put somewhere else, it annoyed me that we seemed to be constantly seeking acceptance and validation by white people—*any* white people at all, anywhere.

· · ·

Shortly before I was to go off to teach at Douglass College, another economist at the Labor Department came by my place for the last of our weekly chess matches. This evening he decided to stay to watch the television program "Open End," which was one of my favorites. It was a round-table discussion, hosted by David Susskind and featuring a different group and a different topic each week. This week's discussion featured a group of young college women.

As we listened, I was appalled by their ignorance, shallowness, and dogmatic self-righteousness. My friend enjoyed a good laugh at my obvious consternation.

"*This* is what you are going off to teach," he said.

One of these young women, whose name meant nothing to me at the time, was Jane Fonda.

· · ·

Douglass College had a lovely little campus, which I could see from my studio apartment on the top floor of a building across the street. It was "a small college, but there are those who love it," as Daniel Webster said of Dartmouth, and I was one of those—at least for a while.

My first few days in New Brunswick were almost too good to be true. The building was new, the neighbors nice and the view from my apartment magnificent, encompassing the Raritan River as well as Douglass College. When I arrived, I also found mail saying that an article I had submitted to a British scholarly journal—published at the London School of Economics—had been accepted and would be published the following year. It had been a couple of years since my first article appeared in the *American Economic Review,* and it was good to see that it was not just an isolated fluke.

A few days before classes were to begin, three of us who were to teach introductory economics met to discuss coordinating our classes. The main textbook and a supplementary book—*The Worldly Philosophers* by Robert Heilbroner—had been selected the previous spring, before I was hired. I was asked what I thought of them.

"The text is fine," I said. "I am familiar with it from having learned introductory economics from it myself, years ago."

"And *The Worldly Philosophers?*"

"Well . . ."

"It's a very popular book."

"True, but . . ."

"You have reservations about it?"

"I don't think it's worth the paper it's written on."

"Why?"

"It's not only that it is wrong on a number of things—which is true of any book—but that its whole *way of thinking* leads the student *away* from economic analysis and away from intellectual development generally."

"Well, the students like it!"

This phrase was to become a familiar one in justification of many questionable educational practices—at Douglass College and elsewhere.

• • •

My first day of teaching began with my getting mixed up on the directions to the building where the class was meeting, so that I arrived about ten minutes late. The students were still there, I was relieved to find.

When I handed out copies of my long reading list for labor economics, there were audible groans. When I tried to point out that it really wasn't so much reading, there was a certain undercurrent of derisive laughter. And when I added on the blackboard another article that had come out since the list was mimeographed, there was a shocked silence and exchanges of glances among the students.

Over the next few days, I was braced to receive notices of students dropping the course, and anticipated an evacuation like Dunkirk. However, not one student withdrew. A few days later, another student came around to my office for a copy of the reading list and subsequently joined the class. It was a very heart-warming beginning to my teaching career and I grew very fond of my classes, though you would never know it from the grades. My salary was now 20 percent lower than it had been in the government, but nevertheless I decided that this was how I wanted to spend my life, perhaps all of it at Douglass College.

From my apartment, I could see the girls lining up outside the library before it opened up at 8 AM. They were conscientious students, by and large, and many were quite bright. But the focus of their efforts were good grades to take home, not a drive to understand or to develop their own analytical powers. They wanted to *receive* a prepackaged education—and that was not what I offered.

My teaching was directed toward getting the student to think. The reading assignments often contained conflicting analyses of a given economic problem. Some students responded to this but others found it very disconcerting. This was brought home to me one day when questioning one of those students who clearly preferred a more conventional approach. In the assignment on which she was being questioned, Heilbroner's book, *The Worldly Philosophers,* asserted that the classical economist David Ricardo had denied the existence of depressions. Along with this chapter, I assigned a chapter of Ricardo's *Principles* in which Ricardo explores the causes of depressions.

"Miss Robinson," I asked, "what were Ricardo's views on depressions?"

"Well, Ricardo denied that there could be any depressions because . . ." and she went on into an almost verbatim repetition of Heilbroner.

"What did Ricardo say about depressions in his *Principles?*" I asked.

"Ricardo said that depressions were caused by changes in the patterns of demand, such as when you convert to peacetime production after a war, or where——"

"Wait," I said. "How do you reconcile this with the previous statement that Ricardo denied the very *existence* of depressions?"

"Well. . . . I hadn't really thought about that."

"Are the two statements compatible?"

"I guess . . . I don't know."

"Well, what is your opinion then?"

"*My* opinion . . . ?" she said, as if it were the strangest and most shocking concept in the world.

"Yes, your opinion."

After a puzzled moment, she said: "Why would Heilbroner say that if it wasn't true?"

• • •

Personally, my relations with the students were pretty good on the whole, though I was not a big participant in student-faculty get-togethers. I was surprised one day when one young lady told me, with some pique, that she had noticed that I was not present at a recent student-faculty picnic—because she had looked for me. A colleague more in tune with things said to me:

"The students seem to like you, Tom. There's just one complaint I hear about you personally."

"What's that?"

"You never invite them to your home, the way other faculty members do."

"My home is a bachelor apartment," I said. "I don't think that's the place for me to be inviting these young ladies."

"How did you get to be such an old fogey at such a young age?" he asked.

• • •

With all the exhausting work involved in preparing every lecture from scratch for the first time, and with all my misgivings about the students' view of education as a spectator sport, still I looked forward to my classes and felt a certain regret when I finished the last one on Thursday afternoon and realized that I would not see the students again until Monday. Part of this may have been the sense of fulfillment at beginning at last the teaching career that I had looked forward to since graduate school. Part may also have been due to my meager social life.

Friends and colleagues in Washington gave me names of people in New Brunswick and in New York, but nothing much came of it—at least nothing that would induce me to cut ties with my girl friend in Washington. However, I kept up a lively correspondence with friends, colleagues, and family, scattered here and there, and talked on the phone regularly with a black sociologist named Al, who taught at one of the New York City colleges.

Al was a real character. He was the epitome of the 1960s radical and militant—except that he had a sense of humor. Like many black radical intellectuals, he was from an affluent family, lived his life almost entirely among white intellectuals, and had little direct knowledge or experience with "our black people," as he liked to call them. He knew that I thought this kind of talk was as phoney as a three-dollar bill, but he was a decent sort and was helpful in providing me with information and insights about the academic world, and with social contacts.

Al was "politically correct," long before that term was coined. For example, he sent me a Christmas card on which all the people were black. The next time we talked on the phone, I said:

"Al, I'll bet those were the only black people you have seen all year."

A mutual friend who introduced us recalled that, in graduate school, "Al always had a blonde on his arm and militant slogans in his mouth." To needle him, I went out of my way to be "down home." I remember one day in particular when he phoned.

"Hi, Tom," he said, "just thought I'd chat a little. What are you doing?"

"I'm eating watermelon," I said (which I was).

"Water——melon?" Al asked, somewhat squeamishly.

"Yes, Al, watermelon!" I said enthusiastically. "Pardon me while I wipe my ears."

"Oh, Tom."

One of the highlights of the year for Al was having lunch with Malcolm X in Harlem. However, before heading up there, he phoned me to double-check the directions. For years afterward, whenever Al forgot himself and engaged in racial breast-beating around me, I would remind him that I had once had to give him directions to Harlem. At that point he had already been living in New York for years—in Greenwich Village.

· · ·

At Douglass College, there were only three economists and we were part of a department of economics and sociology combined. One of our sociology colleagues was an attractive matronly woman named Emily. She told me that my kind of teaching was completely foreign to many of the students.

"They've been taught to memorize and recite for twelve straight years. Now you're asking them to *think*. It's not easy for them."

"But Emily," I said, "isn't that what education's all about? You can get 'facts' out of an almanac."

"Tom, look—I started out teaching with the same ideas you have. In fact, I still believe in them. But I can't keep butting my head against a stone wall, year after year, frustrating myself and the students."

"What do you do?" I asked.

"Well, I've seen a lot of interesting things in my life. I tell them about them. I listen to their experiences. It makes a better relationship all around. You can't cram abstractions down their throats all the time."

"I try to lighten it up a little sometimes."

"Yes, but they know that the grade—the almighty Grade—will depend on how well they've mastered those abstractions."

"Why are grades so important around here?" I asked. "Are most of these girls going on to graduate school?"

"No. A lot of them are going into teaching, in fact. Each girl will teach 1.5 years, get married, and have 2.8 children."

"Then why is the grade so important? They can study what they like, read the material with their minds at ease, and get whatever development or stimulation education has to offer."

"Grades are important because they *think* grades are important. So do their parents."

"What a mess."

"Don't get discouraged."

Some time later, while riding a bus into New York, I overheard some students praising Emily as a teacher. Every point they mentioned in her favor was in fact a condemnation, not only by my standards but by the standards she herself would prefer, if she could afford them. But she was doing what the students liked and it was a success in those terms.

• • •

Assuming that teaching young women is not fundamentally different from teaching young men or a mixed class, I proceeded at first in utter disregard of their sex. However, somehow I sensed that this approach was not always what they wanted, that some occasional acknowledgement of their identity would be better. Accordingly, while explaining some principle of economics one day, I deliberately made a gratuitous remark:

"Since this product is purchased mainly by women, the demand for it is obviously unstable."

Instantly, there were boos and hisses, followed immediately by raucous laughter. In a later era, this would be a *cause celebre,* if not a federal case.

One of the sex differences I took more seriously was the tendency of so many of the students to be planning to go into school teaching, when I thought that a number of them had minds capable of much more intellectually challenging work. When I asked my colleagues why more of the girls did not go on to graduate school, I was told that it was harder for women to get fellowships.

At first I was incensed that they would be arbitrarily discriminated against in this way, but I was told that women were much less likely to complete graduate school, so that those entrusted with awarding financial aid felt an obligation to put the money where it was most likely to produce successful Ph.D. students. When I did some research in the library, I found that women did in fact drop out of graduate school moreso than men.

While I developed more relaxed relations with the students as time went on, and grew quite fond of some of them, I also maintained a sharp line that neither of us was to cross. I had the feeling that a couple of them might have had some non-academic inclinations, but it is hard to distinguish that from a sort of trying out their new adulthood. One day, one young lady came to my office and, instead of sitting in the chair by the desk, sat up on the desk itself, striking a pose with her little buns toward me.

"Miss Wilson," I said quietly, "if I had a hat pin right now, do you know what I would do?"

Instantly, she was off the desk and into the chair.

This is not to say that I was oblivious to all the attractive young women around me. As I wrote to a friend at the time, I felt like the Ancient Mariner, when he said:

> Water, water, everywhere,
> Nor any drop to drink.

• • •

Generalizations about "the students" cannot be carried too far. Not only did individual students differ greatly; so did whole classes. During my first semester at Douglass College, I taught labor economics and two classes of introductory economics. Obviously the upper level classes differed from the introductory classes. But the latter differed between themselves as well. Whether judged by classroom participation or examination results, one introductory class was clearly better than the other.

I wondered at first if there were something that I was doing differently in the two classes. The way the schedule was set up, one introductory class was taught the material before the other and took the exams before the other. I deliberately varied the order in which the two classes were taught material and examined on it, to see if that made any difference. It didn't. One class was simply better than the other.

The difference might have been due to a couple of gung-ho students in one class and the contagiousness of their enthusiasm. Whatever it was due to, the difference was quite real. Recognizing that whole classes differ in performance made me impervious to the lure of grading on a curve. Why should a good performance be rated better or worse because of the performance of the other people in class? How can valid letters of reference be written in later years for people who studied in classes with different ability levels, if they are graded on a curve?

Within each class, there seemed to be growing differences—almost polarization—between those who were responding well to my teaching and those who were becoming progressively more alienated. The latter began going to the department chairman (a sociologist) with their unhappiness. Toward the end of the first semester, he and I had a talk about this in his office. Inside the door of his office was a chart showing enrolments in economics declining over the past several years, a trend which he was anxious to reverse.

"Tom," he said, "the feeling I get from talking to a number of students is that you aim your course at the A and B students—and let the C and D students go to hell. We know the students exaggerate, so I wanted to get the real story from you."

"No, I think that's a pretty fair summary of my approach."

"Well, the A and B students can pretty much get it without our help. It's the people further down who need us."

"That depends on how you conceive of education," I said. "If education is just an accumulation of information, then of course the A and B students can read as well as we can. But if education is learning to *systematize* your thinking, then the A and B students need someone to help them as much as anyone else."

"But you've got to 'scoop lower' and bring the C and D students up there. If the others get restless, give them some extra work to do to keep them quiet."

"Look, we're talking about C and D students as if they were born into the world with those letters on their foreheads. Anybody who can get into Douglass College can make a B in my course. The students you want me to concentrate on are those who don't *want* to get an education. As for giving the good students something to keep them quiet, that would be treating those who came here for an education as a special problem!"

"Well, we're a state university and we can't just serve the elite. I think you ought to see Joe Talarico—maybe have several sessions on teaching with him—and get some pointers on teaching here. He's been a very successful teacher."

"I respect Joe as a teacher and as a person," I said, "but I can no more adopt his methods than he could mine."

"Well, what *do* you intend to do?"

"I don't know."

A few days later, I left my resignation in his mailbox. The next time I saw him, he seemed neither surprised nor dismayed.

• • •

Although resigning was a tough decision to make—there was no other job offer on the table at the time—once that decision was made, I felt a great sense of relief. One sign of my greater relaxation was that my bowling scores, which had dropped as low as a 101 average for a three-game set, now shot up. I had at least one 200 game in each of four successive outings, hitting my all-time peak of 279. Sometimes you don't realize how much tension has been built up until after it has been released.

Ironically, I had turned down a firm job offer—signed contracts with an "x" indicating where my signature was to go—from the La Jolla campus of the University of California, back in the earlier part of the academic year, when things looked good at Douglass. Two other inquiries came in, early in 1963, both from Washington—Howard University and American University. Other things being equal, I would have preferred to try my hand at a black college, but other things were far from equal. Most important, it was hard to get a straight answer out of Howard as to basic facts about their offer.

A remarkable set of events unfolded at American University. They invited me down for an afternoon of conversations with the economics department chairman, a couple of deans, and the president of the university. This was a lot of top brass to be interviewing a junior faculty member and it all went very well. I had expected a brief courtesy call with the university president, but he was warm and talkative and our conversation lasted half an hour. He told me quite frankly that I would be the first full-time Negro faculty member in the institution's history, and both he and the deans made it a point to say that they were prepared to rubber-stamp the department chairman's decision.

The chairman was equally friendly and straightforward. As soon as he and I got back to his office, he said that he would waive the usual rigmarole and make his offer right then and there. I told him I would send him my answer shortly after returning to New Brunswick and we parted, both in good spirits.

Just a couple of days later, I received a telegram from the department chairman—*withdrawing the offer*—and promising a letter of clarification to follow. When the letter arrived, the closest thing to a clarification was a statement saying "additional information has been brought to my attention which indicates that you might be well advised to seek a post where your keen interest in research will be given greater scope than it can possibly be afforded here."

Since I had taught at only one institution, there could be no mystery about the source of this "additional information," branding me as someone who neglects his students to do his own research. The galling irony of all this was that I had had no time to do any research at Douglass College, and had spent most of my waking hours during the preceding weeks preparing my new courses for the spring semester.

Articles of mine were accepted for publication in three scholarly journals during my year at Douglass College, but every one of them was written before I ever set foot in New Brunswick. In my naive pleasure at getting the acceptances, I had shared the good news with my colleagues—without realizing that some of them would never appear in even one journal of the same calibre in their whole careers. Whether prompted by envy or by resentment of my independence, the "additional information" supplied to American University was a knife in the back that could only represent vindictiveness, since my

resignation had already relieved the department of any practical problem. It was another painful lesson in academic ethics.

• • •

The exodus of students, which I had feared on the first day of the fall
semester, in fact occurred at the beginning of the spring semester. The
bottom halves of my two introductory economics classes disappeared.
This turned out to be an enormous blessing in disguise. The classroom atmosphere in both classes improved noticeably, and the class
which had lagged behind the other during the fall semester now
caught up and held its own. The spring semester at Douglass College
turned out to be one of my happiest teaching experiences anywhere.

Not only were the classes more intellectually stimulating for all,
we enjoyed ourselves immensely in the process. There were so many
outbursts of laughter in the classroom that one girl said, "The teacher
next door must wonder what is going on in here." Years after I left
Douglass College, some of these students continued to write to me, or
to send me Christmas cards, sometimes with little notes about their
jobs, their marriages, or their children.

• • •

The intellectual, political and social ferment associated with the 1960s
were already underway, though there was not yet the galvanizing issue
of the Vietnam war. People were beginning to praise a new drug called
L.S.D. for its "mind-expanding" qualities, though the only evidence
that their minds had expanded was their own belief that it had—a belief that some ordinary drunks have also had, at least until they
sobered up and realized that they had just been making damn fools of
themselves.

The great issue of the 1960s, however, was race. As the media gave
increasing coverage to racial issues, this not only gave increasing
prominence to leaders of traditional civil rights organizations; it also
brought to prominence more or less free-lance black "spokesmen,"
who owed their position precisely to their own ability to project themselves and their ideas in the media.

The charismatic style of the new black spokesmen was dramatized

for me one day when I was watching television and saw a program begin with a very close close-up of James Baldwin, who glared out of the
screen with intense bitterness and said in a quiet but charged voice:
"I've just come from seeing a dead boy—and you killed him."

"Not me, Jim," I said. "I've been here in the apartment all day."

It turned out that this "dead boy" was a man in his twenties who
had died from an overdose of drugs. Apparently "society" was to
blame, or more specifically whites in the society. However, Baldwin
was a master of images, not logic. Psychological warfare was the stock
in trade of the new charismatic leaders, and the tactic of putting others on the moral defensive was sometimes used against blacks as well
as against whites, who were the principal target.

My views were certainly not in tune with the spirit of the 1960s.
However, they were expressed publicly only in occasional letters to
The New York Times, some of which were published and some not.
Throughout the 1960s, my articles dealt with things for which I was
professionally trained—economics in general and the history of economic theory in particular. Because the history of economic theory
was of far more interest to scholarly journals in England and Canada
than to those in the United States, most of my professional work was
published outside the country. Though I did not realize it at the time,
this was a long-term blessing, for the economists who ran these journals in other countries had no way of knowing what color I was, so I
was spared the doubts that became increasingly common over the
years among black academics, as to whether their achievements were
really their own or were due to tokenism or double standards applied
by whites.

* * *

On the job front, I still had an offer from Howard University on the
table—and was still trying to get some straight answers as regards the
conditions of employment. The most available alternative was to return to the government but teaching was preferable to me, if it did not
ruin me financially. At Douglass College, I had to draw on my savings
to stay afloat and I could not continue to do that. Finally, the department chairman at Howard said that my salary would be supplemented

by a summer research grant, which would be enough to enable me to make it. I accepted.

Although I had been thinking about teaching at a black college since my days in graduate school, my contacts with officials at Howard, and earlier at Tuskeegee and Morgan State, left me with grave misgivings. So did my memories of my student days at Howard. On the other hand, my conscience would rest easier if I at least gave it a try. But I had no illusions. As I wrote to my brother Charles in April, 1963:

> I do not expect Howard to be better, but the problems should be different, and I would rather waste my time in Washington than in New Brunswick. I am more or less resigned to marking time until I get the doctorate and can look forward to teaching in the kind of place where I can remain. Of course, if it turns out that I can do something for those kids at Howard, there would be nothing I would rather do, but teaching people who do not want to learn is not something that appeals to me.

• • •

I began teaching at Howard University during the summer session in 1963. I was very much on guard against drifting into lower standards, for the students or for myself. I knew, from my experience in the government, that Howard students had a tougher time getting jobs than students—black or white—from other universities in Washington. Howard students often started lower when they were hired, and tended to get promoted more slowly. The *price* of lower standards was quite clear and vivid to me. I deliberately kept all the Douglass College students' examination answers, so that I could check from time to time to see whether I was still giving the same grade for the same quality of work.

The summer class in introductory economics was held at night, and so probably attracted a more serious student enrolment. I spent most of each day preparing for the evening class. Although the students were obviously less educated and less polished than the Douglass College students, they gave a good account of themselves and I was very heartened to find that their examination answers were as good as those at Douglass. It looked as if I had made the right decision to come here, and I allowed myself to believe that I had found my niche in life.

* * *

Although most students in my summer course in introductory economics were doing well, one student presented a serious problem, both educationally and philosophically. She was a shy young African girl who had just arrived in the United States from Guinea and was thoroughly overwhelmed by everything. She knew only the route from the International House to the university, and on campus she traveled always in the company of a small group of other African students. Her shyness approached fright. In class, she seemed wholly unaware of what we were doing or were trying to do. She failed the first two weekly tests in the course, and when I spoke with her about it after class, she was thoroughly ashamed and hopeless, and quietly began to cry.

It so happened that Mrs. Gadsden, my English professor when I was a student at Howard, knew this girl and had in fact taught her English back in Guinea. I decided to talk with Mrs. G about her, to see if she could suggest something.

"This poor girl is a thoroughly miserable human being, Mrs. G," I said. "You can't imagine how crushed she is by everything."

"Yes, I can. I have talked with her here and I knew her and her family in Guinea. She is in a hellish situation."

"Exactly. I don't see how she can learn anything as long as she is in this emotional turmoil. And with summer school being only six weeks long, and the course moving at breakneck speed—classes every night for two hours—it's too much to expect her to catch up."

"So you think she's going to fail the course?"

"Well, she's not going to learn the material. Whether I can bring myself to give her an F is something else. That's really hitting somebody who's down."

"You're thinking of passing her even if she does not do passing work?"

"Well, you know I'm against that, Mrs. G, but there are exceptions to everything."

"Why is this an exception? Because it's *you* and an African girl, instead of one of those guilty white liberals you're always denouncing for their paternalism to Negro students?"

"No, I don't think it's just that."

"How many times over the years I have heard you criticize teachers who pass unqualified Negroes 'so that they can go back to the black community and mis-educate a whole new generation of Negro students.' Do *you* want to pass someone to go back home and mis-educate a whole generation of African students?"

"But you know how impossible her situation is—"

"Yes, I know. And my heart breaks for her. But what you're suggesting isn't going to help anything. It means that in another ten years *her* students will be over here unprepared and there will be twenty or a hundred other teachers faced with the same situation you're facing now—or *ought* to face now. I'm ashamed of you, Tom. You know better!"

I was thoroughly shaken when Mrs. Gadsden finished with me, and was no closer to a solution than before. It was now intolerable to pass the girl, but still intolerable to fail her. As a desperate measure, I urged her to come to my office every day for an hour before class for private tutoring.

She came and sat frozen with apprehension. The first couple of days, it was like talking to a stone wall. In the next few sessions, she began to understand some of the simplest concepts that the rest of the class had mastered weeks before—and meanwhile the course was moving on. It looked hopeless, but there was no graceful way to cancel the sessions and tell her that I had given up on her as a lost cause. So we kept meeting and I kept going through the motions of tutoring.

One day, she suddenly began to grasp some of the subtle points of economics, and to connect them to what we had studied at the beginning of the course, as well as to what the class was doing now. I was clearly amazed and relieved. She smiled for the first time.

Once the spell was broken, she quickly made up lost ground. Her final examination grade was a solid B. At the beginning of the term, I had made my usual announcement that grades for the course would be based on a strict numerical average of examination grades, with no special allowance for a spectacular finish—all this to discourage loafing at the beginning of the course and dawdling in the middle—but it seemed to me that this was a special case where that rule should not apply. However, I thought of Mrs. Gadsden and of the bad effects of such concessions on the individual who receives them. So I simply averaged the African student's B in with the rest of her scores and came up with a C for the course. The next time I saw Mrs. G, she said:

"Our friend was *overjoyed* at getting a C in your course! She was proud because she knew she earned every bit of it."

* * *

Financially, things were becoming dicey. The summer grant, which was supposed to bring my income up to some reasonable level, was said by the department chairman to be moving slowly through channels. I borrowed money from a bank to keep going while the administrative wheels were supposedly turning. Finally, I went over the channels, directly to the university official in charge of grants, and asked what was holding up my money. He informed me that (1) there was *no* grant being processed for me, that (2) I was ineligible for any university grant, as I would officially become a member of the faculty only in September, and that (3) he had told my department chairman all of this very explicitly *months* ago.

The department chairman was safely out of the country for the summer by this time, but I sent him a note to let him know that I had discovered that he was a liar. Then I began looking for another job. No academic appointment was likely to be available this late, but I was by no means convinced that I wanted to remain in the academic world anyway. However, the fall term opened before anything that I wanted materialized.

During the first week of the fall semester, a job offer came in from the American Telephone & Telegraph Company in New York. It would pay me about double my academic salary. I was prepared to quit on the spot, but friends, colleagues, and both George Stigler and Milton Friedman at Chicago urged me in the strongest terms not to do it.

To walk out during the first week of the academic year would be considered a violation of all academic norms, and would be held against me for years, if I ever wanted to teach again. I listened to them and stayed, much against my better judgment. The appointment had been accepted on the basis of fraudulent misrepresentations. In retrospect, I am convinced that I should have walked out and let the chips fall where they may.

• • •

When the fall semester got under way, it became clear that my students were not as good, on the whole, as those in my summer evening classes. Even so, each class had at least a few students who were first-rate by any standard. But there was also a sizable contingent of students who were just not going to do any work, as well as some who were behavior problems, such as you might expect to find in some high schools. What was most depressing of all, however, was to discover how rampant cheating was. As a student at Howard, I had known about many isolated instances of cheating, but only now did I realize how blatant, how pervasive, and how organized it was. Statistics from other colleges have shown that many students cheat at some time or other during their four years of college. But at Howard, cheating was a way of life.

It seemed to me that no attempt to get the students to learn a difficult subject had any chance of success, unless the cheating could at least be drastically reduced. For this, the university rules were worthless. Procedures for making a charge of cheating stick were such that no instructor could afford to waste vast amounts of time on such a chancy project. The only real control would have to be in the classroom.

I began to make up two or three versions of every exam, and to pass them out in such a way that people sitting next to each other would not have the same test. Because the pervasive corruption extended to typists and secretaries, who leaked or sold exams to students in advance, I had to type up my own exams and use the reproduction machinery myself. Time-consuming though this all was, it was not an excessive precaution. One day, as I entered the economics department office, I overheard a secretary on the phone saying, with some exasperation:

"Don't you understand? He does all the exams *himself.*"

Some people argue that those who cheat are only cheating themselves, while those who are serious will do an honest job. However, the great bulk of the students at Howard were neither incorrigible nor saints. The problem with this large middle group was not that they could not do the work but that they would not do it, unless they had to face exams where they could not fake it. Moreover, it was not just a matter of their success of failure as individuals. These were *black* students and what they did or didn't do meant too much to others for me to let them flounder in their own immaturity and weaknesses. I knew that, whatever "front" they might put up on campus, behind many of these kids was some father driving a cab at night, after working all day, or some mother down on her knees scrubbing some white woman's floor, in order to send their children to college to try to make something out of them.

My tightening up on standards and on cheating initially meant massive failing grades on exams. This in turn meant massive complaints—to me, to the department chairman, and to the dean. One girl who received a very low grade burst into tears and ran into a colleague's office.

The department chairman only reluctantly discussed anything with me, in view of our very strained relations. (I had called him a son of a bitch to his face, and took off my glasses when I said it.)

The dean, however, jumped in with both feet.

"For God's sake, Sowell," he said. "You're not teaching at Harvard!"

"I never thought that I was," I said. "But how are we supposed to reach those higher standards you're always talking about if everyone who comes here is expected to conform to existing standards?"

"We need higher standards, but we have to be reasonable. Kids from these backgrounds can't handle a lot of abstractions, graphs and things like that."

"Yes, they can—but they will not do it as long as they have sympathetic administrators to intervene in their behalf."

"It's my job to intervene when a teacher isn't doing his job."

"If you think I'm not doing my job, you can have my resignation—anytime. We don't even need to wait until June."

"We can talk about that later. Right now, my concern is to get through this term and then this academic year. Now, when I see students line up outside my office, day after day, to complain about one teacher, I know that something is wrong."

"Of course something is wrong! What's wrong is that cheating and intrigue are easier ways of getting by around here than doing the work."

"I am willing to accept the fact that the students have their faults, or that the institution has its shortcomings. But you're unwilling to believe that *you* could be wrong. How do you justify your teaching methods which have produced all this uproar?"

"I don't intend to justify them at all," I said. "The proof of the pudding is in the eating. Now, you give exams to graduating seniors in their major field. Good. When the students from my courses take their exams in economics, compare their results with those of students from the rest of the department."

"That's all you have to say?"

"What else is there? We're here to produce results, not popularity."

"And you intend to keep on with the same teaching methods, the graphs, the abstractions, come what may?"

"Come what may."

Later on, it was leaked to me—no doubt deliberately—that the dean had never taken such instant and total dislike to anyone in all his years at Howard University. We had a number of encounters and a number of acrimonious words. In October, I typed up a four-page, single-spaced letter of resignation, effective the following June, but suggesting that we could, by mutual agreement, terminate my appointment in February.

When the students began to realize that I was continuing on the same path as before, some dropped out, some still tried to cheat or hoped that I would relent at the end, but the bulk of the students started applying themselves. Many were even surprised at their own success at mastering what had seemed an impenetrable subject. Grades began to rise—some dramatically—and by the end of the semester the class work was comparable to what had been done at Douglass College or in the summer session. One group of students, in one of the four courses I taught, held out to the end, apparently on the assumption that I could not fail that many students. Thirty percent of that class flunked.

In the second semester, the bottom half of my introductory economics classes disappeared, as at Douglass College. However, unlike the situation at Douglass College, I not only retained the top half but also gained additional students who had heard about my approach and who wanted to try it in preference to what they had been getting. My introductory economics class that spring was a delight that I looked forward to. The students seemed to like it too, and I can remember at least one occasion when we held classes voluntarily on a university holiday.

As word of my resignation spread, a number of students came to me to express their appreciation for what I had done, many confessing that they had misjudged me, a few urging me to reconsider, and a couple getting angry that I was "copping out" by leaving. One young man said:

"How are we ever going to advance, if people like you come here for one year and then leave?"

The question really hit me. I had no answer for him then—or now. But I did know that the role I played could be successful for one year, with everyone aware that I was leaving, but was not a viable role for the long run.

At the end of the term, a young couple taking my graduate seminar on Marxian theory came to me to express their appreciation for the course, but added:

"We still don't know what *your* opinion is on Marxism."

I took that as an unintended compliment—the best kind.

. . .

These were historic times for civil rights and for racial issues in general. While I welcomed the dismantling of the old Jim Crow laws in the South, I was increasingly disenchanted with the Utopianism which I had first noted back on the day when the Supreme Court announced its decision in *Brown v. Board of Education*.

The idea seemed to be that white people's sins were all that stood between us and economic and social parity throughout American society. The enormous amount of *internal* change needed within the black community—in education, skills and attitudes—seemed wholly un-noticed, as people rhapsodized about the brave new world to come, if and when white people became less sinful, courtesy of the federal government. Neither whites nor blacks had run out of room for improvement, but I expected no dramatic change in the relative economic positions of the races as a result of civil rights laws.

Civil rights were important in and of themselves, and we should have equality before the law as a matter of justice. But to expect civil rights to solve our economic and social problems was barking up the wrong tree, it seemed to me. When the Civil Rights Act of 1964 became a big political issue, my hope was that it would pass without any crippling amendments, not only for its own sake, but also in order that we could turn our attention away from such distractions and toward our own self-development as a people. In February 1964, I wrote to a friend:

> Perhaps if the omnibus civil rights bill goes through Congress undiluted, the bitter anti-climax that is sure to follow may provoke some real thought in quarters where slogans and labels hold sway at the moment.

Although the Civil Rights Act of 1964 wrought dramatic legal and political changes across the South, its economic consequences were in fact a bitter anti-climax. Economic progress continued, but at no faster pace than in the past. Additional blacks entered professional and other high-level positions in the five years following passage of the Civil Rights Act—but these additions were *fewer* than in the five years preceding passage of the Act. The civil rights organizations, with an obvious vested interest in magnifying their own achievements, created an enduring myth that all blacks were indebted to them for economic progress, but the statistical data simply do not support this claim, however often it has been repeated in the media.

When civil rights legislation, school integration and other such policies failed to produce the expected economic and social miracles, this did not produce any of the fundamental re-thinking I had hoped would follow. On the contrary, it provoked renewed efforts for more of the same kinds of things that were not working, eventually leading to bitter struggles over school busing and "affirmative action," both of which led to more anti-climaxes in the wake of political and legal "victories." The underlying assumptions behind such crusades remained absolutely unquestioned.

At this point, I questioned those assumptions only in letters to friends or in letters to newspapers. My professional training and my professional work was in other areas, so I had no background at this point on which to base a wholesale challenge to the orthodox "experts."

⋅ ⋅ ⋅

In my personal life, this was also a period of change. I accepted a job offer from A.T.&T., at that time the world's largest corporation, and moved to New York, where I lived in Greenwich Village, not far from my radical friend Al and within walking distance of my job. My old friend Jim, from Labor Department days, was already working for A.T.&T., in the same unit where I was assigned. The biggest change, however, was that I got married.

It was good to be out from under financial strain for a while, so that my wife and I could go out to a nice restaurant occasionally or see some plays on Broadway. One of the most memorable evenings at the theater was spent watching Lorraine Hansberry's last play, "The Sign in Sidney Blustein's Window." Not nearly as well known as "A Raisin in the Sun," it nevertheless had moments that showed Miss Hansberry's great talent and it also showed that she could move beyond the racial genre. What had the greatest emotional impact, however, was the appearance of her husband on-stage after the play, to tell us news of his wife, who was dying. My wife and I resolved that if we ever had a girl, we would name her for Lorraine Hansberry.

⋅ ⋅ ⋅

At A.T.&T., my job title was "economic analyst," but much of what I did had little direct connection with telephones. I was almost a scholar-in-residence, doing a wide variety of assignments. One assignment I dreaded initially was to write an article on the international balance-of-payments situation for the company magazine. I had never taken a course in international economics, nor even taken much interest in the subject, so I was hardly gung-ho for the assignment. However, I was given ample time to study up on the economics of international transactions. The final product, written for a popular audience, was later recommended, by an authority specializing in international economics, as a good introduction for laymen. I ended up being glad that I had done this assignment, for it broadened me in a way unlikely to happen in an academic setting, where sticking to one's specialty and sub-specialty are the rule.

Since I had just come from academia, some of the A.T.&T. brass wanted to know if I had any students whom I could recommend to be hired. A number of names came to mind, but I did not know how easy it would be to contact them, especially since the Howard University administration's incompetence was exceeded only by its apathy. However, I somehow managed to get the addresses and phone numbers of some of my former students. When I phoned the home of one of my brightest students, his mother said that he had been looking in vain for a job after graduating from Howard, but had just gone out to California to take a job with Pacific Bell. This was a subsidiary of A.T.&T., so the company wouldn't touch him. My second choice was a bright fellow also, and he was very much in the market.

After the C & P Telephone Company in Washington interviewed my former student, as a courtesy to the parent company, one of their officials phoned me to say how impressed he was—and what a contrast this young man was to the other people they had interviewed on the Howard campus, where they had gone recruiting three times without finding anyone even minimally qualified. It did not surprise me in the slightest that very bright students from Howard would be out walking the streets for weeks, looking for a job, at the very same time when major corporations were interviewing on campus without finding anyone who met their standards.

To the narrow, shallow, and petty people in charge of such things at Howard, opportunities were goodies to be handed out to favorites—if they bothered to bestir themselves to mention these opportunities to anybody. Bright students were often not among the favorites, and were in fact sometimes among those most alienated from the administration. You only had to know the people in charge at Howard, and the general attitudes prevailing there, to understand how golden opportunities for the next generation went right down the tubes. Changing such people and such attitudes was only one of the forms of self-development that I wished we had been putting some of our energies into.

My former student was hired immediately to work in another division of A.T.&T. Officials of that division were enormously pleased with his work and never ceased to thank me for having sent him there. And he was my second choice.

● ● ●

A.T.&T. was a nice place to work. The people were thoughtful and considerate, and the company tended to look out for its employees. The first time I ever wore a tuxedo, it was a tuxedo rented by A.T.&T., so that I could attend some business-related gathering at the Waldorf Astoria. When I went out on my own to give a couple of talks on campuses in Pennsylvania, they gave me time off to do it.

A.T.&T. had its own mores, however. When my wife and I went to lunch at a company cafeteria at Western Electric (an A.T.&T. subsidiary), she looked around the huge room and said:

"Do you know that you and I are the only man and woman having lunch together here?"

I looked around and suddenly realized that it was true. All over the cafeteria, men were having lunch with men, and women with women. This pattern was pervasive in company activities. Men and women were on separate bowling teams, and when a gathering was called at the office, they automatically gathered in separate clusters. The only coeducational company activity I can remember was the chess club, probably because there were not enough women to have their own club.

By the time I got back to work at my office, which was about half a mile from Western Electric, word had already spread like wild fire that I had had lunch with a woman. In order to disappoint the gossips,

I let it be known that she was my wife and that we lived within walking distance.

Some months later, I had lunch at the A.T.&T. cafeteria with a former student of mine from Douglass College, who was seeking my advice on a some career move that she was considering. It was long after I was gone from A.T.&T. that my old friend Jim finally told me of the gossip unleashed by my being seen with this pretty young blond woman.

• • •

Nineteen sixty-four was an eventful year, with ghetto riots and the Presidential candidacy of Barry Goldwater, the most clearly ideological candidate in years. Even among those of us who shared some of Goldwater's views on the role of government in the economy were put off by his tendency to shoot from the hip in his public statements, and by a truculence which made it possible to wonder if he would get us into a nuclear war with the Soviet Union. I composed a little couplet, entitled "The Goldwater Administration":

> Fifteen minutes of *laissez faire,*
> While the Russian missiles are in the air.

I thought of trying to get this published, but didn't—which was probably just as well, because it was no doubt unfair to Senator Goldwater. Still, he should have realized that he had only recently become well-known nationally, so that the image he projected was crucial.

More generally, my views were by this time pretty much what they would remain in the decades to come, though quite different from what they had been during the 1950s. In July 1964, I explained to an old classmate from Harvard how my outlook had changed drastically since we were in college together:

> The same problems and the same people are important to me, but the old solutions have crumbled on contact with reality. Recently, in unpacking my belongings after moving to New York, I came across some old scrapbooks in which I had a few letters to

the editor from an earlier period. I was pleasantly surprised to find that I still agreed with most of the particular points I had made, but since then other points not originally seen or not sufficiently appreciated had shifted the over-all balance.

* * *

On the academic front, I had by 1964 put aside the idea of writing a doctoral dissertation on Say's Law and instead was exploring the possibility of writing one on the effects of minimum wages on unemployment in Puerto Rico. For a number of reasons, Puerto Rico was a better place to test the effects of minimum wage laws than was the mainland of the United States. Moreover, I already had some familiarity with the subject, dating back to my first professional work as an economist in the Labor Department back in the summer of 1960.

The real question was whether I could get enough statistical data, with sufficiently consistent definitions over time, to do the study. I was busy writing to all sorts of people, both in the continental United States and in Puerto Rico, trying to get copies of all sorts of government documents. I was also in contact with two distinguished labor economists at the University of Chicago, hoping to get them to approve the dissertation topic and to serve on the committee to direct it. All this meant that I had not abandoned the idea of returning to the academic world, the only place where the ordeal of getting a Ph.D. was likely to be worth it.

* * *

In December 1964, A.T.&T. paid my way to the annual meetings of the American Economic Association, held that year in Chicago. My only specific assignment was to bring back the economic forecast to be given by one of the leading pooh-bahs in the economics profession. It seemed like a small price to pay to get a free trip and have my expenses paid in a fancy hotel.

During the convention, I was interviewed by the chairman of the economics department at Cornell University, and was offered an opportunity to fly up to Ithaca to see and be seen by the department. I told him that I was interested in returning to the academic world, but that I was not prepared to put up with the kind of interference with my teaching which I had already encountered at two other institutions. He assured me that such would not be the case at Cornell.

• • •

By 1965, there were Vietnam war protests and I counted myself among those opposed to the war. My old college room-mates Nort and Ralph were among those who signed a public statement opposing the war. I wrote to Nort in April 1965:

> I hope the Viet-Nam protests do some good. It is almost un-
> believable that we could have gotten involved in this mess . . .
> McNamara's air of papal infallibility is beginning to wear a little
> thin.

I don't recall whether I signed the same statement that Nort and Ralph signed, but I wouldn't be surprised if I did. The idea of some economists that you could "fine tune" the economy had already been discredited. The idea that you could fine tune a war—neither winning it outright nor losing it—was to take longer to be discredited, and was to be immensely more costly.

• • •

Moving from New York City to the little town of Ithaca, far upstate, meant a major change in life style. So did a pay cut of nearly 25 percent. Perhaps the biggest life style change, however, was due to the fact that I now had a son. Still, the move was one that I was looking forward to. As I wrote to a friend:

> We are just living to get away from this place. It is not only the at-
> traction of returning to the academic world but the repulsion of
> New York. There are a lot of cultural attractions here but there is
> also a lot of wholly pointless rudeness and sick people walking
> around with chips on their shoulder. One of these started a fight
> with me in the subway about a month ago. Fortunately, there was

nothing bad about him but his intentions. However, I still suffered a swollen hand, a slightly sore shoulder the next day and blood splattered on my clothes.

Fortunately, it was his blood. Even so, I was happy to be leaving New York, because the next time it could be my blood.

When my friend Al heard about the episode, he immediately asked:

"Are you all right?"

"I'm fine," I said. "I wasn't hurt in the slightest."

"What happened?"

"Well, this fellow stepped on my toes in the subway—and when I complained, he blew up. I didn't believe he was going to start a fight about it, but he did."

"What did you do?" Al asked.

When I described what I did, Al (who had a much more sheltered upbringing) was squeamish.

"Oh, Tom," he said, "how could you do that to a fellow human being, a fellow black?"

"He wasn't black," I said.

"Oh."

Suddenly it didn't seem quite so terrible to Al.

7

Cayuga's Waters

The little town of Ithaca and the lovely campus of Cornell University seemed idyllic in many ways, especially when combined with the friendliness of neighbors and colleagues. My teaching load was the lightest it had ever been—just two courses. One was an introductory economics course for engineers and the other was a graduate seminar on the history of economic thought. The latter represented the first time I had ever taught the subject in which I had specialized.

As someone returning to academia, I was welcomed back by my new colleagues as a prodigal son returning from the dog-eat-dog world of business. I had to tell them that the worst rumors I had heard at A.T.&T. were not as bad as what I had personally experienced in the academic world. They thought I was joking.

Although I was apparently the only black professor on campus in 1965, I was not pioneering because there had in fact been a black economist in the department before me. If there were any suspicions that I was a "token" black appointment, such suspicions were probably minimized by the fact that I had published more than any of the other assistant professors of economics, and perhaps more than all of them put together.

There was a small black community in Ithaca, but Ithaca itself was so small that its whole population was less than that of the university. Moreover, few people at Cornell had any social contact with the people in town. We were located "far above Cayuga's waters," as the school song said, and our social life as well as our work was centered in the highlands where students and faculty alike lived. This was in fact so far above Cayuga Lake that we could feel the changing air pressure in our ears when going down to Ithaca.

Blacks were so rare where we lived that one evening, when my wife and I encountered another black couple while leaving a restaurant, all four of us stopped dead in our tracks and then burst out laughing. It turned out that he was one of two eye surgeons in town—and was more in demand than the white eye surgeon. We visited with them a couple of times but they were way out of the financial league of an assistant professor. Our only other face-to-face contact with blacks during my first couple of years at Cornell were with our relatives, when we visited Washington, or my wife's trips to her hairdresser in Ithaca.

Whether because of this or in spite of it, I tried to maintain or establish whatever contacts I could by mail in the black community. One of the first letters I wrote from Cornell was to the secretary of the economics department at Howard University, asking her to help me locate some former students, so that I could see if they might want to be recommended for jobs at A.T.&T. or in the government. Later, I exchanged lengthy letters with a teacher in Harlem, whom I had heard about through the media, chiefly advising his students on various college possibilities and financial aid. On campus, I did not have a single black American student enrol in my classes, though there was a black student from Guyana who enrolled during my second or third year.

●　●　●

The euphoria of my first days at Cornell could not, of course, last. The first of a number of flies in the ointment was my pay. Not only had I taken a hefty cut in salary; some fringe benefits paid for by the company at A.T.&T. were now deducted from that smaller salary, shrinking my take-home pay even more. When I showed my first paycheck to my wife, she looked stunned and then said:

"Did they misplace the decimal point?"

Still, I was feeling pretty upbeat. I was teaching again, now at a highly reputable institution, and had an opportunity to resume work on my doctoral dissertation. When I talked on the phone with my friend Jim in New York, he could detect my good spirits, which he attributed to my being married.

"Marriage has made you almost *human,* Tom," he said. "In another five years, when you see an old lady fall and break her leg, you'll feel sorry for her." Jim was a liberal and, to him, those who opposed liberals were just mean.

• • •

Neither of my two courses put me in touch with the regular liberal arts undergraduates at Cornell. In one course I taught graduate students and in the other I taught engineering students.

The graduate seminar had twelve students enrolled, apparently twice the usual or expected enrolment, and was very well received by the students—too well received, as it turned out. Although the course took an exhausting amount of preparation, it was a real pleasure to conduct the seminar, which had an atmosphere of serious thought combined with good humor. Once, when I was trying to illustrate the great prestige which John Stuart Mill enjoyed in his own lifetime, I recounted an episode in which Mill walked into the midst of a dangerous mob and got them to disperse. One of the students said:

"He probably gave a lecture on economics. That would disperse any crowd."

Some students mentioned to me that they had been waiting for a long time for someone to teach a "real" graduate course in the history of economic thought. Word of the enthusiastic reception of my seminar may have gotten back to a senior professor in the same field, for I was told that he objected vehemently to a new and junior man being assigned to teach such a course in his field. Rank has its privileges. I was never assigned to teach that course again in my remaining years at Cornell.

A much more serious, or more immediate, problem arose in connection with my teaching of the introductory economics course for engineers. This course had been a source of contention before I arrived but, for reasons not at all clear, it was felt that things would go more smoothly with me teaching it. In fact, there developed more contentions than ever.

My whole approach was at the opposite pole from what the engineering students wanted. They were used to mathematical courses, lecture courses, and courses taught out of a textbook. None of this was my style. Not only was I not a mathematical economist, I refused to use even as much math as I knew, nor even as much math as I had used at Howard University. My theory was that education should supply what people lack, not let them coast on what they already know. Howard students needed to conceive of economics as a system of relationships, in a manner which mathematics forced them to do. Engineering students, however, could easily run through all the equations and graphs without really understanding what it meant as economics applied to human beings.

A further problem was that I expected even a large class like this one to have some discussion, which in turn meant that the students would have to be prepared to be called on in class. The engineering students had entirely different ideas. They were used to listening to lectures and to using their liberal arts courses as "breathers" in a demanding schedule, not something they had to keep up with day by day. Moreover, they were convinced that the "real" reading assignment in a course was the textbook material and that anything else— so-called "outside readings"—were just frills on the reading list.

A real tug-of-war quickly developed as to whether the engineering students would in fact keep up with the assignments as they were due, including the readings that were not in the textbook. On more than one occasion, when it became clear early in the class period that no one had read anything, I announced:

"Well, since I teach by discussion rather than lecturing, and since no one here can discuss what he hasn't read, there is nothing further to be done with this topic. Class is dismissed. Next time we will go on to the next topic. Of course, you are still responsible for this topic on the exam."

This created some stir, but little change. When the exam came, there were widespread failures and of course widespread com-plaints—to me, to the department chairman, and to officials in the en-gineering school. One of these officials phoned me:

"Mr. Sowell, I am in no way trying to influence the way you teach your class—"

"I'm not worried about your doing that."

"——but I just wanted to understand the situation, so I can know how to advise our students."

"I see."

"They say that scores were very low on the exam—many fail-ures—but that you refused to take that into account in the grading, and stuck to an absolute scale."

"That's right," I said. "I have never graded on a curve, and have no plans to do so. Moreover, I informed them of this very plainly on the first day of class, as I do in all my classes."

"Well, it looks right now as if great numbers of them are going to fail the course," he said.

"Not at all," I replied. "The exams remaining, including the final exam, count a high enough percentage of the course grade that a stu-dent with a zero at this point could still pass the course—and none of them has a zero."

"Yes, but it will be very hard for some of them to get a good grade."

"Of course. That's one of the penalties of failing an exam."

"But some students will fail the entire course unless they improve dramatically."

"That's true, but it doesn't take much effort to improve dramati-cally from scores of 20 or 30 percent."

"Well, realistically, some students are not going to improve that dramatically. Some are now alienated from the course, from your teaching methods, and from you as an individual."

"That's unfortunate."

"Realistically, do you have any idea how many will fail if you con-tinue to use an absolute grading scale?"

"No, I don't. Frankly, I never try to figure that out in any class. It's entirely in the student's hands. He knows arithmetic as well as I do, so he knows what he will have to do to pass the course."

"But are you prepared to flunk half the class if they don't come up to your expectations?"

"I have no expectation of flunking half the class. Most students have enough sense to do the work, once they find they are getting nowhere complaining to me or to other people."

"But how many *are* you prepared to flunk?"

"*Whatever number* have scores below 55."

There was a long pause, and then a weary "Thank you, Mr. Sowell."

Some time later, the acting chairman of the economics department came to my office. He was a personable enough fellow, quick-witted and ingenious, though by no stretch of the imagination a disciplined or systematic thinker. He was active in various causes and movements, among them students' rights, and was a very effective speaker, from a theatrical point of view. I could see one of his better performances coming on as he burst into my office.

"Tom, I want to talk to you, not as *chairman*," he said with an emphasis, a gesture, and an expression that conveyed his disdain for such conventional authority, "but as a colleague and friend—and as someone who believes that students have rights, too."

"Go on."

"Look, I know some of the engineering students goofed off," he said. "But others have not goofed off—and they have some *valid* arguments, which I think deserve respect."

"Doug, did Frank tell you that, when he offered me this appointment last December, I told him then that I didn't want it if it was going to mean this kind of interference?"

"*What* interference? I'm not trying to dictate to you. But I think we ought to all sit down and work something out."

"Doug, I can save us all a lot of time: *I don't plan to budge an inch.*"

That really left very little to be said, and he had the good sense to make a graceful exit.

Some days later, I found a note in my box from another senior colleague with whom I was on good terms, asking me to stop by his office when I could.

When I walked in, he said genially, "Hi, Tom," and motioned me to a chair. "Thanks for stopping by. Listen, something has come up. I really feel rotten even having to bring up something petty like this with you, but I have a kind of special involvement from the past."

"What is it?"

"Well, when I was chairman a few years ago, I set up this course for engineers, and I felt a sort of personal responsibility for some of the problems it's had from time to time."

"I see."

"Those kids don't always understand what a liberal arts course is supposed to be, and let's face it—some of them won't do the work. I'm glad to see that you're putting up a fight to maintain standards."

"Well, I'm glad to see that you agree with me."

"Now I think they've gotten the message," he said. "Along with it, unfortunately, they've gotten some very low grades, and it's going to be *very* tough for some of them to pull up and get a decent grade."

"Not *that* tough, I don't think."

"Did you ever think of this, Tom? Give some of them—or all of them if you wanted to—an opportunity to do a paper to make up for the bad grade on that exam. Then you could either substitute the grade from the paper for the exam grade or else just average it in to give them a better chance. You wouldn't be changing your grade, you would just be giving them a chance to do extra *work* for a better grade."

At last I saw where this meandering discussion was leading. *"Marie, the dawn is breaking,"* I said, quoting some old song lyrics.

"Hmm?"

"Fred, when you announce standards at the beginning of a course, it doesn't mean anything if you're going to figure out 'outs' for those who don't meet them."

"But you're not *giving* them anything. You're making them *work* for it."

"That really doesn't change the principle," I said. "That's just face-saving."

"Tom, there's a lot of things involved here, and I don't want to take up your time going into all of them. But, for example, the economics department benefits from this course."

"How does the economics department benefit from giving this course?"

"Well, it's an involved story, but what it amounts to is that the engineering school is paying us for teaching it."

"I'm afraid that doesn't make any difference to me."

"Well, it makes a difference to a lot of other people in the department. And frankly, some of those other people—myself included—will be among those who vote on whether to renew your contract when it expires in a couple of years."

"Since I intend to keep on making my own decisions as I see fit, I assume that others will make *their* decisions as they see fit," I said as I got up and walked out.

When my wife picked me up after work, I told her as I got into the car:

"Well, you needn't worry any more about our settling permanently in Ithaca."

After hearing what had happened, she said:

"Suppose you get *fired?*"

"Then I'll go back to work in private industry. We can use the extra money."

"In that case, give 'em hell."

• • •

My doctoral dissertation—the crucial reason for returning to the academic world and a major factor in determining whether I would stay in it—hit a snag after several months. After collecting masses of statistical material and discussing it by mail and by phone with my adviser at the University of Chicago, I found that the data I really needed was just not available. I was back to square one, after two years of futile effort.

Rather than try to come up with another dissertation topic right away, I decided to take a breather and instead work on fulfilling my language requirements for the Ph.D., starting with French. This proved to be surprisingly difficult at first. I hadn't read anything in French for years. However, once I slowly worked my way back into it, it became easier and I decided to read a nineteenth-century Swiss economist named Sismondi, who wrote in French.

As I began to read what Sismondi had written about Say's Law, it became clearer than ever to me that my original interpretation of that controversy was the right one, George Stigler to the contrary notwithstanding. By July, 1966, I was writing again to Stigler, to see if there was any chance of my resurrecting Say's Law as a topic, now that I had more material to support my interpretation. My letter to Stigler ended:

> Since we decided last time that it might be better if I wrote the dissertation under someone else's direction, perhaps we should do the same in the current attempt. However, I should like to get your opinion on the prospective topic in any case.

Stigler responded helpfully with a suggestion of an alternative dissertation chairman at Chicago, but also expressed his opinion that I would be better off trying some other topic, which had not already been written about as much as Say's Law. My reply to him ended:

> I cannot believe that re-interpreting a major episode in the development of economics and showing how a promising line of thought was put out of court (both glut theories and supply-demand analysis by the same economists) is less important than exploring some topic which no one has thought worthy of exploring before and in which I might become the world's authority by default.

Stigler was famous for many things, both as an economist and as a person. One of the things he was *not* famous for was patience. However, I must say that he showed patience with me (most of the time). By the fall of 1966, I had resumed work on a doctoral dissertation on Say's Law, with his blessing, though tentatively under someone else's direction.

* * *

Frank, the regular department chairman, returned from leave to resume his duties in the fall of 1966. Despite my run-ins with other senior members of the department in his absence, which he undoubtedly heard about, he was fine with me and in fact surprised me with the news that my teaching load would be reduced to one course during the spring of 1967, providing me more time to work on my doctoral dissertation. This windfall gain was of course welcome, but it was also a reminder that the department was ruthless in not renewing the contracts of assistant professors who did not finish their dissertations before their contracts ran out.

Another aspect of the reduced teaching load which caused me mild qualms was the notion that accepting it might seem to imply a long-run commitment to Cornell. Although things had quieted down after my first-year confrontations, the bloom was definitely off the rose. I had misgivings, not only about Cornell, but about the whole academic world. If my current dissertation effort did not end with my getting the degree, I had no intention of trying again. Moreover, I was not certain whether I would stay in academia, even if and when I did get my doctorate.

As early as January 1967, I was sending a resume to a "head-hunting" firm specializing in finding people for professional jobs in private industry. I also stayed in touch with various people at A.T.&T., where I was told that I would be welcomed back if I wanted to return.

None of this was a result of despair at my academic prospects. The writing of my dissertation was going well and two long articles of mine were accepted by scholarly journals during 1966 for publication in 1967. When the University of Toronto Press asked me to review a book-length manuscript on Marxian economics for them, it suggested to me that I might be beginning to get something of a reputation.

I liked teaching but I didn't like the cheap expediency and petty intrigues of academia. The kind of thing I despised was exemplified by an episode at the end of the spring semester. A student was absent on the day of an exam, without authorization, and I refused to excuse it, even though he had been absent to play on one of the Cornell athletic teams. Frank, our department chairman, told me that there was a rule under which the student was to be excused. When I asked to see the rule or be referred to it, he refused.

Frank was a crusty old fellow, who apparently was not used to having assistant professors giving him a lot of back talk. He couldn't do anything about my decision, but he suggested that maybe teaching was not something that I was cut out for. That did it. I started going to interviews for jobs in private industry during the summer and eventually found a couple of good prospects, including one back at A.T. &T.

Although I knew that walking out just before the beginning of the fall semester might mean the end of my academic career, that did not seem like such a big loss any more. When I went down to the economics department office to inform the chairman that I was leaving, I discovered that Frank was not there. Another colleague named Tom was now the new chairman. He said that he had no idea that problems between Frank and me had reached this point, and added that the only reports he had heard about my teaching were good. This cut the ground out from under my intended resignation, especially so close to the beginning of the fall semester. I decided to stay and finish out my contract at Cornell.

• • •

While I was in New York City during the summer of 1967, I arranged to meet my radical friend Al for dinner. It so happened that I arrived shortly after Israel had inflicted a crushing defeat on a coalition of Arab states in the Six Day war. Al was a passionate "anti-Zionist," as he called it, so I knew that he would be getting his defenses ready, in anticipation of my razzing him about what had happened. Knowing how important it was for Al to be verbally one-up, I could just imagine how much time and effort he was putting into preparing his rejoinders. Therefore I studiously avoided the subject, to add to his frustration, by providing no occasion for his *bon mots*.

Joining us was another old friend of Al's named Mark, whom I also knew and who I believe was Jewish, but who in any case had a very different set of views on Israel. We had a happy reunion and caught up on what was happening in each other's lives. When time came to go out to dinner, Al asked:

"Where do you want to eat, Tom?"

"I don't care. Wherever you guys want to eat is O.K. with me."

"But you're the visitor," Al insisted. "You get to pick the restaurant."

"Really, I don't care," I said. "One restaurant is the same as another with me." Then I could not resist adding, "——so long as the food is kosher."

"Tom," Al replied with a certain quiet and grave dignity, "Mark and I agreed, before you got here, that we would not discuss the Middle East this evening."

• • •

At Cornell, it was time for the economics department to make its decision as to what to do about my contract, now in its last year. The options were non-renewal (almost inevitable in my case, I was told by another assistant professor, who was close to one of the senior men), a one-year extension (given sometimes to those near to completing their Ph.D.s), or a three-year renewal.

I was voted a three-year extension, contingent on completion of the Ph.D., and a one-year extension with a raise, not contingent on anything. A senior professor present at the voting later told me:

"A couple of guys apparently thought they could knife you in the back at the outset, but when it became clear that the others wouldn't stand for it, they shut right up. You had a lot of defenders," he said. "Frankly, I was surprised!"

The worst term of opprobrium used against me in the meeting, I was told, was that I was "uncompromising."

• • •

In March 1968, I was scheduled to give a paper in a symposium on Marx at the University of New Hampshire. Predictions of a large snow storm made it unlikely that I could fly out of Ithaca, so I rented a car and set out on the highway.

Things went fine for perhaps a couple of hours. Then a light snow began to fall. It later became a heavier snow and finally it made the crucial change from snow to sleet. I was not having any great difficulty controlling the car until suddenly, perhaps hitting a patch of ice, it went completely out of control and began spinning and sliding sideways off the highway. Neither the brakes nor the steering wheel made the slightest difference in what the car did as it spun out of control.

While the car was in a backward position, I could see in the rear-view mirror a huge concrete pillar hurtling toward me.

Once it was clear that I had absolutely no control over the car, I resigned myself to whatever was inevitable, which at that point looked like death. However, I didn't care to have a steering wheel driven through my body, so I lay down across the front bench and curled up on the passenger side, to give myself whatever small chance of survival there might be.

By the luck of the spin, the car crashed into the concrete pillar while facing backward, which meant that I was thrown into the seat cushions, instead of into the dashboard or out through the windshield. The impact—very loud—pulverized the rear window on the right side of the car, sending a fine spray of glass over me. But, when the car came to rest and I sat up to check for injuries, I was surprised to discover that I was completely unhurt.

The car was a total loss, but I rented another one and continued on to the University of New Hampshire. When they welcomed me to the conference and I replied "I'm glad to be here," I really meant it. I was glad to be anywhere.

●　●　●

At Cornell, by this time there was now a substantial presence of black students, most brought in under lower admissions standards, though I did not know that at first. Not one of them enrolled in any of my courses, however. Nor was there any response when I told the administrator in charge of the special minority program that I was available to offer advice and counseling to any of the students that might need it. Although I was still one of the very few black faculty members at Cornell, I was never consulted on any aspect of the program. I could not help wonder if the black students were being steered away from hard-nosed professors, as athletes often were.

In March 1968, I went to a meeting at which some of the black students and their various white faculty patrons were trying to gather support for a program of research on the ghetto by the minority students. Although the meeting was billed as an attempt to get advice on how to help the education of black students, this was a misrepresentation. It was a meeting to line people up behind plans that had already been formulated. The black students, or at least the more vocal of them, wanted education that was "relevant," such as research in the ghetto.

Much of what the students said was sophomoric, but that is what to expect from sophomores. What had me aghast was that the white faculty members at the meeting were not only going along with it, but also were encouraging the students in a wholly paranoid vision of the "repressive" academic establishment, arbitrarily standing in the way of these wonderful ideas and projects.

I tried to argue that the most urgent educational needs of the students were for a solid foundation in academic skills, that any "research" that they could do at this early stage of their education would be of no use to them or to the black community. But the students clearly didn't want to hear that. Neither did the white activist professors. It was a long and acrimonious meeting that lasted four hours. As the only person present to question what was being said, I quickly became the villain—the representative, if not the tool, of the evil establishment. You would think that I had "sold out" for an assistant professorship, while these tenured white activists were their only real friends.

After the meeting finally broke up, I encountered a colleague from the economics department who had been at the meeting, and began arguing that the students' proposals were self-defeating. He just listened as we walked across the parking lot. Finally he said, "Of course," got into his car and drove off. He knew better all along. It just wasn't politic to say so.

· · ·

A more personal concern was building during this period. My little boy was now three years—and still could not talk.

With all the small children growing up in the development where we lived, it was impossible to avoid noticing how far behind his development was in this area. Children who had been conceived and born since we arrived were now talking. But not my son.

Our little boy himself did not seem particularly unhappy or frustrated at not talking. Whenever he wanted something to eat or drink, he would simply open the refrigerator door and point to it. He also clearly understood what was being said to him. If I asked him to go into his room and bring me the red pillow, that is what he would do.

He seemed normal in other ways and we had him tested by all sorts of doctors, who could find nothing wrong. In some ways, he seemed like a bright kid, but he was also a kid who marched to his own drummer. If his mother tried to kiss him while he was absorbed in something, he would stiff-arm her, without even looking up from what he was doing. He also had an uncanny knack of picking the child-locks we tried to use to keep him out of the kitchen or the open stairwell in our upstairs duplex apartment. He could do this before he could walk. Sitting in his little walker, he picked the best child-lock, the one on the lattice device guarding the stairwell, and tumbled down the stairs in the walker, fortunately without any serious injuries.

His ability to pick these locks was not just a matter of trial and

My son John when he was a year old. He was already figuring out how to open child locks, but it would be almost three more years before he would begin to talk.

error. Once, when I bought a new child-lock for the lattice gate guarding the kitchen, to replace one that he had learned to open, I watched as he scooted his walker over to the kitchen doorway and began to study the new lock. He looked at it for a long time without touching it. Then he reached out and opened it on the first try. After he became old enough to walk, he did something similar with the doorknob, which he could barely reach. He began studying a door that was ajar, feeling the door knob and the tongue of the lock, then inspecting the door jamb where the tongue of the lock fitted. After a long pause, he suddenly slammed the door, turned the doorknob, and opened it up again.

There were other things that sustained our hopes. After he learned to walk, he liked to check the reflection of the sunlight from a window in an outside door that we sometimes left ajar in warm weather. He would go over to the door and inspect the small window in it, then run over to the opposite wall to inspect the reflection. Then he would go back and move the door slightly, changing the angle, and then run back to the wall to see how the reflection had moved. This process seemed to fascinate him and he did it on a number of occasions.

There was also a remarkable reaction on his part one day when a Presidential seal filled the television screen, just before a speech by President Lyndon Johnson. The little fellow immediately turned and ran back to his room, returning with a Kennedy half-dollar that his grandmother had given him. He then compared the Presidential seal on the back of the coin with the pattern he saw on the television screen.

Perhaps the most remarkable of his achievements during this period was revealed accidentally. Once, while I was on the telephone in the kitchen for a long time, he seized the opportunity to play with my chess set in the living room, which I had always forbidden him to touch. When I returned and found my chess pieces scattered all over the floor, I angrily ordered him to pick them up and put them back. He put all 32 pieces back—in exactly the same positions they had been in before.

All these things might seem to be sufficient to sustain hopes for his development, but they occurred at long intervals, and in between there were weeks and months of silence. As the passing months turned into years, worry about his not talking grew like a dark and foreboding cloud over our lives. Eventually, even his mother told me that I was just being stubborn in not recognizing that he was retarded.

Beginning when he was about two, the little fellow said a few words occasionally, but his whole vocabulary did not exceed half a dozen nouns like "wayo" (radio) or "wah-ee" (water), and he did not even attempt to speak a sentence. At age three, his vocabulary stopped growing and eventually it declined until it consisted of only two words "wah-ee" and "rocky"—a word he repeated with amusement when the television weatherman on the "Today" show referred to weather conditions west of the Rockies. However, I realized that he used the word "wah-ee" only to refer to bodies of water, as in a lake or a stream. Whenever he wanted a drink of water, he pointed to the water in the refrigerator or to the faucet.

One night, when I had him with me as I went to my office, he pointed to the water fountain, indicating that he wanted a drink, and I thought that this might be an opportunity to get him to see that the water from the fountain was the same as the water he saw in ponds and lakes.

"Wah-ee," I said, pointing to the fountain, but he said nothing. As I kept repeating it, he just kept pointing more insistently. Finally he became so frustrated that I had not picked him up to get some water that tears appeared in his eyes. I immediately scooped him up in my arms and held him so that he could get a drink. He stopped crying— and I began crying.

. . .

The long and disturbing meeting I had had with the black students made me want to find out more about them and about the whole special admissions program that had brought them to Cornell.

As I learned more and more about the special program for black students at Cornell, it became increasingly apparent that black students were virtually a special preserve for a small clique of white activists and black militants. This clique emphasized the recruitment and selection of black students by sociological or ideological criteria, disdaining "conventional" or "academic" standards.

I was not the only black on campus who was never consulted about any of this. A black assistant dean named Pearl Lucas was also not consulted. Her efforts to become involved in these decisions were repeatedly rebuffed and resisted, though she did eventually get a foot in the door. Her views and mine were well known to some members of the in-group, and obviously were not welcome. However, at my request, I was given access to some files that indicated that the average black student at Cornell had test scores significantly above the national average for all students—and considerably below the average for Cornell students.

About half of the black students were on academic probation. They were not "unqualified" by any means. But they were mismatched with the other students at Cornell. At most other American colleges and universities, they would have been prospects for the dean's list. As it was, they were under great academic pressure and had serious social adjustments to make in an environment essentially geared to a very different kind of student.

It was not that Cornell necessarily covered so much more difficult material than other institutions, though it no doubt did so to some extent. It was the *speed* with which we covered whatever we did cover that played a large role in leaving these students falling behind. The amount of reading assigned, the amount of verbal facility and mathematical preparation presupposed, the quickness with which explanations were expected to be understood without much elaboration—all these were geared to a student body which, in the liberal arts college, was within the top 5 percent in the nation.

I caught a revealing glimpse of the agonizing experience that Cornell was to many black students when I attended a meeting of the Afro-American Society. Listening to an impassioned speech by one of the leading militant figures in the organization, I could sense that he was going through a personal hell at Cornell. A proud young man, he faced a crushing load of work in a difficult subject, with humiliatingly poor results. In addition, he was submerged in a sea of white people, who did not even understand what he was going through. He bitterly resented those black students who found the educational and social adjustments much easier.

His personal plagues were fused in his mind into a general, world-wide political and economic vision of white oppression, black "traitors," and an evangelical mission to set all this right. He was a complex individual—intelligent but under-educated, naturally charming but calculatingly vicious, shy but arrogant, blunt but devious. With an adequate education behind him, he undoubtedly could have mastered the work at Cornell, and even without an adequate education he could probably have done well at a less demanding institution. As it was, he found Cornell a sour experience, he was the focal point of much turmoil on campus, and ultimately he left the university in disgust without getting a degree.

· · ·

Black students were not the only people at Cornell who did not really belong there. In our own department, there was a visiting professor whose qualifications for being there were not apparent to me, except that he was a crony of Frank. He was a soft-spoken, mild-mannered priest, Father McPhelin. I had no occasion to get to know him, and my only information about him was indirect, though disquieting. First, the bookstore's collection of books for his course in introductory economics seemed only tangentially related to the subject. Secondly, an African friend of mine who was enrolled in this course observed that the visiting professor seemed "ethnocentric" to him, and apparently believed that everything worthwhile in the world was a product of Western civilization. My friend was a man of mature years who was a government official in his own country, so he regarded these views more with amusement than concern.

One day, as I was working in my office, two black students approached rather hesitantly and asked if they could see me. I welcomed them in, probably rather excessively, since they were the first black students to come to see me in three years. They said that they were enrolled in Professor McPhelin's course and were upset by remarks of his which they regarded as "racist." I told them that this sounded like something they should talk over with some administrative official—perhaps a dean—but confessed that I did not understand the administrative maze well enough to tell them exactly who to see and what to do. We talked for a few minutes and then they thanked me politely for my suggestions and left. I was still disturbed after they left, but more by the fact that they had let McPhelin upset them—and distract them from their work—than by the remarks he was supposed to have made, which sounded thoughtless rather than vicious.

* * *

Out of the blue, an alternative way to become involved in the education of black students came up. An official from the Rockefeller Foundation approached me with an idea for setting up a summer program that would bring students from the black colleges up to Cornell for intensive training in economics. The idea was to find promising Ph.D. prospects, in order to increase the number of black economists. Although I had been planning to make 1968 my first year of *not* teaching summer school after the academic year, this was something I could not pass up. Since time was short, I accepted and started work on the project immediately, even before a salary could be determined.

The summer economics program was essentially a one-man operation. I designed the forms and posters, answered the mail, arranged for housing for the students, and emptied the wastebaskets. I worked well into the night many nights—and lost twenty pounds in two months. But I felt that I was doing something that really needed to be done, and my feelings as I waited for the black students to arrive can only be likened to those of a small child waiting for Santa Claus.

* * *

Another bolt from the blue was a message I found at the office. It was a telephone message from a secretary at the University of Chicago. When I phoned back, she asked:

"When will you be prepared to come out here and defend your dissertation?"

"Did you say defend the dissertation?"

"Yes."

"I didn't know it had been accepted by the committee."

"Oh, didn't you get a notice?"

. . .

On Tuesday, April 2, 1968, I went to the departmental office to talk with the chairman about my summer program, and saw a small delegation of black students sitting soberly but quietly, and apparently not angrily, outside his office. A couple of them recognized me and nodded. They went in to see him, while I waited my turn. After several minutes they came out, obviously angry, and stalked away.

A couple of days later, I was staying at home, as I usually did on Thursdays, when I had no classes to teach. Usually, I spent the day with my son, taking him around to places we liked. This particular Thursday, however, I was preoccupied with other things, since I had an appointment to go see my doctor, who would tell me the results of tests to see if a lesion on my arm was a minor skin disease or cancer. In the middle of the morning, a colleague phoned to tell me that a group of black students had seized control of the economics department office and were sitting in there. We both laughed, for it seemed as good a way as any to get attention, in a situation where established procedures were vague and an administrative run-around seemed inevitable.

The phone continued to ring as other colleagues called, with various reports and reactions, some thinking that I should "do something." Since neither the students nor the department had authorized me to speak for them, it seemed futile and probably counterproductive. However, as more and more reports came in, some suggesting the possibility of violence, I decided that I had better go there, after all.

When I knocked on the door of the economics department office and asked to be let in, the students refused, but they did crack the door a little and talk to me. I could see the department chairman sitting at his desk in the inner office, working quietly on some papers. The outer office, occupied by the students, looked in good condition. The worst of the rumors were obviously false.

One of the black students was very distrustful of me and my motives, and he began to spout some of the usual rhetoric. I just looked at him in disbelief. I was stopping here on my way to find out if I had cancer, and was in no mood to answer cheap absurdities. Another black student, one of those who had been to my office, stepped in and talked calmly and rationally to me.

"What's going on?" I asked him. I had heard at least three different stories about an episode in McPhelin's class that offended the black students and sparked this take-over of the economics department office.

"O.K.," the student said. "Can I talk to you in strict confidence?"

"Yes," I said. "But before you do, consider this. A confidential statement will make it necessary for me to disqualify myself if there is a committee formed to find out the truth of all this. The one thing I won't do is be a double agent."

"I understand that," he said. "We're not worried about anything."

After he explained things to me, I was satisfied and left—and made it a point to have nothing further to do with the matter.

My doctor found that my lesion was not cancerous and began treating it.

After several hours, we received word that the sit-in was over. We had barely breathed a sigh of relief when we heard that Martin Luther King had been killed.

• • •

My summer program absorbed increasing amounts of my time, sometimes keeping me away from home too late at night to put my little boy to bed, which was perhaps the most painful sacrifice, as I knew he had grown used to it. Usually, when he became sleepy in the evening, he would take me by the hand and lead me into the kitchen. Then he would pat the refrigerator door and, when I opened it, he would point to his bottle.

Recruiting students from the black colleges was a special challenge, especially with so little time available before the summer program would begin. Moreover, I knew that the administrators at these institutions could not be relied on for any help, as the telephone company had discovered at Howard University. What I hoped to do was to find one or two individuals at each college who took a real interest in the students and would want them to know about an opportunity like this. I wrote formally to the administrators, asking for their help, just so their petty vanity would not be offended when they found me contacting people on their campuses.

Going through my grapevine, I was able to reach a number of good people on a number of black college campuses. There are usually some good people, even in the worst institutions, and it is just a matter of trying to locate them. Howard University turned out to be one of the hardest places to get anything done. Fortunately, the Rockefeller Foundation gave me a small revolving fund, to be used directly by me, without having to go through the Cornell bureaucracy, as I had to do for the rest of the Rockefeller grant money for the program. I took some of that money with me, flew down to Washington, went straight to the offices of the student newspaper and paid cash to take out a full-page ad, saying what the program was about, and when and where I would be available on campus for interviews.

The response was tremendous, both quantitatively and qualitatively. On a campus where officials said that I would not be able to find students who could qualify, I found not only students who would qualify but even some students with test scores comparable to those in the Ivy League.

Many special programs for black students were being set up, all across the country, in the wake of the assassination of Martin Luther King. Most were centered on admitting less qualified or "high risk" students, or students from "disadvantaged" backgrounds. My program was focused on getting the best black students I could find, in the time I had available. The difference in orientation became almost painfully apparent during a long discussion I had with a Cornell colleague whom we had over for dinner. He was a fairly typical white, liberal activist in behalf of various campus "causes" involving black people.

He was surprised and skeptical when I told him that I expected to come back with far better black students than those recruited by other programs at Cornell. My feeling was that people usually come back with what they are really looking for—that those who are looking for black people to feel sorry for will find them, while those of us who are looking for blacks with ability would end up with a goodly share of those.

This was, in effect, throwing down the gauntlet to him and what he represented. We argued hot and heavy from suppertime on past midnight. He was convinced that there was no such pool of undiscovered talent as I envisioned at the black colleges. He argued that the recruiting efforts of major universities had already skimmed the cream of academically able black students. I then asked him whether, if he had 100 places available for black students, he would pick the 100 best black students he could find.

He followed a familiar pattern by asking what I meant by "best" and elaborating various possibilities. I told him that I meant best intellectually, by *whatever* measure he preferred—but not by social or ideological standards. He shifted and dodged some more, but when finally cornered, said "no," he would not pick the best black students. That was it, as far as I was concerned. It made all his other arguments meaningless.

• • •

After all the years of struggle to complete my doctoral dissertation, the end came quickly and surprisingly easily. My defense of the dissertation took fifteen minutes—ten minutes of presentation and five minutes of questions. Then George Stigler and my other professors took me to a fancy restaurant in downtown Chicago to celebrate.

It wasn't all over yet. The requirements for the Ph.D. included passing two foreign language examinations. But even with such unfinished business ahead of me, life looked pretty good at this point. The biggest hurdles on the long road to the Ph.D. were now behind me.

At Cornell, I felt vindicated by the vote of my senior colleagues to renew my contract with a raise. It was also a good feeling to have lost more than twenty pounds of excess weight by walking all over the hilly Cornell campus to check out the living quarters and make other preparations for my summer students from the black colleges. Moreover, just the feeling of being involved with something like this, after three years living out of contact with blacks other than family members, was a boost. In addition, even though I had started work on this job without any salary being set, or even discussed, the Rockefeller Foundation did well by me when they finally decided what they would pay.

There was only one real cloud on my horizon. My little boy still couldn't talk. I was no longer able to spend as much time with him, and his mother insisted on resuming her career, putting him in a nursery school. Although the little fellow had no way of telling us how he felt, I could see some symptoms. Before, he used to love to have me throw him up in the air and catch him. Now it made him afraid, so I had to stop it.

. . .

As the time grew near for the students from the black colleges to arrive at Cornell, I tried to make sure that everything would be just right on the first day of their arrival. This seemed important, not only to have them begin the program with a positive attitude, without distracting problems, but also because of the way I intended to begin the program in high gear, to squeeze as much as possible into 8 weeks of work.

I planned to test their knowledge of economics on the first day of the summer program and again on the last day—each time using a test prepared by the Educational Testing Service in Princeton, which would score the results, independently of me. I was sick and tired of reading about experimental educational programs which were a "success"—as judged or tested by the people who ran it. But in order to have the "before" and "after" tests be comparable, the students had to arrive at a time and in a way that would allow them to get a good night's sleep and be well-rested and alert when they took the first test the next day.

My first run-in with the Cornell administration came when I refused to use the university's travel agent to arrange the students' flights to Ithaca. I insisted on using a private travel agent in town, because I knew that I could tell her what I was trying to accomplish, and that she would arrange the travel accordingly. But the campus bureaucracy, like all bureaucracies, thinks in terms of standard procedures and rules—not results. I could easily imagine Cornell's travel agent bringing in some students by a roundabout route, with long and tiring lay-overs between planes, in order to get a fare 10 percent lower.

The only reason I had to argue with Cornell bureaucrats in the first place was that they were in charge of disbursing the money which the Rockefeller Foundation provided to support the program. My revolving fund of $500 freed me from their control up to that limit, so that I could do things like flying down to Howard University and paying for an ad in the student newspaper, without needing their approval. But there was not enough money in the revolving fund to cover the costs of bringing in students from the black colleges, located predominantly in the South.

I won that battle with the bureaucracy, but there were more. The most important thing the students would need to have on their first day was money. Since this was provided for in the Rockefeller grant, I went to the Cornell administrators more than a month before their scheduled arrival to tell these officials that I wanted to have the students' living expense money ready for them before they got here. Then, about a week or so before the students' scheduled arrival, I went over to the administrative offices to again remind them that I needed to have the checks in my hand before time for the students to begin arriving. The bureaucrats told me that this was "impossible" because of the way their computer was programmed. I went from person to person in the financial aid office, explaining that it would be disastrous to the morale of a program of this sort to begin with the students' being forced to skimp or borrow money for meals and other necessities. No one budged. Finally, I said:

"I am damned tired of this run-around. If I don't get that money before those kids get here, I am phoning the Rockefeller Foundation to tell them how I am being hamstrung by bureaucrats around here."

When I said, "Rockefeller Foundation," it was like saying the magic words in a fairy tale. The whole scene changed. Voices became sweet, sympathy and understanding flowed. More important, I got the money.

. . .

When the summer program students began arriving—from Howard, Spelman, Morehouse and other black colleges—I met them at the local airport and drove them to their campus dormitories in my little Volkswagen bug. When several arrived on the same plane, we may have set a record for the most people riding in the same VW.

The summer program got off to a good start. I taught the economic theory course and found the students as a whole comparable to those in my regular Cornell classes. They were apparently doing good work in various other courses they were taking at the same time. A colleague with whom I had lunch regularly asked if I had sent him the cream of the crop for some reason.

"No," I told him, "just a representative sample."

Another colleague with an office near mine asked the same question and got the same answer. I was regarded as some kind of miracle worker, when I had simply come back with the kind of students I went looking for. At least, most of them were that kind. A couple of the students were doing nothing, except exhibiting a negative attitude that could threaten the whole program, if allowed to continue unchecked.

Discussion with the university legal counsel brought out that the program could discontinue support at any time, if a student was not doing the work in good faith. Discussion with the economic department chairman brought instant and insistent agreement from him that any student who was failing to do the work must leave—"voluntarily" if possible, but leave in any case. However, by simply talking earnestly with one of these students, I was able to get him to change sufficiently to avoid the need for any further action. The other student was a different story.

I offered him an opportunity to withdraw voluntarily, with partial payment of a stipend which students received on successful completion of the program. He made no real response to my offer or to my specific complaints about his attitude and behavior. Instead, he telephoned a white faculty member at M.I.T. who had taught at his college in the South. This professor had as his guest at the time one of Cornell's white liberal activists. This Cornell professor—the same colleague who had been at the bizarre meeting on "relevant" education, and who had argued at dinner against my idea of getting the best black students—phoned the economics department chairman on behalf of the student. At the same time, the student's home institution was contacted and the officials there were urged to put pressure on Cornell to keep the student in the program.

The net result was that, the next day, the department chairman reversed himself and said that the student must stay.

I was both astounded and furious. It was not enough that the chairman had to knuckle under to pressure; he had to rationalize this reversal by making it appear somehow nobler or more far-sighted.

"Well, you know, he *is* a human being and has feelings," he said.

"Did he *become* a human being since our talk and decision yesterday? Or after the pressure was put on you?"

"Look, it's not the pressure . . ."

"No, it's the fact that you don't have the guts to stand up to it."

The argument raged for nearly an hour. Finally, I said:

"You have my resignation—from the program and from Cornell University. We've talked enough. I'm going to lunch."

Theoretically, the decision about the student was mine alone to make, but my only means of enforcing it was to withhold funds from this student—and the department chairman had joint authority to grant these funds. Although I refused to authorize any further expenditures for this student, the chairman did.

Now that my authority had been undermined, a degenerating atmosphere of non-cooperation and petty mischief developed in my class. Reports began coming in from other faculty members that students from this program were now absenting themselves from class for days, missing examinations, refusing to participate in class discussions, and the like. Some were just goofing off, but others were no doubt responding to the racial militance of the regular Cornell black activists, who had contacted them, and who wanted "relevance" rather than a course taught like mine.

The really dedicated students continued to do good work, but most students were in the uncertain middle between the single-minded workers and those who wanted to goof off or to go "relevant." This middle group was largely lost academically. Test scores in my course, which had been rising steadily, declined sharply. Similar results appeared in the students' other courses.

My personal inclination was to walk out in the middle of the program, but that would have left the good students high and dry. My resignation from the program was made to become effective at the end of academic year 1968–69, like my resignation from the university itself. My original agreement with the Rockefeller Foundation was to run this program two years. I suffered through the rest of the summer session.

●   ●   ●

Shortly after my confrontation with the department chairman, I contacted one of the senior men in the department, to talk over what had happened. By the time I reached him, he had already heard about it, had in fact been briefed on the whole situation, and had a few things to say to me:

"Tom, I know you too well to try to influence your decision. But I am going to tell you some things I have been told, so you will know what your options are, and can make an informed decision as you see fit."

"O.K."

"First of all, you might consider that the pressure—or even the decision—did not necessarily involve just the department chairman. Cornell is involved in a number of ways with the black colleges, and people high up in the administration are very much concerned with the university's image in racial matters."

"If they were as much concerned with the university's integrity as they are with its image, everybody would probably come out ahead in the long run."

"True. But integrity is not 'in' this year, and it may be quite a while before it's back in style around here."

"God knows that's true."

"Now I have been told that you have a great future here. You've finished your doctoral dissertation, you had a couple of good articles published last year, reports on your teaching are good. You can expect promotion and tenure before your present three-year contract runs out. Cornell will match any offer you get from any other university."

"Uh-huh. *But*——?"

"All right. *But* it's going to be hard to get people to go along with this if you wash the department's and the university's dirty linen in public."

"Like telling the Rockefeller Foundation about this?"

"Right."

"I see. Well, this is very encouraging."

"Really?"

"Yes," I said. "You see, one of the things that keeps some of us from saying any more than we do is an overwhelming sense of the futility of it all—the feeling that nobody is listening and nobody gives a damn. Now, if knowledgeable people on the inside are anxious to keep me quiet, it means they must figure someone *will* listen and *will* give a damn."

I phoned the Rockefeller Foundation and told them everything.

• • •

Despite the downturn in the students' work in the second half of the program, the over-all results were good enough to destroy the usual excuses for mediocrity. The students' scores on the Graduate Record Examination in economics rose 70 points, from 28 teaching sessions. I know of no other program that achieved that. Since my goal was precisely to destroy the rationales for failure, I could consider it achieved, and under adverse conditions at that.

Apparently the Rockefeller Foundation liked my work, and even thought that I might still be persuaded to stay on to complete my two-year term as program director. Just to clear up any lingering doubts in their minds, I wrote to the Deputy Director of the foundation on August 24, 1968:

> I have no desire to try to work out a more satisfactory arrangement with the Cornell economics department that would make me willing to continue as program director. In view of the undermining that took place this past summer, no arrangements that can be made at Cornell will have my confidence, whatever the intrinsic merits of the arrangements.

The only other formality required to wrap things up was my letter of resignation from Cornell. Unlike my long resignation from Howard University, my resignation from Cornell consisted of only one sentence. Over the years, I had learned the futility of trying to talk sense to people who don't want to hear it.

8

Movin' On

With the ending of my summer program, my time was no longer so completely absorbed. I could now resume work on my remaining doctoral requirements. The last hurdle between me and the Ph.D. were my two language exams. I had already passed the written examination in French, but still needed to pass an oral examination in French, and both a written and an oral examination in German. The written exams could be taken in absentia but the oral exam had to be administered by a University of Chicago faculty member. Ordinarily, I would have had the expense of flying out to Chicago. Fortunately, however, there was a University of Chicago professor—a distinguished economic historian named Earl J. Hamilton—who was a visiting professor at the State University of New York at Binghamton, about an hour's drive from Cornell, and he was willing to give me the examinations there.

After I took the French orals in September 1968 and passed them, Professor Hamilton and I had a wide-ranging conversation that lasted about two hours. At one point, he asked in a very friendly way:

"How are things going in your life in general, Mr. Sowell?"

"Things are going pretty well in most things," I said. "There's only one really serious problem in my life."

"And what is that?"

"My little boy. He'll be four years old in a few months—and he still cannot talk."

John's early interest in analyzing things is shown as he examines a reflection from a window in a door that led out onto a balcony. He liked to move the door and then run over to the wall and inspect the reflection to see how it had moved.

"Have you taken him to doctors?"

"All kinds of doctors, all kinds of tests. They can find nothing wrong."

"Is he alert, active? Does he seem bright?"

"Yes. That's what makes it so puzzling."

"Have you and your wife been able to give him a lot of attention?"

"Not in the past several months. I have been tied up in my work and my wife took a job for a while, so he hasn't been getting the attention he needs. Now I have had some time lately, and I have been trying to teach him to talk, but it just doesn't work."

"Mr. Sowell," he said in a kind and gentle way, "Don't try to teach him to talk—not right now. You just give him lots of love and attention. Take him with you wherever you can. Let him know that you think he is the most wonderful little boy in the whole world. And when he feels confident and secure—he'll talk."

I was desperate enough to try anything, so I decided to follow Professor Hamilton's advice.

• • •

As word of my summer program at Cornell spread through various networks, all sorts of people began to correspond with me and to talk with me on the phone about special programs for minority students.

Still, I did not consider myself an "expert" on racial matters. At this point, I had done no research on the subject and had not published a single article on race or ethnicity, much less a book, and had never even given a speech on the subject. My professional work was in economics, and whatever I did as regards racial issues was simply a matter of personal interest and concern. Nor was there any thought that this might become a professional activity. As I wrote to Charles in November 1968:

> As a result of my work on the summer program, I have become one of the army of "experts" on race and education who infest the land. Efforts to disavow expertise are regarded as mere modesty, and I am questioned all the more insistently.

A conference was held in New York in the fall of 1968, bringing together directors of various special programs for black students. Although I never intended to direct such a program again, I went to the conference in order to get a sense of what was happening. As I listened to the various speakers from around the country—mostly white—I began to realize that the incredible rhetoric and bizarre notions I had encountered at Cornell were part of a nationwide trend. What seemed even more amazing to me was that none of the blacks present were saying anything to challenge it. After one speaker from a New England university had outlined his school's efforts to recruit under-qualified black students and give them special help, I asked:

"What are you doing to recruit *able* black students who don't *need* your special help?"

From the murmurs and looks around the room, it was clear that this was considered an awkward question, if not an incomprehensible one. A couple of other times I asked similar questions, with similar reactions. One or two other blacks questioned the prevailing views in various ways, but most of the blacks present sat frozen in silence.

After the meeting broke up into smaller groups for food and

drinks, the dean of a leading medical school came over and introduced himself to me.

"I was glad to hear you say what you did," he began. "Makes me feel I'm not alone."

"Do you have the same kind of attitudes at your school that we saw there in the meeting room today?" I asked.

"*Very* much so," he said. "After the assassination of Martin Luther King, some of our faculty members came to me and said, 'We think what we ought to do at a time like this is admit a dozen or so black students to our medical school immediately, to begin in the fall.' When I asked, 'Where do you expect me to get qualified black students in May, after they have all been snapped up by other places?' they said, 'Don't you worry about their being qualified. You just get them in here, and we will see that they graduate.'"

"How can they see that the students graduate?" I asked.

"Well, they give out the grades."

I was too stunned to say anything for a moment. But then I asked:

"Do they plan to send *their* children to be operated on by these 'doctors' that they maneuver through medical school?"

"Never."

"Then why should *my* children be operated on by such doctors?"

"That's the kind of argument I used with them—and I held them off, *this* year. How many more years they can be stopped from doing this is another story."

(A couple of years later, a faculty member from another top medical school told me that his school was *already* turning out black doctors without the proper qualifications.)

That evening, a black caucus was held in one of the hotel rooms. The same people who had been sitting silently through the afternoon, while two or three of us had been objecting, were now suddenly the most vocal of all. They sounded so militant that you would think they were going to burn down the hotel. I left in the middle of it, went back to my room, and fell asleep. The next morning, the leading talkers of the previous night, now fortified by mutual support, began to speak out—wildly, irrelevantly, and sometimes incoherently. Now it was white people's turn to listen in silence to absurdities.

I walked out again, went to my room, packed my suitcase, and went home.

· · ·

As a lame-duck faculty member, I saw no reason to attend faculty meetings or departmental meetings, since the future of this institution was no longer any business of mine. This, together with having both the doctoral dissertation and the summer program behind me, gave me more time to spend with my son, and I seized the opportunity, not only for his sake but for mine. He was a sweet little boy and I enjoyed taking him places.

Sometimes we walked in the woods or along the lake, or went to look at waterfalls. Still a photography buff, I took pictures of scenery or of him. After the project on which his mother was working came to an end, she stayed home and was able to give him more attention as well.

He seemed much happier and more relaxed—but still he said nothing. But now we stopped trying to get him to say anything. Eventually, he reached the point where he again wanted me to pick him up and toss him in the air. I thought it was now time.

One day, I turned on our tape recorder and asked him to say "water."

"Wah-ee," he said.

I played it back, so that he could hear himself, and he seemed to enjoy the novelty of it.

"Rocky," I said.

"Rocky," he shouted.

I played that back to him as well. This was all done in the spirit of play, with no pressure. Gradually, as the days and weeks went by, I began to introduce some of the words he used to say, but which he had stopped saying during the past few months. As I began to play back his voice saying more and more words, he seemed to enjoy his accomplishments.

As the weeks turned into months, his little vocabulary grew to a dozen words, and then two dozen. Still, they were just disconnected words that he could not put together in a sentence. But he knew what these words meant. They were not just sounds. Eventually, he reached the point where we were ready to take him to a speech therapist. She was a young woman who was a student at Ithaca College—attractive and personable, which no doubt helped to get and keep his attention. There in the college facilities, while we watched from behind glass (one-way glass, I believe), she patiently led him through game-like procedures to let him learn to speak, and especially to speak more audibly than in the whispers he usually used.

Eventually, he began to talk, not just as a game in itself, but to express things. For example, he enjoyed it when our car drove across railroad tracks, and would laugh and cry out:

"Railroad tracks!"

As time went on, I began to notice that sometimes he said "railroad tracks" before we reached them, in fact before they became visible from the car. One day, at home, I drew a picture and showed it to him:

"What is this, son?" I asked.

"Railroad tracks," he said.

He had learned that this was the sign he saw before we came to the railroad tracks themselves. In other ways as well, it became clear that he had learned many things, without being about to tell anybody that he knew them. It also became clear that he had a phenomenal memory, that it was not just a fluke when he picked up scattered chess pieces and put them back on the board in perfect order.

From isolated words, he moved on to phrases like "down the drain." More important, he was *using* words to express things, to ask for things. It was now a normal part of his life. His verbal development pattern was that of a child much younger than he was. But he was talking!

The long silence and the long nightmare were over.

. . .

The next large item of unfinished business was completing the German language requirement. After a great deal of study, I could read passages in German, but it was hard to imagine myself sitting down to spend a day reading a book in German, the way I had done with several books in French. The German exam in fact turned out to have more rocky places for me than the French exam had, but in the end Professor Hamilton smiled and said to me:

"You're a free man."

Only someone who has been through the Ph.D. ordeal knows how much its conclusion is like being released from prison. Professor Hamilton was a fine, warm man, but the irony was not lost on me that I was being set free by a white Mississippian.

He had also set my son free—from silence. What if I had been swept up in the racial rhetoric of the hour and refused to talk with him or to listen to him?

. . .

Toward the end of 1968, I became increasingly preoccupied with the job market—and with the question as to whether I should remain in the academic world or move on to private industry. The Ph.D., for which I had worked so long and hard, was officially awarded in December 1968, but now its value and the career it opened up to me seemed more and more questionable. I did not go to the Commencement ceremonies at the University of Chicago, but had the degree mailed to me, like my previous degrees from Harvard and Columbia.

There was a real irony in being approached or interviewed by leading economics departments whose interest I would once have been very happy to receive—but now, instead, I felt ambivalence or even distrust. What I most wanted to know, on each campus that I visited, was the racial atmosphere on that campus. Was I expected to be guru-in-residence to the black students or was I being hired to be what I had trained for years to be, an economist whose work was in his chosen profession? For the first time in my career, I made it a point to try to contact at least one black faculty member at each campus I visited, or was considering visiting.

Often the mere attempt to contact a black faculty member was revealing. I grew used to phoning the professor and getting his wife instead—and hearing how Bob or Ted was off somewhere helping to deal with a campus racial crisis, or was tied up trying to establish a special minority program, or was tutoring individual black students, or was meeting with the Black Students Union over their problems or agendas.

"Who's minding the store while all this is going on?" I sometimes asked. "How is he keeping up with the scholarship in his profession? How is he getting any research or writing done?"

Often the wife's response was that such activities were now virtually a memory, that her husband was tied up fighting brushfires. In some fields—economics among them—you have to work hard just to keep up with the scholarship being produced within the profession. Otherwise, you can become obsolete within a few years of leaving graduate school. When I made campus visits, the husband usually acknowledged that campus politics was interfering with his efforts to keep up with developments in his field, sometimes adding that he was expected to stay within a certain ideological range as well.

"Who needs it?" I asked myself, even after receiving offers of appointment from some leading economics departments. At one point, I phoned my old friend Bernard, from Labor Department days, who was now teaching at the University of Pennsylvania. We talked for more than an hour about whether or not I should stay in the academic world. He thought that I should, that I had something to contribute, and that ways and means could be found to avoid or minimize the toll of campus politics. I trusted his judgment and decided to at least leave the issue open, rather than seek only non-academic posts.

• • •

A couple of small things happened which seemed to be of no special significance at the time, though they turned out to have a decisive influence for my later work.

A book titled *Beyond the Melting Pot* caught my eye and its discussion of various American ethnic groups turned out to be fascinating and eye-opening. It put the experience of blacks in a larger context, permitting a judgment as to what was unique in the history of blacks and what was similar in some respects to the social history of some other groups. The other event was a campus talk by an economics professor from Wabash College named Benjamin Rogge. Although I missed the talk, I was sufficiently intrigued by his subject to write to him later, asking for a copy of his talk.

Eventually, I met Ben Rogge, a big, teddy bear of a man, smart and a fine human being, but someone not known much beyond the range of those who knew him directly, since he did not publish much. By the time I met him, he had decided that his many activities would not leave him time enough to write the book he had conceived on the economics of race. Then he did something of great generosity. He turned over to me the manuscript of what he had done so far, and said that it was mine to use as I pleased. What I gained most from his brief manuscript was the general idea of applying economic concepts to racial issues. Although I still did no research or writing on the subject, the idea had been planted, both by Ben's manuscript and by *Beyond the Melting Pot.*

. . .

Some of the black students at Cornell expressed hostility to me, as a result of hearing about the summer program, but I became better acquainted with other black students and was on good terms with them. Moreover, I had black students enrolled in both of my classes, for the first time. One, a young lady named Wilhelmina, received the only 100 percent on an exam in that course.

One remarkable young man, who can be called Bill, was an interesting study, even though he was never a student of mine in a course. One day, as I was leaving my office, I noticed Bill looking at a list posted outside the door of a radical colleague's office. After going down the list, Bill sighed with relief and then turned away, smiling.

"What's going on?" I asked.

"Just checking the names on that list for the Urban Economics course."

"What's the list for?" I asked.

"Well, admission to the course is by instructor's permission only. That way, they can have an all-black class without technically violating the college rules."

"Oh."

"But they don't accept all the black students either. Just certain ones. I was checking to see if my name was among those accepted."

"Was it?"

"No. That's why I was smiling."

"I don't understand," I said. "Why did you apply if you didn't want to be accepted?"

"I thought it *advisable* to apply," he said knowingly. "Certain people *expect* you to apply. Now I've applied, wasn't accepted, and can take something worthwhile."

As the year wore on, I was to learn more and more about intimidation among the black students.

Bill enrolled in a course taught by a very tough foreign professor who regarded American students in general as very coddled and lazy. Typically, this man would begin the term with about forty students, but after a couple of weeks there would be only about a dozen left. Once, some of us in the department got copies of one of his exams, and then tried to answer the questions, to see how well we would do. The highest score among us was 50 percent, made by the man who taught the same course the previous year. Bill was a bright guy, but I didn't think his background prepared him for this, and said so.

"Isn't that inconsistent?" he asked. "You're always saying that black students shouldn't look for soft courses."

"All right, it's inconsistent," I said. "Be a wise guy. But there are *degrees* to everything."

We talked for a long time, and he said he would consider everything I had said. But, in the end, he stayed in the course. Occasionally, as the term went on, I heard reports from him and from the professor, each indicating that it was rocky going. I wrote it off as a bad gamble that Bill had taken. At the end of the term, as I was walking down a crowded hall, I heard a loud voice calling my name and saw a black arm waving above a sea of white faces to attract my attention. A few moments later, Bill burst out of the crowd of passing students and said:

"I did it, man."

"Did what?"

"Got a C+ in that course!"

He walked on, bouncing and beaming with pride. It would probably be one of his most "relevant" experiences in college, even if he never had occasion to use any of the material from that course.

• • •

During the fall of 1968, I was contacted by the Urban Coalition, an organization headquartered in Washington and concerned with racial and poverty issues. They wanted me to help draft a proposal for a federal financial aid program to help disadvantaged students go to college—and to try to help sell this program to people in private industry, in academia, and in various civic organizations, to line up their political support behind the program.

The Urban Coalition's sense was that Congress was very receptive to some sort of program, and that we needed to get something together that would focus the help on students, rather than have it become another pork barrel program to benefit academic institutions themselves. We were, in short, in a race against a well-organized academic lobby, to try to get something to put in front of Congress, with some political support behind it.

Although I was hired as a consultant to help out on this project, as time went on it became more and more my responsibility to both draft a proposal and to contact people around the country to support it. By February 1969, I had come up with a proposal that would cost the federal government about $5 billion. The general pattern of it was that low-income students would get substantial outright grants and higher-income students would receive less money, with more of that money being in the form of loans.

The Urban Coalition had a list of people and organizations for me to try to win over. They ranged from A.T.&T. to the AFL-CIO, and included the N.A.A.C.P., the Sloan Foundation, and Lytton Industries, among others. My job was not to get a commitment of support but to get them to agree to come to a scheduled meeting in Washington in the spring, to hammer out a final proposal that many of them could then line up behind when the Urban Coalition took it to Congress.

In addition to sending out copies of my proposal, I wrote letters, made personal visits to some of the East Coast organizations, and made phone contacts with people in more distant places like Minnesota and California. The reception of my proposal was very gratifying in most places. In only two places was the reception really disappointing. The Washington office of the N.A.A.C.P. showed no interest. Although I had not always agreed with what the N.A.A.C.P. did, this was the first time that I was truly bitter about them. Roy Ash, chief executive officer of Lytton Industries, agreed to fly in from California for a meeting at the Urban Coalition, but the head of the Washington N.A.A.C.P. did not deign to walk down the street to talk about it. A white millionaire showed more interest in low-income students than our "black leaders."

One of the places I visited in person was the Washington headquarters of the AFL-CIO. I was scheduled to see a union official and his subordinate. As I was entering the office of the subordinate, I had barely gotten my foot across the threshold when he said:

"Your program would help mostly low-income people. Our members are mostly middle class. We're against it."

"Well, there's something in there for middle class people, too," I said.

"Yeah," he said, "but it's mostly focused on low-income people."

He remained unshakable in his opposition—and all on purely selfish grounds. I could not help thinking what a contrast his crass words were to the high-flown public rhetoric of labor unions about the solidarity of working people. When his immediate superior, a black man, became involved in the discussion, it became painfully clear that the white "subordinate" was calling the shots. The net result was that it was easier to get the interest and support of big business for a plan to help the poor than it was to get the interest and support of big labor.

Although all the major groups targeted by the Urban Coalition were not ready to participate in the spring meeting, there was wide enough support for such a meeting to make us optimistic. We knew that there was a rival approach brewing elsewhere, one that would use federal money to help academia itself, rather than low-income students, but we would just have to cope with that when the time came. Little did we know that this would turn out to be the least of our problems.

* * *

During the winter of 1968–69, the word that was heard around campus with increasing frequency and increasing certainty, from a variety of sources, was that all hell was going to break loose in the spring among the black students at Cornell. Partly this reflected the national mood of growing militancy among black students, and partly a very rapid shift of influence within Cornell's Afro-American Society toward more militant leadership.

This internal shift of power was not unrelated to the university administration's policies. Where there is little attention paid to reasoned arguments about legitimate problems and a total capitulation to force, "moderate" or "rational" leadership obviously cannot deliver the results that more uninhibited leadership can deliver. A series of probing actions by black militants—beginning with the sit-in at the economics department office—revealed the hollowness of the Cornell administration.

To the black students' complaints about remarks made by Professor McPhelin, the administration responded by (1) stalling until McPhelin's last class was over, making the issue moot; (2) issuing a ringing declaration of concern over the issues raised—racism and academic freedom—but with no real position being taken on the merits of the case at hand; (3) taking no action against either the disruptive students or the accused professor, and (4) creating the Urban Economics course, taught by one of the militant students' favorite radicals.

A series of larger disruptions in December 1968 brought similarly evasive statements by the Cornell administration—and refreshments provided by the administration to the disruptors. This managed to be simultaneously insulting and cowardly. All this set the stage for the biggest and worst student disruption and confrontation in the country, in a year plagued by disruptions and confrontations, on campuses from coast to coast.

In the spring of 1969, a group of black students seized control of one of the buildings at Cornell University and, armed with shotguns and rifles, issued their demands. When the administration capitulated to those demands, the faculty repudiated the administration's agreement, in effect nullifying it. However, in the face of general threats issued by the militants publicly, and specific death threats received privately by some individual professors, the faculty made a humiliating reversal of its initial vote and approved capitulation to the militants' demands.

Even more incredible than these events was the atmosphere in which they occurred. To admit that they changed their votes because they did not consider the issue worth having a shoot-out about was apparently too much for the faculty to do. They had to find a "deeper" reason, reflecting a sudden "understanding" of black people. Yet it really fooled no one, least of all the black students.

During the tense days of the armed stand-off, with state police cars parked discreetly along the routes to the campus, there were interminable discussions in offices and hallways at work, as well as on the telephone and in homes throughout the academic community. On campus, people whispered and looked around before they spoke, or eased the office door shut behind them, and some began sentences with:

"Don't mention that *I* said this, but . . ."

Thousands of students and faculty members gathered in a huge, armory-like building for *all-night* ideological discussions, some of the participants bringing bed-rolls and food. The immediate "reasons" for the spring crisis were examined in the most minute detail by people who had known that an outbreak was coming, months before any of these "reasons" existed. The most twisted travesties of reasoning became commonplace among people whose careers were supposedly based on scholarship.

One of my colleagues called me a "man from Mars" for not joining in any of these mass discussions or small group intrigues which dominated the campus. A couple of the more shallow junior men even came to my office to voice their feeling that I had a "duty" to "speak out" publicly at a time like this. I replied:

"If I knew something to say that would make things better—perhaps save lives—do you think I would wait until my white liberal colleagues came along and told me to say it?"

When they sensed the wind-chill factor, they left the office, flustered as such people often are by common sense.

Far from escaping the pressures which others felt, I felt them even more acutely. For one thing, I was under increasing pressure from the black militants to sign a wild, sweeping statement to be issued on behalf of the entire black community on campus, including faculty and staff. Only two blacks refused to the bitter end to sign this statement— Pearl Lucas and me.

In addition, a daily reminder of the dangers inherent in the whole situation was a young black woman student whom my wife knew, and who moved out of her dormitory room and into our apartment during the crisis, fearing both blacks and whites who were engaging in mindless acts of violence against innocent people on campus. Since I began each day by escorting her to class and ended it by taking her back to our home, I could hardly be oblivious to what was going on, though I had no interest in the scholastic discussions over fine points which held such fascination for my colleagues.

When it became impossible to work at the office, because of the eternal discussions, gossip, rumors, and philosophizing, I began working instead in a study that I had, back in the library stacks. I took special pride in the fact that my research and writing at the time were about two anonymous pamphlets published in Britain during the 1820s—the ultimate in "irrelevance" by current standards, though very relevant in that these pamphlets dealt with the ways people trap themselves with words.

Unlike some of my colleagues, I refused to cancel my classes or to turn them into discussions of current events on campus. When a small group of radical white students urged that the "real issues" at Cornell be discussed in my introductory economics class, and set forth a few of their views, I listened for a couple of minutes and then said:

"Getting back to economics . . ."

The class burst into applause. Other professors who did similar things received similar responses. It suggested what might have been possible, if there had been just a little leadership at the top, willing to appeal to something more basic than the mood of the moment among the vocal few.

By the time the Urban Coalition held its long-awaited spring meeting, student lawlessness and violence, such as that at Cornell, had soured Congress on the whole idea of new financial aid initiatives. Months of work were down the drain.

• • •

On the job front, I was just about to bow out of the academic world and accept an offer from a think tank in New York, when I received an inquiry from Brandeis University. One advantage that Brandeis had over some bigger and better-known places, whose offers I had already turned down, was that I had met some black student leaders there during an earlier visit to evaluate the university's special minority student program. These black student leaders seemed like reasonable guys and, with their help, I expected to resolve pretty quickly the questions I had. I phoned the head of the Brandeis Afro-American Society and asked him to arrange a meeting between me and the members of his organization. He readily agreed.

"I've had an offer to teach here at Brandeis," I told them, "and it looks like the kind of place I would like, but I came here to find out what the general atmosphere is like—especially what the students, the faculty, and the administrators *expect* from a black faculty member. I understand you want to have more black faculty members at Brandeis. But your own attitudes and behavior are a big factor in whether they will come when the offer is made. I know black professionals who would ordinarily be delighted to be here, who have, however, turned down offers from Brandeis—and from other universities as well—because they think they are going to be expected to play roles that they do not want to play. They don't want to be constantly harassed with requests—or demands—that they engage in all sorts of activities outside their professional field. That's my position. I don't intend to be a guru-in-residence to black students. I also don't believe in double standards for black students and I don't waste my time on campus politics."

"We don't believe in those things either," the head of the society shot back heatedly. "To hell with white paternalism. We may demonstrate, or do whatever else we feel we have to do, but we're not here to play games. We're here to get an education."

This was a particularly refreshing contrast to the politicized rhetoric at Cornell. As the discussion opened up, it became clear that all kinds of opinions were represented in the group, and that all felt free to express themselves publicly, without fear of ridicule or retaliation. This was also in contrast to Cornell. Many of those present disagreed with my views, but our exchanges were always civil, though often sharp. When I looked at my watch, I was surprised to see that two hours had passed, and that it was time to rush to the airport.

After thanking the students for coming to talk with me, I headed out. As I neared the door, a couple of arms were extended to shake my hand. One man said:

"We'll look for you in the fall."

I accepted the offer from Brandeis.

• • •

Near the end of the spring semester at Cornell, a reporter from *The New York Times* contacted me. His story in the next day's paper quoted my charge that academic paternalism was detrimental to black students and my characterization of the university administration as "a veritable weathervane following the shifting crosscurrents of campus politics." The story was picked up by other publications and was something of a passing sensation on campus, especially in the context of a trustees' investigation of the university president and controversies as to whether he should stay or go. My new-found notoriety led to my being asked to testify before the board of trustees.

Now that I had made the decision to remain in the academic world, I was able to accept a long-standing offer from U.C.L.A. to teach summer school there. I was looking forward to seeing California for the first time, and also to seeing much of the country for the first time by driving there.

When the day to begin the trip finally arrived, it was bright and sunny. We drove down the long curving highway that overlooked blue Cayuga Lake, stretching forty miles into the distance. In front of us was the little town of Ithaca, nestled in the valley formed by tall green hills on three sides. It was a scene we had seen many times, but it was never more beautiful. From the corner of my eye, I also saw one of the buildings of Cornell University—the only thing to sadden the mood—and I thought of an old parody of the school song:

> Far above Cayuga's waters,
> There's an awful smell.
> Some say it's Cayuga's waters,
> Some say it's Cornell.

9

California, Here I Come

For a couple of weeks in June, 1969, I had the closest thing to a vacation that I had had in years. It was spent driving across the United States to California—at a leisurely pace of about two to three hundred miles a day, with some days being spent resting and relaxing where we were.

We stopped in Washington, where my wife and I both had relatives, then went out through Ohio, where we stopped to see Lonnie and his family, and then proceeded out through Indianapolis and made a stop in St. Louis, where I visited a summer program in economics for minority students at Washington University. From St. Louis we followed Route 66 and recalled the old song about it, sung by the Andrews Sisters in the 1940s, as we stopped in Joplin, Missouri, Oklahoma City, and Amarillo, among the cities mentioned in the song.

The highlight of the trip was the Grand Canyon, one of the few sights to live up to its reputation. In human terms, the highlight of the trip was the development of our son, who learned to say more words, to read signs, and to count. Among the first signs he learned to read were traffic signs, and among these "No Left Turn" seemed to be his favorite. Being constantly with both parents all day seemed to hasten his development. He learned to play a xylophone, at first playing tunes that we taught him, but later being able to play tunes he had heard by ear.

Both Los Angeles and U.C.L.A. turned out to be very pleasant surprises—the loveliest city and the loveliest campus I had ever seen. A friend from my undergraduate days, now a professor at U.C.L.A., had spent weeks looking for a place for us to stay and had found a perfect little house for us to rent for the summer. The economics department at U.C.L.A. was a stronghold of University of Chicago economists, who shared many of my views on social and educational issues.

One day, a tall black man came to the door of my office at U.C.L.A. and said:

"I understand that you and I have similar views, so I thought I would stop by and see."

"Come on in," I said.

"My name is Walter Williams," he said.

It turned out that our views were in fact very similar. However, in later years, it would be said by the media that he was either a student or a disciple of mine—he was neither—when in fact we got together precisely because we had already independently arrived at similar conclusions. Walter was a graduate student working on his Ph.D. in economics.

My sense of philosophic isolation was also relieved by a long telephone conversation with syndicated columnist Joseph Alsop, who wrote a column about my experiences at Cornell. There was also a letter waiting for me from Bayard Rustin when I arrived at U.C.L.A. He too had read about my views on the Cornell crisis and asked me to contribute a brief essay on black studies for a pamphlet he was putting together. I tossed off a couple of pages for what would be my first published essay on racial issues. Still, there was no thought that I would write on the subject again, much less do research on race or ethnicity.

Another unexpected call I received was one from Kenneth Arrow, a world-renowned economist who was president of the American Economic Association, the national organization of economists. He offered me an appointment to the editorial board of the *American Economic Review,* the Association's official organ and the most widely read scholarly journal in economics. It was obviously an honor, but I asked:

"When was the last time you offered this position to someone who had published nothing during the past two years?"

He was somewhat taken aback by the question, perhaps because not many people look gift horses in the mouth. As I pressed the issue, however, it came out that there was some concern to racially diversify the membership of the *American Economic Review*'s editorial board. I not only turned down the offer, I told him that such double standards were a terrible and harmful idea. In fact, I was so emphatic that I later phoned him back to say that I was not making an attack on him, but was condemning completely the principle involved.

• • •

The relaxed atmosphere and mild weather of Los Angeles, the kindred souls in the economics department, and my son's blossoming, all combined to make my brief interlude in California seem almost like a summer romance. Inexorably, however, the fall loomed on the horizon. It was time to head back east, driving at a much more hectic pace, as the time between the end of summer school at U.C.L.A. and the beginning of the fall semester at Brandeis left little margin to do all the things that had to be done for us to move from upstate New York to Massachusetts.

We drove back home via the northern route, going through such places as Salt Lake City, Cheyenne, Omaha, Chicago and Rochester. In Rochester, we stayed overnight in the home of some friends we knew from Ithaca. When I woke up late the next morning, I heard children's songs being played on a piano. It was my son playing them. He had never had a piano lesson, but he had figured out that the piano keys were in the same order as the notes on his xylophone, so he could play the same tunes on the piano.

Once back in Ithaca, we hastily prepared to leave for Massachusetts. Among the people who came by our apartment to say goodbye was a lady we barely knew, but she brought along a going-away present. All we knew about her was that she had a retarded child.

"I understand you have a boy like mine," she said, "so I brought this toy that my son likes, and hope that your boy will like it too."

"Thank you," I said. "You are very kind."

There was nothing else to say. I felt so grateful within myself that she was wrong. But now I also knew what my neighbors had been saying.

. . .

While we were in California, colleagues at Brandeis looked for a place for us to live, as my friend had done in Los Angeles, but the results were not nearly as good. In Massachusetts, the people who were doing the looking were white, and they did not mention that we were black when they spoke to the landlord in a predominantly Irish neighborhood.

After two weeks of miscellaneous harassment by the landlord, we moved out—and into another house in a different Irish neighborhood, where the harassment was less serious and more sporadic, but still a fact of life. These things were shocking to my colleagues at Brandeis, who apparently thought of racism as something that used to happen down South. When we mentioned some of the petty nuisances we encountered to a neighbor, we were told:

"Oh, that's *nothing* compared to what happened when an Italian couple lived there."

. . .

The atmosphere at Brandeis was a great improvement over that at Cornell. Neither the students nor the faculty were as politicized as at Cornell, nor did my colleagues in the economics department have the factional hostilities or personal back-biting found in the Cornell economics department. Our department chairman was Joseph S. Berliner, a noted authority on the Soviet economy and a gem of a human being. Although the department had no graduate courses, I taught a graduate seminar on the history of economic theory in the History of Ideas department, where I had a joint appointment as a courtesy, though the economics department paid my full salary.

I was now an associate professor without tenure, but with the expectation of getting it soon. My real concern was not with tenure, but with whether conditions would remain reasonable enough for me to stay in the academic world. However, I took advantage of the present calm to begin expanding my doctoral dissertation (only about 60 pages long, about half the size of my undergraduate thesis at Harvard) into a book.

While none of the black students at Brandeis enrolled in my courses, I had something of a sense of their academic and non-academic activities on campus from various sources. As on other campuses, there were racial double standards of admission at Brandeis, leading to a black student body not as academically prepared as their white classmates. Some of the black students coped by avoiding courses in tough subjects like economics and some were rescued by a black administrator whose activities included phoning professors to try to get them to "reconsider" bad grades or to try to "understand" black students, which amounted to pretty much the same thing.

Not all the academic problems of the black students were due to their having less academic preparation than the white students. A major handicap was that they, like myself during my first year at Harvard, simply had no experience with the heavy demands of a first-rate education—or with the study habits and self-discipline required to cope with it. Here, however, in the atmosphere of the 1960s, there was no one to tell them to shape up or ship out. I noticed a sort of microcosm of the problem when I began spending time in the library, doing research.

When I arrived early the first morning and looked around, there was not a single black student there, though there were many white students studying away. After about an hour or so, the first black student showed up. He took a long time to get his books and papers unpacked and to settle down to study. After a while, another black student came by and chatted with him. After perhaps an hour or so of study, they were among the first to leave for lunch. It was painful for me to watch. This was not the last time I would see this kind of scene, either in this college library or in others.

Although I had no black students enrolled in my courses, occasionally I would get a visit at the office from one of them seeking advice, and one fellow came by a few times just to talk.

During one visit, I gave him a passage to read, about a confrontation in the 1840s between Karl Marx and another Communist leader.

The issue was the role of the intellectual in advancing the interests of the poor. After the young man read the passage, he exclaimed:

"We had that argument last Thursday in the Black Students' Union!"

I was pleased to see that he understood that things did not have to be about minority issues to be "relevant" to minority issues.

On another occasion, he came to the office visibly dispirited.

"I just don't understand it, Dr. Sowell," he said. "The Jewish students do *twice* as well as we do."

"Only twice as well?" I said. "When they work three times as hard? What I can't understand is how you fellows do as well as you do, with no more effort than you put into it."

* * *

By the beginning of 1970, the manuscript of *Say's Law* had been professionally typed and was ready for me to begin sending it around to university presses. Since such publishers do not operate at breakneck speed, the process of getting the manuscript evaluated, accepted, and then into print seemed likely to take more than a year, perhaps two, and then the equally leisurely pace of reviews in scholarly journals would push back even further the time when I could expect any professional recognition that might affect my career options.

I was content at Brandeis, but I was not content to be paying high Massachusetts prices on my academic salary. Still, there seemed to be no obvious way out—until I received an unexpected inquiry from U.C.L.A. They had suddenly found themselves with money to hire another economist and wanted me to come out, give a talk, and meet with some people. When I mentioned my manuscript on Say's Law, they were anxious to get a copy, which meant that it could have an effect on my future, much sooner than expected.

Economists trained at the University of Chicago were a sizable contingent at U.C.L.A., so it was perhaps inevitable that my talk led to the kind of all-out intellectual battle common among Chicago economists. A black woman from the U.C.L.A. administration was in the audience, and was so appalled that she later phoned a senior member of the department to say:

"If you don't want to hire Sowell, that's your business. But the whole department didn't have to attack him like that! I have never seen such hostility."

"What are you talking about?" he said. "These guys love Tom. Of course we are going to hire him."

U.C.L.A. made me an offer of an associate professorship with tenure—and I accepted.

This offer and my decision to accept it came late enough in the hiring season to cause me some embarrassment in informing Brandeis that I would not be back in the fall. However, both the department and the dean of the faculty were gracious about it and wished me well. For the first time, I left an academic institution with goodwill all around, and with a sense of regret at leaving a fine bunch of colleagues.

• • •

Having finished writing *Say's Law,* I began almost immediately writing another book—an introductory economics textbook.

Having taught introductory economics more than a dozen times, I had some lecture outlines that I was very proud of, and thought that these lectures would provide the basis for a book that students would find easy to understand.

After writing a few chapters and doing an outline for the whole book, I sent this around to a few publishers. Scott, Foresman offered me a $5,000 advance—a sum of money that was much bigger in those days than today, due to the intervening inflation. It was equal to one third of my annual salary at Brandeis. I signed the book contract and worked at breakneck speed to complete the book before going out to California. We had some financial breathing room again. We would need it. Our second child, a baby girl, was born in June 1970. As planned years before, she was named for Lorraine Hansberry.

Say's Law was not doing nearly as well. As I wrote to a colleague:

My principles book—tossed off during the spring semester—has brought a contract and a sizable offer of advance royalties, while my book on Say's Law—the fruit of a decade of research—is still collecting laudatory rejections. You would think they were nominating me for the Pulitzer Prize. I would rather they said it was lousy but they will print it anyway.

* * *

August 1970 found me in Los Angeles, looking for a place for us to live. While in my hotel room one day, I was surprised to receive a phone call from Washington, D.C.—from Howard University. They wanted me to return and become chairman of the department of economics! Their opening bid was 50 percent more than my salary at U.C.L.A. Flabbergasted, I asked:

"When do you have in mind for me to begin?"

"In September."

"You don't mean next month?"

"Yes, next month."

"Obviously, I can't do that, after making a commitment to come to U.C.L.A. This is awfully late in the year for a job offer."

"Well, we were late getting our budget approved."

"Does that mean that, if I were department chairman, I wouldn't be able to recruit during the regular recruiting season, and would have to hire whoever was left over during the summer?"

"Well, that is one of the problems."

"No," I said. "I won't be able to accept under these conditions."

The one good thing to come out of all this was that I now knew that the old chairman from my days there—a despicable human being—was no longer in charge. The acting chairman was a very decent man and I thought that Howard University would be far better off to let him continue as chairman until they found someone clearly more suitable, rather than try to replace him right away with someone with name recognition and little more. I wrote to the acting chairman, suggesting various people as possibilities. I also explained my own position, that "the chairmanship at Howard—considered by itself—would be something that would represent real fulfillment for myself and for the things I believe in." But not under existing conditions.

Had I heard from Howard last year concerning the department chairmanship I would, frankly, have been delighted. I am convinced that a first-rate undergraduate economics department can be created in a black college out of the materials currently available, and that within a few years its faculty can become respected in the profession for their scholarly work as well. To be instrumental in developing such a department would be something that would mean a great deal to me personally. The great problem is that now I am committed to move to California, and my family has already moved too much for our emotional good, especially for the good of my five-year-old son.

• • •

If I needed any reassurance that I was in a different academic environment, it came in a meeting of the U.C.L.A. economics department to vote on some policy that was likely to be controversial. No one questioned the proposed policy itself, but a couple of colleagues expressed concern over how it would be "perceived." To this the department chairman responded:

"The question is whether we have the honesty and guts to do what we know is right."

In my entire academic career, I had never heard a department chairman pose an issue in terms of honesty and guts. The vote in his favor was overwhelming.

Although I found U.C.L.A. and Los Angeles very congenial, I was still haunted by what was going on, on the racial front, around the country. Some colleagues suggested that I should write about it, perhaps just because they were tired of hearing me talk about it so much. The result was my first article on racial issues, which appeared in the *New York Times Magazine* on December 13, 1970. In it, I attacked the prevailing assumptions behind admissions policies for minority students—especially the practice of passing over highly qualified black students in favor of other black students who happened to fit some sociological or ideological profile.

More than a hundred letters poured in from around the country, the overwhelming majority favorable, with some of the strongest support coming from people who identified themselves as black. Many reported their own vain efforts to talk sense to academics who were on some ideological binge, or who just wanted to be "with it." Three publishers wrote to me, suggesting that I do a book on the subject. Thus began my first book on a racial issue, *Black Education: Myths and Tragedies.*

The most farcical responses to my *New York Times* article occurred at Cornell. Some of the episodes mentioned in the article were not identified as to where they happened. The next day's *Cornell Daily Sun* contained vehement denials that these things had happened at Cornell!

In the days that followed, Cornell administrators and other members of the in-group were quoted in the school paper, denouncing me as uninformed and a liar. A couple of my former colleagues at Cornell wrote to me, *privately* supporting my position, while I was being publicly smeared. The climax of the public attacks was a long, semiliterate letter from an official of the special minority program, assuring everyone that academic standards were being maintained.

The attacks came to an abrupt halt after two members of the admissions committee—people I didn't know—wrote letters that appeared in the paper, substantiating my charges and pointing out that my main critics had themselves been the principal instigators of the policies and practices in question.

*   *   *

My son had a rocky first term in the public school, so I took him out and put him in a private school. This not only turned out to be better in itself, it set the stage for an inadvertent discovery of his mathematical abilities.

Usually I dropped him off at his new school, on my way to U.C.L.A. To give him something to think about during the trip, I would show him the mileage on the odometer when we left and let him figure out what it should be when we arrived. Once we figured out the distance the first day, it would have been easy thereafter, except that sometimes the odometer might be at nine-tenths of a mile when we left and at other times it might be at one-tenth, so his answer could be off by one. With some reluctance, I taught him decimals, so that he could get a more exact answer—and he took to it immediately.

On the way to school, as we drove down the Santa Monica Freeway, he noticed that the numbers showing distance had fractions, so I also taught him fractions as we drove along. Again, he learned them very quickly, though he was only six years old.

• • •

One of the delayed reactions to my *New York Times* article came over the telephone from my radical friend Al:

"You know, Tom, I hate to say it, but you were so damned right in that *Times* article."

"Really? This is quite a change from your original reaction."

"Well, I have just gone through 25 papers from some of those under-prepared students."

"Yeah?"

"I can't teach illiterates!"

"No."

"The university should never have let them in," he said. "They're not getting anything here. They should be in some junior college learning a trade, so they can make a living."

"Why don't you say that in the next thing you write, or in some of your lectures?" I asked.

"Ha!" he replied. "I'll say this to *you*, but if I said it in my class I would never get out of the room alive!"

• • •

One day, for no particular reason, I began to think of Birdie.

It had been nearly 20 years since I had heard her voice. I decided to phone her.

When she answered the phone, her voice sounded subdued, if not dispirited.

"Hello, Birdie," I said. "This is Tommy."

"It's Tommy!" she cried out. "It's Tommy!"

Her voice sounded like the Birdie of old. It was all I could do to hold back the tears.

Later, I went to New York to visit. Mom had long since died, and Birdie and Lacy now lived in her old apartment on 145th Street. Ruth lived over in the Bronx. Jimmy's little sister, Ruth Ellen, was now a grown woman.

We drove over to the Bronx to visit Ruth, with Birdie coming along. After a very warm visit, Ruth walked out to the curb with us. The day was very hot, so I opened the car doors to let in a breeze while we talked and Birdie sat sideways on the passenger side in front, with her feet resting on the curb. After Ruth and I hugged each other and said goodbye, I started walking around the car to get in.

"Birdie, turn around there and get your feet in the car!" Ruth said sharply. "Tommy's getting ready to drive off."

"You're always the big sister, aren't you?" Birdie said.

"Just get your feet in the car," Ruth said.

The main thing was that we were all in touch once more. We never lost touch again as long as they lived.

• • •

One day, I received another telephone call from Howard University:

"Tom, I know you have already turned down our offer to become chairman of the economics department here. But I am coming back again with the offer," and before I could turn them down again, he told me the name of another candidate on their list.

When I heard the name, I said: "Oh, my God! Give me a week to think about it."

The candidate mentioned was a classic hustler peddling racial hype. But he had the backing of a white liberal establishment foundation.

Since the previous offer, I had tapped some inside sources of information about the situation at Howard University, so that I would know what was what if the offer were ever renewed. What I had learned made it painfully clear that there was little hope of accomplishing anything worthwhile there. But the question now was: How far was I prepared to go to block a man who would turn mediocrity into disaster?

The very fact that the university had such a man on its list of candidates for the department chairmanship spoke volumes about the attitudes and priorities of its administrators. After a week of soul-searching, I decided that I could not save an institution with such attitudes and priorities. Certainly it would not be right to uproot my family again and move them back across the country, in the vain hope of saving Howard from itself.

• • •

With the long years in academic limbo now behind me and financial pressures eased, I was now at a stage of my life where I had an opportunity to think about what I wanted to do to prepare for the next stage of my career. Many possibilities crossed my mind, and were discussed with friends and colleagues around the country. Walter Williams was at a Washington think tank called the Urban Institute and suggested that I might join him there. A black man at Stanford, with whom I had been corresponding as a result of his comments on my *New York Times* article, suggested another think tank, the Center for Advanced Study in the Behavioral Sciences, across the street from the university. He also mentioned another think tank right on campus, the Hoover Institution.

Since I was now a tenured faculty member at U.C.L.A., there was no urgency about my making any decisions about the future, except the urgency I felt within myself.

In January 1972, my friend at Stanford arranged for me to make a visit, and to meet people in the economics department, the Hoover Institution, and at the Center for Advanced Study, an independent think tank nearby.

The Center for Advanced Study was for scholars of distinction, in other words, the kind of place that might be a realistic possibility after some of the stuff I had in the pipeline actually appeared in print, especially my book on Say's Law. It was not a waste to meet with them, however, because my understanding was that it was not unusual for some years to elapse between the initial contact and an actual offer of a year's fellowship.

I knew little or nothing about the Hoover Institution, but found the atmosphere there very congenial. However, some of the large, plate glass windows on one of its buildings were boarded up, having been smashed by Stanford students during campus disruptions over ideological issues. That was certainly not something I wanted to be in the middle of.

I had a good visit with the Stanford economics department, but a bad impression of Stanford from a luncheon at the faculty club. During the meal, a group of radical students showed up with a bull horn and proceeded to denounce the faculty for various sins of commission and omission. When some security guards stepped in, the students protested that they had "peacefully" entered the faculty club and were being "violently" resisted by the security guards. In fact, nothing violent happened to the students. Instead, there was one of those "reasonable" compromises so characteristic of academia in the 1960s: Having begun by blasting away on the bull horn at a tremendous volume, the students negotiated an agreement with the security guards to turn the volume down some for the remainder of their harangue.

Among the faculty themselves, there was not one word of protest. When I expressed some surprise at how supinely they were taking it all, I was told that this was not nearly as bad as it had been on another occasion, when the students actually came to the tables and took the silverware away. I asked:

"How many of them were there—and how many of you?"

This question seemed to elicit more reaction than the students' disruption had. I was told:

"Well, I just never thought of it that way."

That told me all I needed to know about Stanford.

The economics department made me an attractive offer of a two-year visiting professorship—teaching half-time, while getting paid full-time—with broad hints that an offer of a tenured position was likely to follow. However, when I phoned around to various people on campus, nothing that they said erased the sour impression I had from that luncheon scene in the faculty club. I declined the offer.

• • •

My growing personal interest in racial and ethnic history finally became a professional interest in the spring of 1972, when I drew up an outline for a book to be called *Race and Economics*.

Meanwhile, I was still looking around for some alternative career move. I was interviewed at two more think tanks—the Rand Corporation in nearby Santa Monica and the Urban Institute in Washington. The Rand Corporation would have been my first choice in terms of location, but the Urban Institute offered me more scope. I would be the director of a research project on American ethnic groups. It was a two-year appointment, which was about the amount of time I wanted to spend on the subject, before turning to something else.

* * *

My daughter Lorraine was now 18 months old, a very affectionate and very spoiled child, but she was already talking, sparing us the long agonizing suspense we went through with my son.

John was now six years old and was very much interested in math. For some reason, however, he did not go to the math class at the unstructured school he attended, but was eager to work out the questions in the math books I bought him. One night I noticed the light on in his room at 3 AM. When I looked in on him, he was working out problems in a third-grade math book.

I have never really believed in unstructured schools, but I do believe in results. For my son, this school helped him come out of his shell as a person. Academically, he was able to develop on his own, to a large extent at home.

As the Vietnam war dragged on and the casualties mounted, my initial misgivings escalated into exasperation, and then bitterness, at the thought of all those young men being sent to their deaths for no clear reason, other than to spare politicians in Washington from being embarrassed by pulling out. I had no respect for the pro-Communist elements of the peace movement, or for those who called for bombing pauses. My feeling was that we had no right to keep soldiers in Vietnam, with their lives on the line, if we weren't going to back them up with everything we had.

By this time, the Vietnam war seemed so much more important than any other political issue that I voted in the Democratic Party primary for George McGovern, simply because he was committed to ending the war. As the election campaign wore on, however, and I saw more and more of McGovern and the people supporting and advising him, I became more and more repelled. By the time of the election in November, I didn't have the stomach to vote for either McGovern or Nixon. In fact, I was pretty disgusted with politics in general, and never again registered as a member of any political party.

* * *

My research project at the Urban Institute began in August 1972 with an initial grant representing a fraction of what would be needed to do all the research that was planned during the two years that it was scheduled to run. However, this initial grant was sufficient to pay my salary and that of a small staff while we developed a formal proposal to take to various funding sources, to try to get the rest of the money needed. I began in very low gear, being more stingy with the money than the Urban Institute administration expected, while I took my time to think through the conceptual problems of the research, design a way of carrying it out, and establish contact with numerous scholars, officials, and others across the country, whose inputs or cooperation would be essential to getting the work done.

At age 42, when I was directing a research project in Washington.

At first, I didn't even have a regular secretary, but from time to time used people sent over from a temporary agency. After about two months, however, the backlog of secretarial work had reached the point where I clearly needed someone on a regular basis. At this point, one of the temporaries seemed like the right person for the job, so I asked to have her hired right away on a permanent basis, so that we could get started. At this point, I encountered bureaucratic delays and ended up in a shouting match with one of the vice presidents of the Urban Institute.

"If I get hamstrung by bureaucrats every time I want to do something," I told him, "this is going to be a long two years for everybody!"

He backed down this time and let me go ahead and make the temporary secretary permanent, but he and the other bureaucrats made themselves a pain on many other occasions, and my run-ins with them became a recurring feature of my stay at the Urban Institute—which was, indeed, a long two years for all concerned.

When Walter Williams commented on my argument with the vice president, I was surprised because Walter's office was on another floor at this time.

"Could you hear us down there?" I asked.

"Tom, you could be heard in any part of the Urban Institute," he said. Then he added: "Do you know why you get into these hassles? When you first meet people, you come on like Mr. Nice Guy—and they try to take advantage of you. You're not Mr. Nice Guy. You're hard as nails. Let *them* know that from the beginning."

More than personality clashes were involved, however. The Urban Institute was a policy-oriented think tank and wanted my project to come up with policy recommendations. I refused. In fact, I had refused even during the negotiating stages before I was hired, and I accepted the appointment as project director only after the Institute accepted the fact that the Ethnic Minorities Research Project would be directed toward adding to our knowledge and understanding of racial and ethnic groups, *not* specifying what policy should be followed. My feeling was that there will never be a shortage of people to come up with ideas for policy. What was painfully lacking was the knowledge and understanding on which to base those policies. We would have our hands full trying to provide that, in the two years available, without being distracted by policy issues ourselves.

Although the Urban Institute had accepted in principle my refusal to direct the project toward policy-making, in practice they kept trying to get me to hire policy-making types, even after I made it clear beyond any doubt that I was looking for people with skills as scholars.

This tug of war over the focus of the research was part of a larger pattern of administrators trying to micro-manage my project. I was new to managing research projects and to raising money, but I was not about to be a puppet, or a means by which particular administrators enhanced their reputation and career prospects by running my project from behind the scenes.

* * *

Things were active on the publication front. *Say's Law* and *Black Education* were both published in the fall of 1972, though the writing of the latter began more than a year after the former was completed. Meanwhile, *Race and Economics* was completed in manuscript by the time these two books were published. However, the copy-editing of *Race and Economics* turned out to be another problem of micro-management, as the copy-editor made massive changes in the manuscript and asked hundreds of questions about particular points made in the book. Both the changes and the questions betrayed the ignorance of the editor, as well as her meddlesomeness.

If the coincidental publication of *Say's Law* and *Black Education* created the impression that I was a faster writer than I was, delays in publishing *Race and Economics* created the impression that it was written later than it was. The publisher and I reached an impasse when I refused to go along with the copy-editor's changes or to answer all the idiotic questions she asked. After a great deal of frustration, I simply informed the publisher that I had no more time to waste, and would do nothing whatever until we began all over again with a fresh manuscript and a new copy-editor. He said that that was impossible.

Several months passed with no further communication between us. Then one day, I was surprised to receive in the mail a couple of chess books from the same publisher, who knew that I was a chess enthusiast (not to be confused with a good player). A few days later, he phoned me:

"Hi, Tom, this is Ed. Did you get the chess books we sent?"

"Yes. Thank you very much. It was a very pleasant surprise."

"What do you think of them?"

"They're wonderful. I'm sure they will improve my game a lot."

"Listen, Tom. When can we get started on publishing that book of yours?"

"Anytime, Ed."

"Really?"

"Yes—just as soon as I get back a new manuscript from a new copy-editor."

Several more months passed.

Another shipment of chess books arrived. Another brief telephone conversation took place. By now, more than a year had passed.

There was a clause in my contract providing that the manuscript reverted to me if it were not published within two years. However, after about 18 months, a new copy-edited manuscript suddenly arrived in the mail unannounced. It had extremely few changes or questions.

After *Race and Economics* was finally published, none of those hundred of questions raised by the copy-editor was ever raised by book reviewers or by readers. In fact, no one even questioned why a book published in 1975 had so few footnotes referring to anything published after 1972.

• • •

A formal proposal, detailing the research agenda of the Ethnic Minorities Research Project, was completed by the beginning of 1973, and I spent the next several months sending it and taking it to foundations and government agencies from which I hoped to get the money to carry out the research.

At one of the foundations, after my formal presentation was over and I was standing in the hall, waiting for the elevator, a member of the foundation staff—a black woman—took me aside and said:

"Officially, the Urban Institute is supporting your request for money. Unofficially, they are doing everything they can to see that you don't get it."

This was both shocking and baffling. Why would they not want me to get the money? It would be money that would go to them, not only to administer, but also to take about half in administrative overhead charges. By this time, I had a confidential contact within the Urban Institute administration, to whom I posed these questions.

"You don't understand, Tom," he said. "You are potential *competition* for the Urban Institute."

"How can I be competition for the Urban Institute, when I am an employee of the Urban Institute?"

"Any time you want to, you can walk down the street and open up your own office, competing with the Urban Institute for grants. They don't want you to get that big by having this project succeed—not after all the independence you've shown. If they can't control you, they would rather get rid of you—and the easiest way to do that, without a messy scandal, is to have you run out of money and leave."

I still did not understand the ruthlessness with which the game was played, until I found myself invited to lunch by a high official in a government agency, a man I had known casually some years before. After the usual pleasantries, he said to me:

"Do you know Bruce Harrington?"

"Yes."

"Would you say that he was 'emotionally unstable'?"

"Bruce Harrington is one of the most emotionally stable people I know—and he was never more emotionally stable than when he decided to leave the Urban Institute."

The official smiled knowingly and we went on to talk of other things.

Bruce Harrington (not his real name) in fact went on to establish his own consulting business, where he competed for grants with others, such as the Urban Institute.

• • •

In mid-February 1973, a conference on race and ethnicity was held in Glen Cove, on Long Island, under the sponsorship of the Ford Foundation. I was invited at the last minute, after the agenda and the participants had already been chosen. As the situation was explained to me, it appeared that the official who invited me was worried about the direction that the conference was likely to take, but did not want to stick his own neck out by opposing it, so he invited me as someone likely to raise objections.

"In other words," I said, "you want me to play the role of Jack Palance in *Shane* and come in to shoot down the homesteaders."

"If you want to look at it that way," he said.

The conference in fact turned out to be the usual mixture of sense and nonsense, both from the academics present and from Ford Foundation officials. One of the big-name black scholars present was disturbed to hear that I was doing research on race and I.Q. He urged me to abandon the idea. He said that it would "dignify" Jensen's theory of genetic differences in intelligence, but I found this argument unconvincing, since so many people believed in that theory before Jensen ever came along. My reading of his objections was that he was afraid of what I might find, that he had no faith in black people himself.

This was by no means the worst of what was said at the conference. Some of the trendy nonsense seemed truly unbelievable, including the statements of some Ford Foundation officials and staff. Afterwards, I talked with the man who had invited me.

"Is the Ford Foundation *serious?*" I asked.

"In the sense in which you mean it—no," he said.

• • •

One of the first sources the Urban Institute management had led me to was the government agency called the Office of Economic Opportunity, better known as the "war on poverty" agency. I didn't even know that O.E.O. gave out research grants, but they did. However, after a pleasant luncheon meeting at an expensive French restaurant (no doubt paid for by the taxpayers under the "poverty" label), none of our subsequent efforts to get money from them got anywhere. Then, months later, I had an unexpected and unofficial visit from a political insider whom I had not met before.

We went to a nearby bar, for discussions better held away from my office, where we might be overheard. We hit it off well, and had many laughs about politics in general and the Washington scene in particular. However, there was more than conviviality involved. He informed me that there had been a shake-up in the Office of Economic Opportunity, with the old liberals with whom the Urban Institute had its contacts being replaced by more conservative appointees—who would be much more receptive to my project if I re-submitted my request.

When I returned to O.E.O., I noticed both new faces and new attitudes. Gone were the nit-picking questions and the pettifogging statements. The new officials seemed to appreciate the substance and value of my research proposals. As time went on, however, I began to sense that hints were being sent, which I was unable to interpret. Eventually, they came right out and said what was on their mind:

"We like you," I was told, "but we don't like the Urban Institute. Moreover, we hear that the Urban Institute is having financial problems, and we don't intend to be the ones to throw them a life preserver. If you could take this project somewhere else, it would make it a lot easier for us to give you the money you need."

After I got back to the Urban Institute, I asked key members of my staff whether they would stay with the project if I moved it to California. They said they would. I made some contacts on both coasts to see if a move was feasible—and it didn't seem to be. However, now I could at least go back to O.E.O. and report a good faith effort to move the project. They accepted it as such and the review process began.

I applied for $325,000 from O.E.O. and for another $100,000 from the Rockefeller Foundation. My contact at the Rockefeller Foundation told me that, even if they awarded me a grant to supplement the money from O.E.O., the Rockefeller money could not be delivered until *after* the O.E.O. money had been received. He and other officials had been warned about giving supplementary grants before the main grant was given. Otherwise, if the main grant did not materialize, then the supplementary grant could turn out to be wasted, since it was not big enough to do the job by itself. That sounded reasonable to me. I could not foresee how that would affect my situation—but it did.

My relationship with the vice president to whom I reported was worsened even beyond its usual level by my re-submission of my grant proposal to the O.E.O. His posture was that his "expertise" was necessary to my fund-raising efforts, since I had no experience with such things and he was an old Washington hand. When I told him that I had a Friday appointment at O.E.O., he asked:

"What time do we go over on Friday?"

"*We* don't go over on Friday," I said. "*I* go over on Friday."

"You don't know anything about O.E.O.," he said. "You don't know anything about raising money."

"We'll see."

Having gotten completely fed up with this character, I asked the head of the Urban Institute to change the arrangement that had me reporting to him. There were plenty of other vice presidents at the Urban Institute—in fact it was crawling with vice presidents—but all sorts of objections were made to the change. When I said that I needed to know what his decision was, so that I could decide whether or not to stay at the Urban Institute, he said that he would give it some thought. After some more time passed and it became clear that he was just stalling, I phoned him.

"Bill, I need a 'yes' or a 'no.' I've got some decisions to make."

"Then make them!" he snapped.

"I will!" I said—and hung up on him. Immediately, I dialed one of my local contacts. He wasn't in, but right after I hung up, I received a call back from the Urban Institute president. He was more conciliatory this time. The net result was that I now reported to a different vice president. I recalled what one of the older hands had told me—that you had to be ready to resign to have any independence, or even self-respect, around here.

· · ·

My book on black education brought me to the attention of a number of people. One was a local television hostess on a New York program called "Straight Talk," where I had my first media appearance in April 1973. A much more substantial contact was Irving Kristol, whose many accomplishments included being editor of the quarterly publication, *The Public Interest*. He invited me to a dinner for people associated with that journal.

During the after-dinner banter, Irving mentioned his youthful days as a Trotskyite. This then prompted Edward Banfield to recall his days as a youthful pacifist and provoked a general reminiscing about the left-wing pasts of virtually everyone present. It was the first of many occasions, at many places, in which I would discover that most conservatives seem to have been left-wingers in their youth, as I had been.

A more serious discussion took place between Irving and me, when he asked, with obvious distress, what could be done to create some first-rate schools for blacks.

"Irving," I said, "you're talking as if this is some hypothetical possibility for the future. There has already been first-rate education for blacks—for decades, for generations."

"Where?"

"Dunbar High School in Washington," I said.

This was news to him and he was very interested. He said that it should be researched and written up. He offered to contribute money and to publish the results in *The Public Interest*. I added this to my Urban Institute project agenda and my article on Dunbar appeared the next spring in *The Public Interest*.

While Irving Kristol was very interested in how first-rate education had been achieved in a black school, no one in the black establishment seemed at all interested, except for a few who tried to discredit the results by saying that Dunbar was a middle-class school for the sons and daughters of doctors and lawyers. My data showed that there were far more Dunbar students whose mothers were maids than there were students whose fathers were doctors.

Although Dunbar had been a fine school for more than 80 years, it was turned into a typical substandard ghetto school within a very few years, after a reorganization of school boundaries.

"How could this have happened?" I wondered. "Did anyone protest or try to stop it?" The answer was "No."

I looked back through the minutes of the board of education during the period of reorganization and found no sign of concern for the fate of Dunbar High School. This was especially puzzling to me, because one of the board members—a feisty woman named Margaret

Just Butcher—was a graduate of Dunbar and a critic of many school board policies. Why had she said nothing about policies that would destroy Dunbar High School?

Eventually, I phoned Dr. Butcher to ask her about this. Was there anything said "off the record" that I missed by reading the minutes? No. It was just that *racial integration* was the crusade of the hour and other considerations simply faded into the background.

What was becoming painfully clear to me was that black "leaders" had a preconceived agenda, and were interested only in such things as advanced that agenda—and were opposed to whatever retarded or distracted from that agenda. In education, the agenda was racial integration in general, including busing. Discussions of first-rate all-black schools were a distraction from that agenda.

• • •

My grant application to the Office of Economic Opportunity was approved in the review process and now needed only the O.E.O. director's signature for disbursement of the money. Meanwhile, however, O.E.O. had become embroiled in a larger legal battle that resulted in a court order, forbidding the director to disburse any such funds.

Times became tense as our project's money began to run low and the supplemental grant from the Rockefeller Foundation was put on hold, pending a resolution of the O.E.O. grant situation. There was no way to know when the legal snarl would be untangled. Meanwhile, the time approached to begin giving lay-off notices to our staff, for lack of money to pay them.

At the eleventh hour, I phoned my contact at the Rockefeller Foundation.

"I know you said that you could not give me a supplementary grant until the main grant was received," I said. "But I think you should know that I am going to have to give lay-off notices next week, if I don't get any money. And once the people have gone, and have found new jobs, we may not be able to get them back after new money arrives."

"I'm going out on a limb, Tom," he said. "You'll get $100,000 next week." That saved the project.

Shortly thereafter, the O.E.O. was authorized to disburse money again—just days before the end of the fiscal year on June 30th. They worked day and night to disburse money to those whose grants had been approved. Even so, not everyone got their money. We were among the fortunate ones who did.

Later, I was told that there was a "good news and bad news" joke going around in the Urban Institute. I forget what the good news was, but the bad news was "the Ethnic Minorities Research Project has been funded."

• • •

One evening I had my radical friend Al to dinner at my house, along with Walter Williams and his wife. Al and Walter had never met each other before, but it turned out that both had grown up in Philadelphia. Walter began asking him if he knew various people, to see if they had any friends in common from the Philadelphia ghetto. As Al kept saying "no" to name after name, Walter grew more puzzled and Al grew more uncomfortable. Finally, Walter asked:

"Well, where did you live?"

When Al told him, Walter said: "I didn't know any black people lived out there!"

"We were the only ones," Al said.

• • •

At the Urban Institute, there was a flurry of hiring activity and an expansion of our research efforts in the wake of receiving $425,000 in grants. Our project now had half a dozen professionals on staff, several secretaries, and perhaps as many as two dozen research assistants scattered across the country, collecting I.Q. data. There were also many consultants, whose expertise was tapped as needed.

It seemed like a new era, with the problems of the past behind us—but it only *seemed* that way.

The Urban Institute management's attempts to micro-manage me directly were replaced by attempts at indirect micro-management, by letting people who joined my project know that they could expect a sympathetic ear among the administrators if they had any trouble with me. This in itself guaranteed that there would be trouble, when people felt that I was a straw man whose policies or instructions they could ignore. A struggle ensued which lasted for months, with the project polarized between those loyal to me and those seeking to undermine my authority.

The administrative burdens and tensions of this period were finally relieved by two factors. The first was the hiring of an administrative coordinator, to assume day-to-day responsibility for managing the various research efforts going on simultaneously within the project. The second factor was the project's rapidly declining financial balance, as we carried out our research agenda. When time came for staff cutbacks, near the end of 1973, I of course got rid of the trouble-makers and the deadwood. It was a very much happier project thereafter. There was a camaraderie among us like that among soldiers who had gone through combat together.

The administrative coordinator was a young woman named Lynn, who was very sharp and very reliable. One of the first things she told me after being hired was: "I understand from talking with the Urban Institute management that my best chance of getting ahead here is to betray you. I just want you to know that I am not going to do it."

Lynn's crucial role was to allow me to divest myself almost completely of administrative chores and to disappear from the Urban Institute to do my research and writing in seclusion elsewhere, free of interruptions and distractions. She became the *de facto* project director for most purposes, while I was able to go off and become in effect a scholar in residence, writing two very long articles for the book we were preparing, in which the research products of the project would be published.

• • •

During the most tension-filled times at work, I was especially glad to come home at the end of the day and find my children waiting by the door for me. Sometimes their sweet little faces looking up at me was all that made life seem worth living. Caesar in his greatest glory never had a more triumphant welcome.

Often I would kneel down and gather them both into my arms

and kiss them. Little Lorraine would sometimes run off into the kitchen to cry out:

"Mommy—it's Daddy! It's Daddy!"

She was probably too young to realize that her mother was not nearly as thrilled as she was. A marriage that had long been rocky was now starting to come apart.

• • •

As the year 1974 began, the agenda of my research project was now essentially to bring to completion all the studies already under way. Now that I was surrounded by a loyal staff, the ability of the Urban Institute management to create mischief was much more limited. An additional $100,000 grant from the Ford Foundation in March 1974 eased our financial strains.

Although we were doing more work than anyone thought possible in two years, it was also clear that some of this work would not be completely finished by the time of my scheduled departure at the end of July. Despite an attempt to get me to extend my time until everything was wrapped up, I insisted on making my resignation effective July 31st, as originally planned at the beginning of the project. A couple of members of my staff made their resignations coincide with mine. A secretary and a research assistant stayed on after my departure to finish up the project's work before leaving. My biggest regret at the end was that I could do so little to reward those who had remained loyal to me and dedicated to the work, despite the distractions of office politics. I rented a small dining room at a local hotel for a farewell luncheon, which everyone seemed to enjoy, including a couple of former project members who joined us.

None of those who stood by me was offered a job elsewhere in the Urban Institute when the project ended, though places had been found for some of the troublemakers I got rid of. A high government official happened to contact me to ask if I had anyone to recommend for a special job he had. This gave me an opportunity to recommend Lynn, who was hired. For the others, the best I could do was to give them my highest recommendations when they applied for jobs elsewhere.

At the end of the project, I gave some parting advice to Lynn, who had carried the daily burdens of administering the project and borne the brunt of internecine fighting, without getting the credit she deserved: "Don't ever take another job like this." She assured me emphatically that she would not. Years later, I learned that she went on to set up her own consulting company with *Fortune* 500 clients and was well on her way to becoming independently wealthy in her forties. She could never have done that if she had remained at the Urban Institute.

• • •

My own future was by no means clear. I was returning to U.C.L.A., where I had been promoted to full professor during my absence, but I did not know how long I would stay. Other options had been discussed, including a visiting professorship at Harvard, and I had been notified that I was now eligible to be a fellow at the Center for Advanced Study, but each of these was a one-year appointment and I did not think that frequent moves were good for the children.

Returning to California now was radically different from my first trip there in 1969, or my relocation there in 1970. In those days, which now seemed so far away, I was full of hope and anticipation. This time, I was returning to U.C.L.A. by default and remaining in my marriage by default—both for the children's sake, rather than my own. Still, whatever the circumstances, I was glad to be returning to California because it felt like home, the place where I wanted to spend the rest of my life.

10

Arrivederci

It was good to see the sights of Los Angeles again, including the U.C.L.A. campus and my old colleagues. It felt like a homecoming. But little did I know that this was going to be the closing chapter of many aspects of my life.

• • •

One of my black colleagues told me about a conversation among black students at U.C.L.A. Someone had a theory about the black professors there, but someone else mentioned me as an exception to that theory. To this the reply was:

"Yeah, but Sowell came in the *front* door."

On one level, it was good to know that they thought of me as someone who got where he was legitimately. On a deeper level, it was disturbing to realize that they thought of other black faculty, and perhaps students, as having come in the back door. If black students felt this way, what did white students think?

One of the ironies that I experienced in my own career was that I received more automatic respect when I first began teaching in 1962, as an inexperienced young man with no Ph.D. and few publications, than later on in the 1970s, after accumulating a more substantial record. What happened in between was "affirmative action" hiring of minority faculty.

Even when students at U.C.L.A. came to me at the end of the term to express thanks for what I had taught them, there was often some revealing phrase that let me know they had been pleasantly surprised.

One young man, early in the term, came to me with a question about a passage in the textbook that he was having difficulty understanding. After I explained what it meant, he asked:

"Are you sure?"

"Yes, I'm sure," I said. "I wrote the textbook."

He then noticed my name on the cover and was obviously embarrassed. It was one of the signs of the times, one of the fruits of "affirmative action."

• • •

A couple of small grants enabled me to begin research for a couple of papers I was preparing to write. It was a great relief to have grants in my own name, so that the money could be spent in the most effective way, without having to go through the kind of bureaucratic maze I had to fight through at the Urban Institute. I bought some office supplies and rented an office in the Venice section of Los Angeles. Although it was advertised as an office, it was actually an efficiency apartment with a nice view, and some people in the building used such places as living quarters rather than offices.

One of my projects involved collecting I.Q. data from a handful of schools, so I phoned a couple of people who had been part of my research project in Washington, to see if I could hire them before they found new jobs after they left the Urban Institute. Margo and Yolande had already found new jobs, but both volunteered to quit them to work for me again, even though the work would last only a few months.

The grant money for this particular mini-project was not yet in hand, but I needed to get started in order to meet a publication deadline, so they volunteered to put their air fares and hotel expenses on their own credit cards until I could come up with the money to reimburse them. The more I thought about this remarkable arrangement, the more heart-warming it was, and the more grateful I felt.

Before the grant money reached me, Yolande reached the limit on her credit card and the manager of the hotel where she and Margo were staying in New Orleans was understandably concerned about the bills being run up. I had to withdraw several hundred dollars from my personal bank account to send to Yolande by telegram. Fortunately, the grant money for this project was in my hands not long afterwards, so we could all breathe a sigh of relief.

A great deal of mutual trust was involved in this effort, for I actually saw them in person only once, during a brief visit to New Orleans to interview people at the school where they were collecting data. Still, it worked out fine and the resulting article appeared in *The Public Interest* in the spring of 1976.

This article was a sequel to my earlier article on Dunbar High School. Now several first-rate black schools were researched, to see what general lessons might be learned from their history. The school that impressed me the most was a ghetto school in Brooklyn, where many youngsters were reading a year or more above their grade level. I sat in on several classes, chosen at random by me, and was amazed and gratified by the high quality of the work being done.

The obvious question was: If this could be achieved here, with children from broken homes and on welfare, why couldn't it be done elsewhere? At the end of the day, when I waved goodbye to the children in the school yard, I was on the verge of tears.

● ● ●

Back in California, life settled into a routine of teaching large classes, making long drives to and from work on the Ventura Freeway, and a growing estrangement between my wife and me. In hopes of giving a fading marriage as much chance as it could have, I had acceded to her desire for a more expensive house than we could afford to rent, located much too far from U.C.L.A. One day, an argument between us—one that was not very important in itself—suddenly made me realize the utter futility of our situation. I simply packed some things and left.

On the way to my little office/apartment in Venice, I stopped in a grocery store and bought some things to eat, as well as a six-pack of beer and a small packet of aspirin. In the months that followed, I con-

Here I was back in California in my mid forties and beginning various transitions in my life, the most painful being my divorce and the most promising being exploring avenues to move beyond my career as professor of economics.

tinued to live in that little efficiency apartment, in order to economize while supporting two households. As long as I lived there, I never finished off either the six-pack of beer or the little packet of aspirin. Neither was needed. There was just a great sense of relief.

Although never a heavy drinker, I had gotten up to about a bottle of wine a week when I had both the Urban Institute and my marriage weighing on my mind. That was cut in half after I returned to California. Then, after I left my wife, most of the other half disappeared. At a party I attended, I passed up so many offers of drinks that someone asked if I were a teetotaler.

The greater peace in my life made me think back to a remarkable phone call I had received some years earlier from an older person whom I did not know particularly well. That caller very plainly and very strongly advised me to divorce my wife "before she destroys your life." Now I sat down and wrote a letter expressing my gratitude for that advice, which I was belatedly following. The separation may have saved my life literally. I had cardiovascular problems, which were common in my family. That spring, Charles had died of a heart attack while in his 50s. A year earlier, William died of a heart attack in his 40s. In the fall of 1975, Mary Frances narrowly escaped death from a heart attack—and she was only a year older than me.

I continued to visit the children twice a week at scheduled times, taking them out to dinner on Wednesdays and spending the day with them on Sunday. To avoid contact with my wife, I would simply park in the driveway a few minutes before the appointed time. When the children came to the window to look for me, they would see the car and come running out. It was a very bittersweet time.

The divorce was a classic case of both parties losing and the lawyers winning. My offer of alimony and child support was rejected out of hand as inadequate, and a long, expensive litigation followed, draining my bank account dry. At the end of it all, the judge awarded less alimony and child support than I had originally offered. But, by then, I was financially drained by the costs of the litigation, so the smaller amount was harder to pay than the larger amount would have been earlier.

The real issue for me, however, was custody of the children. I was convinced that I could raise them better than their mother could, but my attorney and others warned of the damage that could be done to them by a custody battle. I wrestled with this dilemma right up to the eleventh hour. On the day before the scheduled custody hearing, I told my attorney to be in court at 9 o'clock the next morning—and if I didn't show up, to call it off. That night I stayed up well past midnight, weighing every consideration, until finally—in the wee hours of the morning—I decided that it was best not to have a custody fight. Once the decision was made, I was at peace with myself and fell asleep, waking up long after the 9 AM deadline.

• • •

Among the people I talked with about my divorce was my radical friend Al in New York. After I explained the situation to him over the phone, he asked:

"Do you have a Jewish lawyer?"

"Al, with all the things that are going on, I really haven't had time to ask my attorney what day he goes to church."

"Tom," he said impatiently, *"get a Jewish lawyer!"*

For the first time, I realized that Al—like many people hostile to Jews—was awed by Jews. That was no doubt part of their hostility.

• • •

In February 1975, I was unexpectedly invited to have lunch with President Ford at the White House, along with half a dozen other writers, including Edward Banfield and Gertrude Himmelfarb. In honor of the occasion, I took my one good suit to the tailor to be repaired.

It was a very pleasant experience, primarily because President Ford was such a down-to-earth man, with a natural graciousness about him.

The lunch was moved up to an earlier time than that originally scheduled, but the White House staff was unable to contact me, so I came in late. A staffer whom I had met some time before leaned over and whispered to me:

"I'm not going to ask where you were last night, but we know that you were not in any hotel in Washington."

The President himself immediately put me at ease. He simply held his hand out and said:

"Hi, I'm Gerald Ford."

This little meeting made the media. Among those who phoned to comment on it was my old friend Al. Our political differences were old stuff, but now I could tell from the tone of his voice that he was truly upset.

"How *could* you go there and be with *those people?*" he asked. "They're anti-black!"

Al seldom got upset over our ideological differences but now something was clearly bothering him.

• • •

Much of my spare time in 1975 was spent closing out old chapters in my life—both the divorce and preparing to publish the research from the Urban Institute. Intellectually, I turned my attention away from racial and ethnic issues to begin planning a new book on decision-making processes in general. It was a major departure in my work, a large challenge, and something I had been thinking about for more than a year. Now I was ready and anxious to move into this new area.

Midway through the year, things began to sort themselves out. With the divorce terms finally settled, I could begin to put my life back together. I moved out of the efficiency apartment in Venice and into a very nice one-bedroom apartment in Marina del Rey, a more up-scale community nearby. However, I rented furniture for the apartment because I could not afford to buy any, and did not know how long I would be staying.

With my time no longer being tied up in litigation, I could earn some extra money with my writing and speaking engagements, and try to recuperate financially. I also took the fall quarter off on sabbatical leave from U.C.L.A., which gave me more time. Both the Hoover Institution and the Center for Advanced Study in the Behavioral Sciences expressed interest in having me become a visiting fellow during the coming year, and both offers were tempting opportunities to begin writing the book on decision-making processes. The only holdback was my reluctance to leave the children, though air fares were low enough that they could visit me in northern California with some regularity.

• • •

In September, I was invited back to the White House, this time as part of a group debating the merits of "affirmative action" before the President and several members of his Cabinet. There were intellectuals on both the "pro" and "con" side. The former included Kenneth Arrow, Nobel Prize–winning economist.

On the night before the White House discussion, one of the organizations critical of affirmative action wanted to have a strategy session in the hotel where we were staying, but I thought a good night's sleep would do me more good than a cram session.

"I'm going up to my room, watch Johnny Carson, and go to bed," I said. The leader of the organization seemed incredulous.

"Tomorrow you're going to be debating a Nobel Prize winner in front of the President of the United States!" he said.

"I don't mind debating smart people," I said. "It's debating stupid people that's hard. Arrow is both smart and honest, so he knows the limitations of his position."

I had just completed a study on affirmative action, with one of my mini-research grants. The facts uncovered in that study went completely counter to most of the basic assumptions behind the policy, and I laid this out in my presentation at the White House. One of the Cabinet members was a former professor of mine. He had a wry smile as he hefted my paper and considered what I had said.

"Some years ago," he said, "we came to a cross-roads. Perhaps, if we had known then what we know this morning, we might have taken the other path. But today we can't go back to that cross-roads."

His words were politically prophetic. Nothing changed as a result of our debate.

• • •

One of the chapters of my life that I had not intended to close out was my relationship with my radical friend Al. However, it seemed to me that there was a real change in that relationship after my White House luncheon meeting with President Ford. Still, when Al mentioned a family situation that had tied him up, I accepted that as the reason for not hearing from him for a long while. In January 1976, I wrote to him:

> It was good to hear from you after all this time, and your response to the personal tragedy in your life seemed to exemplify the best in you.

Then I turned to some of our long-standing philosophical differences:

> Obviously you and I have differing visions of the way the economic and social system functions. This in turn means that when

we want to accomplish the same objective, we often advocate opposite means. This is not very surprising, and I think the same general principle applies to the differences between the liberals and radicals, on one side, and Kristol, Banfield, et al., on the other. Adolescent self-righteousness has become so fashionable in the past decade that common sense and common decency have suffered a kind of environmental pollution that hurts everybody and makes all social problems more difficult to understand and deal with rationally. As an historian of ideas, I am especially struck by how far we have gone down the road to mindless labelling and almost bogey-man talk. In the 19th century, for example, in Karl Marx's numerous references to Adam Smith there was not the slightest suggestion that Smith had done anything other than call them as he saw them, just as Marx was calling them as he saw them. Smith's arguments were answered by other arguments, not by calling him "anti-worker," which would simply have been a lie.

Younger people are especially vulnerable to simplistic visions spun out by older people who keep their reservations, sophistication, and humanity discreetly in the background, rather than spoil the rhetorical effect. The later agony of withdrawal of many young people from these visions can be dreadful—and some young people come out of it with permanent disabilities, including felony convictions, as the high price of someone else's rhetoric. One of the things I liked about Marx was his utter condemnation of this kind of parlor revolutionism, for just these kinds of reasons.

I don't think it was any secret to Al that I considered him to be a parlor revolutionary. If that was what ended our friendship, so be it.

• • •

During the winter of 1975–76, a Washington insider asked me if I would be interested in being appointed a Commissioner of the Federal Trade Commission. I said that I had never given it any thought, so I wouldn't rule it out, just off the top of my head. Some time later, a

White House staffer phoned me to ask if I were prepared to be nominated by the President to that post. After a brief discussion, I declined.

"We respect your decision," he said, "but don't be surprised if we get back to you."

Later, other people phoned me to urge me to accept, having been prompted by the White House. One argument was that I had been critical of agencies like the F.T.C., so that it was time for me to put up or shut up, as far as going to Washington and doing a better job myself. Andrew Brimmer was one of those who phoned me, and though he was gentlemanly as always, the clear implication of what he was saying was that he thought I was a damn fool not to take the appointment.

When the White House staffer phoned back, I told him that I was willing to be nominated only under certain conditions.

"What are they?" he asked.

"Well, this is an election year," I said, "and strange things can happen to nominees in election years. If any opposition to my nomination develops, let me know and I will withdraw immediately, so that I don't get left dangling."

"All right," he said, "but there isn't going to be any opposition."

With that, the nomination process began. I had to fill out all sorts of forms and submit to an F.B.I. investigation. Among all the questions put to me, those about my financial assets were the easiest to answer—unfortunately.

Weeks passed without a word.

My White House contact assured me that all was going well, even if slowly. However, I heard a different story from a different source—that Senators were being fed questions with which to ambush me during the confirmation hearings by "enemies you may have forgotten, but who have not forgotten you."

That did not worry me very much, because whether or not I was confirmed did not worry me much. However, the dragging out of the process itself created many problems and complications. The department chairman at U.C.L.A. wanted to know if I were going to be around to teach in the spring quarter, as scheduled. The Center for Advanced Study and the Hoover Institution wanted to know whether

I would be joining them, or whether they should offer my fellowship to someone else. My ability to earn outside income with speeches or writings was restricted by the need to avoid receiving money from anyone subject to the Federal Trade Commission's jurisdiction, or in any other way that would create the appearance of a conflict of interest. Among the complications introduced into my personal life were those revolving around the prospects of having one or both my children relocated to the East Coast, perhaps by my acquiring custody of my son.

When the weeks of delay turned into months, I phoned my White House contact, who said that it was just routine bureaucratic delay, but no opposition.

During a trip to Washington on other business, I decided to go to see my White House contact in person. He was as upbeat as ever, and said that he didn't know why the Senate committee in charge of such things was so slow to schedule confirmation hearings. Since I knew what committee that was, I decided to go up to Capitol Hill to find out for myself. Another White House staff man was headed that way and gave me a ride in his limousine.

I found a senior legislative aide to the chairman of the committee with jurisdiction over the confirmation, and asked what was happening. He was quite candid that they were not going to confirm my nomination. Moreover, it had nothing to do with claims or charges made about me by others, none of which checked out.

"We've gone over your record with a fine tooth comb and can find nothing to object to," he said. "So we are simply not going to hold hearings at all."

When I looked puzzled, he continued:

"If this were not an election year," he said, "your nomination would have sailed right through. But we think our man is going to win the Presidential election this year, and we want him to nominate someone in tune with our thinking."

"Does the White House know this?" I asked.

"We told the White House *months* ago," he said.

"Thank you," I said. "You've given me the first straight answers I've gotten."

I went back to my White House contact and said:

"I've just been talking with Chuck Michaels up on the Hill—and either he's lying or you're lying. Which is it?"

He began to hem and haw. I had my answer, so I turned on my heel and walked out the door. I don't recall whether or not I slammed the door on the way out, but I believe that a press account later said that I did. I must have been walking pretty fast in my anger because, when I stopped for a red light at the corner of 17th Street and Pennsylvania Avenue, I saw my White House staffer running to try to catch up with me.

"I really didn't understand what was going on," he said.

"It's your job to understand," I said. By then the light had changed and I walked on across the street, leaving him standing there. I went straight to my hotel room and wrote him a one-sentence note on hotel stationery:

> As a result of my discovery that I had been grossly misled on my nomination to the Federal Trade Commission, I am no longer willing to continue as a nominee.

Why had they nominated me, when they knew that the nomination was likely to be held up, so that the next President could name his own people? As I thought about it, I now realized that, politically, my nomination was a heads-I-win-and-tails-you-lose situation for the administration. Either they would get someone with the kind of philosophy they wanted on the Federal Trade Commission or they would have a political issue, with a qualified black man being rejected by the Democrats. I was the only one who could lose.

* * *

In mid-1976, after the Federal Trade Commission fiasco was behind me, I was ready to move up to northern California. The plan was for me to be at the Center for Advanced Study for 9 months, and then go on to the Hoover Institution for the next 5 months, until the beginning of the following academic year. What I would do after that was unclear. I could return to U.C.L.A., or perhaps accept another academic appointment somewhere, or leave the academic world entirely. That would depend on what turned up in the meantime.

By this time, *The New York Times* wanted me to write an article for their magazine section, setting forth my views on racial issues. They chose the label "black conservative" for me, though I expressed negative reactions to it. In the title of the article, they did put "conservative" in quotation marks, but a lasting label had been created nevertheless. As I was packing up my belongings in a trailer, for the 300-mile drive up to Palo Alto in northern California, a photographer hired by *The New York Times* came around to take pictures of me to accompany the article. In the midst of all the details that go with moving, the photographer and the article seemed incidental. In reality, it would turn out to have surprising repercussions.

After a long drive, I knew that I was nearing San Francisco when I heard a news report on the car radio, excitedly saying that the temperature in the city was up in the 80s! Only in San Francisco was a temperature that high considered surprising in the summertime.

I moved into an apartment complex located near the Center for Advanced Study and right across the street from Stanford University. I could now afford a two-bedroom apartment and planned to buy some furniture. However, pending delivery of the furniture, all I had was an empty apartment with a desk, a cot and a portable television set sitting on the floor. In this condition, a few days after my 46th birthday, I watched on television the national celebration of the 200th anniversary of the founding of the United States on July 4, 1976. As I looked around the bare apartment, I realized that I was almost one fourth as old as the country itself, and had very little to show for it.

● ● ●

Although I was unaware of it at the time, 1976 marked a number of turning points in my life. Intellectually, I was moving beyond my professional work in the history of economic thought, and beyond my work on race and ethnicity, to develop a broader social analysis on decision-making in general, for a book to be called *Knowledge and Decisions,* the largest and most ambitious of my books at that time. I was also becoming used to a life as a scholar in residence at a think tank, with none of the administrative responsibilities I had at the Urban Institute nor any teaching chores as in academia.

My time was my own and I intended to keep it that way, free of interruptions and distractions. Soon after I began work at the Center for Advanced Study, I informed the young lady at the switchboard that I would appreciate it if she would leave me notes at the front desk about any phone calls that came in for me—but not put the calls through to me and avoid interrupting me for anything that was not an emergency.

"What do you mean by an 'emergency'?" she asked.

"I mean like the place is on fire—and by that I don't mean that you smell smoke. I mean that you see the flames with your own eyes."

Very few phone calls were ever put through to me, and I got a lot of work done on *Knowledge and Decisions*.

Another way in which 1976 was a turning point was socially. As a result of my *New York Times* article, a woman who was an attorney in Palo Alto began discussing my ideas—somewhat critically—with a mutual friend at Stanford. He suggested we all get together for lunch to hash things over on September 8, 1976, another turning point in my life. It turned out that she was a very interesting and attractive woman, and our philosophical differences seemed to fade into the background. I invited Mary to dinner the following week and she accepted.

Another new feature of my life was Yosemite National Park. I took the children there for the first time for a few days in August 1976, but it rained the whole time—very unusual for California in the summer. A month later, I went back alone and again it rained—still unusual for the time of year—and I learned that it was the first rain since I was there before. On the morning when I was scheduled to drive back to Palo Alto and take my new-found friend to dinner, the sun came out bright and clear. Everything looked beautiful and I now had a chance to take pictures of it for the first time—except that I had to leave. When I phoned Mary to check last-minute details, I mentioned the weather situation to her—and she suggested that I stay there until I got the pictures I wanted, that we could go out to dinner later in the week. I was very pleased at her suggestion, not only because it gave me an opportunity to take some pictures, but also because it was such a pleasure to discover that she was such a considerate person.

Although I didn't know it at the time, both Mary and Yosemite were to become permanent features of my life.

● ● ●

Although I had moved beyond racial issues in my research, I was still concerned personally about such things as school busing and affirmative action. My concerns about busing and affirmative action were that both had become *symbolic* issues, which were no longer judged by whether in fact they were achieving what they set out to achieve, or by whether they were making things better, rather than worse. When black kids in Boston were bused to a white school whose educational standards were even lower than those in the ghetto, that to me was the decisive sign that we were going in for pure symbolism, rather than results. My research on affirmative action likewise convinced me that it was counterproductive for its avowed purpose, except for a relatively few affluent individuals.

What was frustrating in both cases was that people with different opinions seldom even wanted to debate the evidence. Their motto seemed to be: "I've made up my mind; don't confuse me with the facts."

I got some sense of the emotionalism surrounding busing when I had my first encounter with the national press, after a White House conference among various academics and school board people opposed to busing. The hostility of the reporters in the White House press room was transparent, and our motives were questioned, along with our conclusions. One reporter made a flat accusation:

"You're not here to talk about education. You are here to help President Ford win his Republican nomination battle with Ronald Reagan!"

During the hours of private discussions that morning, no one in our group had even mentioned election-year politics, but now that this inflammatory charge had been made, each member of the group who came to the microphone to express his views on busing found it necessary to preface his remarks with some statement of his partisan politics. It turned out that there were both Democrats and Republicans in our group, and one of the Democrats was a local official of his party who said:

"I expect to be walking my precinct in November, getting out the vote for Jimmy Carter."

It turned out that those who identified themselves as Republicans were all supporters of Ronald Reagan. There was not a single political supporter of President Ford in the whole bunch. When my turn came, I prefaced my remarks by saying:

"I represent those vast millions of Americans who neither register nor vote."

•   •   •

My children began flying up to visit me on a regular basis, and these visits were supplemented by my seeing them when I was in Los Angeles. We had good times together, as always, but I began to be concerned about my son's longer-run situation, especially when he said during the summer of 1976 that he would like to come live with me. His mother and I had already discussed the possibility of my taking custody of him during the period of my nomination to the Federal Trade Commission, but nothing came of it, though the question resurfaced sporadically during 1976 whenever relations between my ex-wife and me permitted reasonable discussions. She sometimes said that she would relinquish custody, at other times not, and at still other times would not even discuss it.

Meanwhile, Amherst College approached me about becoming a visiting professor there during academic year 1977–78. The offer was attractive, both in itself and as a way of determining whether being at a small college again would make teaching a satisfying activity again—as it was not at U.C.L.A.—and thereby help me decide what to do with my future. However, I did not want to drag John across the country if I had custody of him, because I thought he needed stability in his life. Finally, in February 1977, I told his mother that if she could not give me a decision by March 1st, that I would accept an offer to go to Amherst. When no decision was reached by that date, I sent Amherst my acceptance. Later, in May, she finally decided to relinquish custody of John.

. . .

Now that I was writing on public policy issues, I was surprised to discover how fast and how easy it is to become known as an "expert" on a number of subjects. The only subject on which I considered myself an expert was the history of economic theory, but others apparently considered me an expert on all sorts of other things.

Someone associated with the writing of *The Harvard Encyclopedia of American Ethnic Groups* phoned me at the Center for Advanced Study because, as he put it, "You are considered the leading authority on West Indians in the United States." Taken aback, I replied:

"Everything I know about West Indians in the United States could be said in ten typewritten pages, double spaced."

"But who else could write five typewritten pages?" he asked.

Apparently, there must be an expert for every subject, even if no one knows very much about it.

. . .

Another lesson in Washington double-dealing came when I joined Walter Williams to testify against a popular bill in Congress. The legislation was supposed to be beneficial to blacks but Walter and I were convinced that its effects were just the opposite. As we and the witnesses on the other side were waiting in the committee hearing room for the proceedings to begin, I was surprised to see another black man that we knew appear on the scene, though he had no official connection with the hearings. He greeted Walter and me, as well as the witnesses on the opposite side. Then he went over to join those witnesses in discussion—which was perfectly understandable, since he was publicly identified with their position.

As the hearings got underway, the opposing witnesses sat down to testify first, with their backs to the audience, while Walter and I waited our turn. At this point, our black colleague came over and sat down in the seat directly behind me. He leaned forward and began to whisper to me as his allies were testifying. He told me what was wrong with the arguments they were making and the studies they were citing. He told me about other studies which showed the opposite of what they were saying. I was silent through all this and had no idea what was going on.

Eventually, Walter and I had our turn to testify, though most of the Committee seemed unreceptive and impatient with what we were saying, which represented a highly unpopular position. After we finished and got up to leave, I noticed that our colleague was nowhere to be seen in the hearing room.

"I wonder what happened to our old buddy," I said to Walter. "I thought we might have a beer with him after the hearings."

"He can't afford to be seen with us, after what we have said this morning," Walter replied.

It was now clear that our colleague understood that the legislation we opposed was harmful to blacks. He just couldn't afford to say so publicly. So he came to the hearings to feed me information to use against it, no doubt figuring that I had no popularity to lose.

● ● ●

In April 1977, I gave a talk on racial issues at Purdue University. Unknown to me, but well known to those who invited me, a local black studies class devoted two weeks before my talk to turning the black students against me. Fortunately for me, they overdid it. They portrayed me as such a monster that if Attilla the Hun had showed up, people would have thought that he was not such a bad fellow after all.

During the question-and-answer period after my talk, a black faculty member and a few black students tried to give me a hard time, but I dealt with them. When it was over, various other black students gathered around me in a friendly manner, one young lady among them with tears streaming down her cheeks, because she realized that she had been lied to.

On a lighter note, one of the black girls asked me a question obviously designed to needle the black male students present.

"Dr. Sowell," she asked, "why do you suppose that black fellows, after they get to college, start dating white girls?"

"Maybe they don't have enough money to date black girls," I said.

From the instant and opposite reactions of the guys and girls, it was obvious that no explanation was necessary.

. . .

One day, I was invited to join a group of Hoover Institution scholars going over to the faculty club to have lunch with former California governor Ronald Reagan, who was visiting on campus. It so happened that I sat next to him, and so had a better opportunity to ask him questions than some others did. He struck me as a man of much more substance than he was usually credited with in the media—then or later.

The discussions were wide-ranging and somewhat revealing. What struck me most was his story of being Governor during the last execution to take place in California at that time. Having the power of clemency or pardon, Governor Reagan was brought all the papers on the case to review, and was also being asked by various groups to stop the execution. Reagan said that he went through the papers looking for anything that would justify stopping the execution—and could find nothing. He wasn't prepared to stop it just on his own notion, so the execution went forward. As the time of the execution approached, protest groups gathered outside the Governor's mansion and some knelt to pray. Reagan said:

"I don't mind telling you, inside the Governor's mansion, I was on my knees praying too."

. . .

In the fall, John and I moved to Amherst. By and large, I liked teaching there, but there was one episode that left a lasting negative impression on me, as a sign of where the academic world was heading. One of the students in one of my courses was a young woman from either Smith or Mt. Holyoke. Her low grades made her highly indignant and she asked for an appointment to see me in my office. When I mentioned this to a colleague, he said:

"Don't close the door while she's in there."

It took a moment for this to sink in on me.

"Have we come to that?" I asked.

Obviously we had. Now suddenly I understood why a colleague in the economics department had students wait in a chair placed down the hall from his office door. That was his way of having private conversations with whoever was in his office *without closing the door.*

The whole thing turned my stomach, especially when I thought back to my first year of teaching at Douglass College, where I was considered prudish for not inviting the students to my apartment. Now we dared not close the office door, for fear of vindictive charges of sexual harassment. What all this implied about the career I had chosen, and about which I had growing doubts, weighed so much on my mind that I in fact forgot all about the practical advice I had been given and closed the door automatically after the young woman entered. Fortunately, she just blew off steam about how she deserved a higher grade and I simply told her that none of her grades was going to be changed.

I had come to Amherst, basically, to find reasons to continue teaching. What I found instead were more reasons to abandon an academic career.

• • •

Before going to Amherst, I had taken on the task of preparing a paper for a gathering of scholars at the University of Miami's Law and Economics Center in January 1978. The Director of the Center, law professor Henry Manne, wanted a paper critiquing the legal concept of "state action"—a phrase and a concept that meant absolutely nothing to me at the time, but which he was sure that I would master in no time. The more I struggled with the legal literature and court cases on the subject, the more I wondered about the source of Manne's optimism.

The nearest law library was in Springfield, Massachusetts, so it was a day's trip to go down there to read and xerox relevant court cases and law journal articles. Although I now knew what the concept of "state action" meant in the abstract, I couldn't make heads or tails of the whole string of legal cases on the subject. One day, however, I suddenly began to see a pattern running through it all and was ready to write my paper—but just then, I noticed the clock and realized that it was time for me to go to school for a conference with John's teachers and counselors. After school, John and I were off to the laundromat, to do our washing, and from there it was off to the supermarket to get a supply of food. By then, it was time to go home and cook dinner.

By the time dinner was over and the dishes washed, and John and I spent some time with each other before he went to bed, I was too exhausted to do any serious intellectual work that day. My paper on "state action" moved very slowly. The only consolation was that, once I understood what it involved, I realized that it also belonged in my larger project, the book *Knowledge and Decisions,* which was taking longer to write than any other book I had done. Being a single parent was part of that. The only consolation was that John seemed happier and more at peace. That was, of course, worth a lot.

His intellectual abilities were also developing, though narrowly focused on analytical areas, such as mathematics and chess. John had already won a local chess tournament for kids down in southern California, and one weekend I drove him down to New Haven to take part in another chess tournament there. In mathematics, I taught him some elementary algebra and we played a game in which I gave him three numbers in a series, leaving him to figure out the fourth number and the general formula behind the series as a whole. It went like this:

"The three numbers in the series are 4, 11, and 32. What is the fourth number, John?"

"It's 95—and the formula is $3x-1$."

It so happened that the chairman of the math department at Amherst was my old college roommate, Norton. When he had John and me over to dinner, Nort was amazed to see a twelve-year-old boy doing such problems in his head—and he took pencil and paper to check out the answers himself.

● ● ●

Despite my growing misgivings about the academic world, no sufficiently attractive offer elsewhere had turned up since I went on leave from U.C.L.A. in 1976, so now I returned there in January 1978, by default.

My choice of a place to stay now had to be governed by where John would have a good public school to attend, since I could not afford a private school for him. After getting a recommendation of a junior high school in Santa Monica, I went to that school to obtain a map showing their attendance boundaries, and then proceeded to look for an apartment within those boundaries. I found a two-bedroom town-house on Second Street in Santa Monica, much like the townhouse we had had—and liked—in Massachusetts.

Now that I was back in California, I could resume seeing Lorraine on the same schedule which I had used with both children before—dinner every Wednesday and a complete weekend every other week-end. I was back in a routine, both at home and at work. It was comfortable, even if it wasn't what I really wanted.

For John, our new home had the advantage that it was within walk-ing distance of a chess club, where he played regularly. Occasionally, he also competed in tournaments as far away as San Diego, where I drove him one day. These were all local tournaments, with different age and ability divisions. He sometimes won prizes of ten or fifteen dollars and, over a period of about a year, won a total of more than a hundred dol-lars. Sometimes I competed in the same tournaments, just to have something to do while waiting for him, but I never won any money. When our official chess ratings arrived from the U.S. Chess Federa-tion, his was a couple of hundred points higher than mine.

• • •

California's Senator S. I. Hayakawa assembled a group of economic advisers to help him when considering various legislation. Arthur Laf-fer, myself, and a number of other people were part of this group. Af-ter a meeting in San Francisco, he invited us to join him for dinner at a nearby Japanese restaurant. He was in high spirits, as usual.

"You barbarians all have to take off your shoes when you come in here," he said at the entry to the restaurant—and we did.

As we were finishing up a very pleasant meal, the Senator tapped his spoon on a cup for attention and unveiled his latest idea.

"I think Art Laffer and Tom Sowell ought to enter the next Re-publican primary," he said. "The winner to run for the Senate and the loser to run for the governorship."

"Senator, you really do have a great sense of humor," I said.

His staffers immediately assured me that the Senator was serious, that they had all given this a lot of thought. A honcho from one of the big banks said that raising money would not be a problem. Art Laffer said that he wouldn't run, but that he would support me.

"Senator," I said, "I've never thought about any such possibility, so I'd like to take some time to consider it."

I was more stunned than anything else. At the same time, I felt an obligation to give it some serious thought, in case there was something worthwhile that I could contribute in Congress. I arranged to talk with a number of political professionals, to get some idea of what practical politics was like.

"Whatever minor influence my writings may have," I said to one political pro, "would I have any more influence as a freshman Senator, one out of a hundred? Would the public interest be any better served if I were in Washington?"

"If you are thinking about this from the standpoint of the public interest," he said, "then you don't belong in politics. You've got to want that job so bad you can *taste* it."

What bothered me most about what the political professionals told me was the enormous amount of time that went into campaigning.

"Who's going to be taking care of my son while I am running around every day trying to get votes?" I asked.

"Look," the political pro said, "to a real politician, his family exists to help him get elected. If you see it differently, then you don't belong in this business."

Most of the people who knew me thought that I was not cut out to be a politician. Irving Kristol gave me the worst-case scenario:

"You might get elected! You'd hate it."

The more political pros I talked with, the more convinced I became that Irving was right. It took these pros very little time to decide that I was not the stuff of which successful politicians are made.

• • •

In 1978 I finally finished the first draft of *Knowledge and Decisions*. It was much longer than I had planned, took longer to write, and was not as easy to read as I wanted it to be. Nevertheless, it was to me clearly the best thing I had ever written at that point. I sent out copies of the first half of the manuscript in June to various people, including my editor Midge Decter—one of the few editors I have ever liked or respected. When she responded enthusiastically to the first half of *Knowledge and Decisions,* that was the frosting on the cake.

I was so concerned that this book must appear in print, regardless of what might happen to me, that I wrote Midge, giving her my home address and directions as to where in the apartment to find my manuscripts and footnotes if anything happened to me.

• • •

In February 1978, I went out to Washington University in St. Louis to take part in a symposium at the law school. Nothing that happened at that gathering seemed particularly memorable at the time—certainly not the fact that a young black man came up to me after the presentation and asked me to autograph a copy of *Race and Economics.* It was years later when he showed me that autographed copy again in his office in Washington. His name was Clarence Thomas.

On the same panel with me was a professor from the law school at Columbia University: Ruth Bader Ginsburg. On another panel was another law professor, from the University of Chicago: Antonin Scalia. One-third of a future Supreme Court was in that room that day.

• • •

Although my career was going along well enough, in terms of academic recognition of my work and invitations to give talks and write papers, teaching at U.C.L.A. was becoming less and less satisfying.

The best students there were top-notch, but there was too little interaction with them in a large class setting, and the number of students who seemed incapable of thought, or wholly lacking in interest, made the whole teaching experience something of a downer. One student who took three courses from me said that he could see my morale decline over time. Increasingly, I began to notice the contrast between the interest and lively interaction in the audiences I addressed on the lecture circuit and the lackadaisical attitudes in the classes I taught at U.C.L.A.

Ordinarily, the problem might have been alleviated by teaching more graduate courses, but the history of economic thought was not a field that attracted many graduate students, and those who enrolled at U.C.L.A. seemed to think that it was a place to rest up from the rigors of macroeconomics or econometrics.

Worse than all of this, however, were those U.C.L.A. students who were constantly trying to manipulate their way to better grades, often with the help and connivance of academic administrators. I found myself repeatedly writing memos explaining to students or administrators that I was not going to have double standards to favor those students who had clever excuses, moral indignation, or who just made a nuisance of themselves in order to extort a passing grade. To do so would be a betrayal of those students who played it straight, as well as a general disincentive to all students, as far as doing conscientious work was concerned. It was bad enough to have to explain such basic realities to students, but it was worse to have to explain them to academic administrators, who were supposed to know such things already.

What was politic, however, carried much more weight with deans and the like than what was a matter of principle.

Symptomatic of the attitudes among the officialdom at U.C.L.A. was the appointment of someone called an ombudsman, whose official role was to champion student rights and whose actual role was to help them get whatever they could from professors. A typical conversation between an ombudsman and me went like this:

"Professor Sowell, a student named Bill Smith has come to me with a problem in your course."

"What problem?"

"Well, he would like to discuss his grade with you."

"What is there to discuss?"

"Well, he'll go into all that with you if you will give him an appointment."

"If there is a mistake in adding up his test score, he can just leave the test in my mailbox and it will be automatically corrected."

"It's not that."

"I didn't think it was. Then what is it?"

"As I said, he'll go into that when he sees you."

"What you're telling me is that he doesn't really have anything concrete to say, but thinks that he can make enough of a nuisance of himself that I will give him a higher grade to get rid of him."

"That may be the way you look at it."

"That's exactly how I look at it."

Almost never was there any legitimate reason to change a grade through third-party interventions, though I readily changed grades whenever I discovered errors in grading by either myself or my teaching assistants, or found that an exam question was ambiguous. Nor was there any need to go through third-parties to get to see me, since I was in my office at regularly scheduled office hours, which were printed on the front page of each course syllabus. What some students hoped to gain by going through third-parties was pressure on me to give them an advantage over other students who played it straight.

Some students went to the department chairman with their complaints, and occasionally a student would even bring his mother with him to talk with the department chairman. The chairman would lend an ear and then relay what they said in a memo, without urging any particular course of action. We understood each other very well. One day, when I happened to encounter the chairman while walking across the campus, he said:

"Did you get my memo, Tom?"

"Yes."

"And is your answer what I think it is?"

"Yes."

"Good! Now we have both done our jobs."

One day in April 1979, while I was in my office seeing students who were enrolled in my spring quarter class, a student who had gotten a bad grade in the previous quarter came in, full of indignation, and vowing to sit in the office until the grade was either changed or he was thrown out by a security guard. I phoned for a security guard.

It was 20 minutes before the guard showed up. During all that time, a whole line of other students had to wait outside my office while this jerk sat inside, mouthing off. I was tempted to throw him out myself, but I knew that this would only open me up to a lawsuit, and nothing I had ever seen in courts gave me any confidence in judges.

What was even worse than this distasteful episode itself was the way it was handled by the U.C.L.A. administration. The long delay in sending a security guard was only the beginning. They did nothing to this student—but it was elaborate, clever, academic nothing. Officially, he received a reprimand. When I asked the dean who handled the case what this meant concretely (and cross-examined him, as he tried to evade), it turned out that this meant simply that a letter of reprimand went into the student's file *temporarily* until he graduated, that its very existence would never be known to anyone without access to those files, and that no one thereafter would ever know about it.

This episode was another landmark on the road to my rejection of teaching—or rather, my rejection of what teaching had come to mean.

• • •

The final draft of *Knowledge and Decisions* was completed in 1979. Although I regarded it as the best thing I had done up to that time, I had no idea how it would transform my career.

Copies of the manuscript were sent around to people who were interested in hiring me. After reading *Knowledge and Decisions,* the economics department at the University of Virginia made me an offer of an endowed chair in economics. The Hoover Institution then topped Virginia's offer with a Senior Fellow position, requiring no teaching at all. I accepted Hoover's offer and began my career there in September 1980. It would turn out to be the longest job I ever held and the most satisfying. It would allow me to devote my time entirely to research. Although teaching was initially what attracted me to an academic career, the atmosphere surrounding teaching now made it something to get away from. I now said goodbye to another feature of my past life.

11

September Song

After you turn fifty, it becomes harder to think of yourself as "middle-aged." After all, how many people live to be a hundred? My fiftieth year brought me far more notoriety than ever before, largely because it coincided with the 1980 election year that made Ronald Reagan the fortieth President of the United States. The media chose to depict me as having some serious involvement with his administration. To say that my actual involvement was modest would still be to overstate my role considerably.

In August 1980, the phone rang in my apartment and someone whom I did not know identified himself as a member of the Reagan-for-President campaign office in Los Angeles. They were preparing a speech for the Governor to deliver the following week to the Urban League in New York, to begin an effort to get the black vote, and they wondered if I would be willing to come down to the campaign headquarters to give them my opinion or advice. My response was to tell them that I would be willing to do it, provided that everyone understood that I was not a member of any political party and would not be doing this from the standpoint of partisan politics, but rather from the standpoint of how this would affect the black community. That was fine with them, so I went down to the Reagan campaign headquarters.

Although I did not know the people who had invited me, I did recognize some of the staffers at the headquarters, some of whom were Libertarians, so I did not feel quite so out of place as a non-Republican. The speech which I came to critique was not yet ready when I arrived. One of the black aides, a man I had not met before, showed me a copy of an alternative speech which he had written, but which had been rejected. When I read it, I found it a very well-written, sharply focused speech which addressed key points that a black audience would be interested in, while being completely consistent with the Reagan philosophy.

"This is a great speech," I said to one of the campaign honchos. "With a man like this on your staff, what do you need me for?"

Staffers said that the speech wasn't the Governor's style and that he had to be comfortable with a speech in order to deliver it. As more time passed and the official speech still did not appear, the black speech-writer and another black aide and I decided to go have a bite to eat—and to talk privately among ourselves. The two men had quite different attitudes. The man who wrote the speech can be called Mr. Skeptic, broadly in favor of the political philosophy that Ronald Reagan represented, but with some troubling doubts about how it was being expressed and carried out. The other aide was a total loyalist, whether from conviction or expediency.

After we went across the street to a hotel restaurant, to get a snack and something to drink, Mr. Skeptic expressed some serious misgivings about both the conception and the execution of the campaign to reach black voters. He didn't think the Governor or his aides knew what they were doing on racial issues, and wondered how much they understood black voters or were comfortable with them. Mr. Loyal defended Governor Reagan but Mr. Skeptic wasn't buying it.

"Look at that last speech he gave to a black audience," Mr. Skeptic said. "You have to admit that it really did not go well."

"I thought it went very well," Mr. Loyal said staunchly.

"It went *as well as could be expected*," Mr. Skeptic said. "But it did not go well."

"What do you *want* from him?" Mr. Loyal asked, with some exasperation. "He was a little ill at ease. He's not yet used to addressing black audiences. How would you feel if you had to address the Ku Klux Klan?"

Mr. Skeptic looked pained at the analogy, so Mr. Loyal turned to me in desperation:

"Wouldn't you be nervous if you were addressing the Ku Klux Klan?" he asked.

"Not me," I said, "because I would be on tape."

We had a laugh and changed the subject. But it was clear that Mr. Skeptic had some real problems with what was going on around him. Some of the hastily thrown-together arguments of Mr. Loyal might suggest that he too was not quite as immune to doubts as he wished to appear.

After we went back to the Reagan headquarters, the draft of the Urban League speech finally arrived. It was truly awful—vague, irrelevant, striking the wrong notes and not hitting any of the right ones. When the honchos asked my opinion, I hardly knew where or how to begin. But, since there was no point being anything other than candid, I gave my honest assessment of it, causing some of the Reagan aides to wince at my comments. The two black aides added their criticisms.

"All right," one of the honchos said. "Why don't we all go into a room here and work it over, cutting and pasting?"

We all sat down around a table and went at it, commenting freely and developing a camaraderie in the process. One line in the speech really got my goat, because it seemed to epitomize the whole wrong-headed approach of the talk. It was a quotation from black Air Force General Chappy James. No doubt Chappy James was a fine man and, in context, his remark was probably a fine thing to say—but in a political campaign speech, it did nothing to address the concerns and allay the fears of black voters, to whom "conservatism" was at best unfamiliar, if not foreboding.

Time passed quickly, and suddenly I realized that it was time for me to be home with my son. The others seemed surprised that anyone could walk out in the midst of this operation, but I was adamant.

"Just one question before I go," I said. "What about that quote from Chappy James?"

"Chappy James is on the cutting room floor," the Reagan honcho assured me.

"Thank you," I said. "I can go home now and sleep well tonight, knowing that that remark will not be made to the Urban League next Tuesday."

Like so many predictions made by economists, this one turned out to be wrong. When I came back the next day, I was told that the Governor was really attached to that quote and wouldn't give it up. For reasons unknown, I was invited over to his hotel suite to join a group having lunch with him. There were some big-name economists there, including former professors of mine. Reagan's suite was quite modest, however, and the lunch consisted of dry sandwiches and drinks in styrofoam cups. I couldn't figure out why I was there, since I had taken no part in the prior discussions of economic policy issues, and heard nothing in the present discussion on which I felt any desire to comment, since none of it was in areas in which I had done any research. However, it was a pleasant enough gathering and did not last too long.

When I went back over to the campaign headquarters, the honcho there said that they would like to invite me to come along with Governor Reagan on this trip, as the campaign went around the country to touch base with various black organizations and black leaders. This invitation was wholly unexpected and I hesitated, much to the astonishment of Mr. Loyal. I had already been drawn further into the political process than I ever intended to go when I first agreed to come down here to look at a speech, and I had no desire to go any further. The honcho apparently sensed this and sought to overcome my reluctance by pointing out the historic opportunity before me.

"You will have an opportunity to spend several hours in a plane with a man who will probably be the next President of the United States," he said. "You will have a chance to present to him your views on what kinds of policies the next administration should follow."

I thought: God knows *somebody* ought to talk to him about racial issues and about addressing the concerns of the black community. Since I was the one who was given the chance, it was up to me to try to do it.

"All right," I said. "I'll come along."

"Great," the honcho said. "Here's an itinerary. After the Secret Service checks you out, we'll get back to you with some more details."

After I got back home and thought about the itinerary, I found it troubling and decided to phone another, higher-up Reagan aide, whom I happened to know from before.

"This itinerary," I said. "The first stop is in *Philadelphia, Mississippi!*"

"Yes," he said. "There's a state fair going on there and the Governor wants to make a brief stop there to address some local supporters."

"Philadelphia, Mississippi," I reminded him, "is where the three civil rights workers were murdered back in the 1960s—and where those who were accused of the murder were turned loose laughing."

"I know," the aide said.

"And that's where you are making your first stop on a trip to try to get the black vote?"

"I have already raised the same objections," he said, "and I was over-ruled."

"Then I won't be able to go," I said.

"I'm sorry to hear that."

"I'm sorry too."

*   *   *

With my two-day political career now behind me, I returned to my research and writing—I was putting the finishing touches on *Ethnic America*—and to making my final preparations for the move to Palo Alto. Joining the Hoover Institution would mark the decisive break with academic teaching that I had been contemplating for more than a decade. Moving to Palo Alto also marked the beginning of a new life in another way: Mary and I were married. In many ways, the years ahead would turn out to be much more fulfilling than the years behind me. One of the immediate signs of the change was that my doctor took me off medication for high blood pressure.

With the manuscript of *Ethnic America* now in the mail to the publisher, I turned my attention to research for a book on Marxism that I had been wanting to write for many years. However, during this period, I also borrowed a book from the library for my personal reading enjoyment on a subject I had heard just enough about to want to look into. This book was *The Chinese in Southeast Asia* by Victor Purcell. It was a monumental study of the Chinese minority in Thailand, Malaysia, Indonesia, Vietnam, and the Philippines. It was an absorbing story. In fact, it began absorbing more and more of my time and interest, eventually pushing the study of Marx to one side. Now I began to think of writing something like *Ethnic America* on an international scale. This now became my primary project, one that would last far more years than I anticipated at the time.

*　*　*

Two unexpected things happened right after Ronald Reagan won the Presidential election: Stories began to appear in the media that I was being considered for a Cabinet position in the Reagan administration and other stories featured bitter denunciations of the Reagan administration that did not yet exist by so-called "black leaders." There had been no contact between me and the Reagan entourage since my two-day misadventure during the campaign, so the talk of a Cabinet post caught me by surprise. What was even more surprising was the variety of Cabinet posts for which I was rumored to be under consideration—Secretary of Housing and Urban Development, Secretary of Education, Secretary of Labor, not to mention the Council of Economic Advisors.

The story that gave me the best laugh appeared in *The New York Times.* It described senior officials of the Labor Department as being "sunk in gloom" at the rumors that I might become Secretary of Labor. These senior officials no doubt included people who knew me when I was an economist in the Labor Department back in the early 1960s. To them, the prospect of having me return as an economist would have been bad enough, but to have me return as Secretary of Labor must have seemed like the end of the world.

Although I had no way of knowing whether any of these rumors had any substance, and I had no desire to be in Washington in any capacity, there was one Cabinet post that would trouble my conscience to turn down—Secretary of Education, simply because American education was in such terrible shape, especially among low-income minority children, and because I knew that something desperately needed to be done about it. I talked with a few friends and colleagues as to what I should do if that post were offered to me—whether what I could realistically expect to accomplish was worth the aggravation of Washington politics and the risks to my health of being under constant stress.

The sweeping denunciations of the still non-existent Reagan administration by black "leaders" who were regarded in the media as speaking for all blacks was another story. I was incensed that such irresponsible rhetoric could help freeze blacks into the position of being a one-party group—a group whom neither party would have to take seriously, because their vote was already so committed to the Democrats that the Republicans wouldn't see much point in bidding for it. When I voiced this concern in a phone conversation with a friend in San Francisco, he expressed complete agreement and suggested that we get together at the home of a knowledgeable colleague of his, to talk over what might be said or done about this media picture of a monolithic black community.

At the San Francisco meeting, I happened to express my amazement at rumors that some people within the Reagan camp were pushing me as a prospect for Secretary of Labor.

"I cannot even *imagine* who would be pushing me for such a job — or why," I said.

"*I'm* the one who's doing it," our host said.

"Then stop doing it," I said.

"I think you'd make a great Secretary of Labor."

"Look, the President of the United States has better things to do than having to be constantly going around saying, 'Well, what Tom really meant—'"

"No," our host said, "I think your outspokenness would be an asset."

"If nominated I will not run; if elected, I will not serve," I said, repeating the formula that General Sherman made famous.

With that out of the way, we turned to the business of the evening—what to do about the media depiction of one viewpoint as being *the* monolithic viewpoint of the black community. After batting around various ideas, we suddenly all agreed that what was needed was a conference, bringing together alternative viewpoints within the black

SEPTEMBER SONG ———————————————— 281

community, and showcasing such a conference to the media. We also decided that time was of the essence, to get some different ideas out there before the myth of a monolithic black community was set in concrete. In our enthusiasm for the idea, we decided to hold the conference in just a couple of weeks. We called it "The Black Alternatives Conference," but the media called it "The Fairmont Conference," because it was held at the Fairmont Hotel in San Francisco. The media also referred to it as a meeting of "black Republicans," even though neither I nor a number of other participants was Republican, and at least two participants were officials in the Democratic Party (Percy Sutton and Charles V. Hamilton). There were also whites on the program.

Throwing together a conference on such short notice proved to be an adventure, to say the least. However, by some miracle, it was done. Even more miraculously, it was a bigger success than we expected—whether measured in terms of the caliber and diversity of the people who attended, the media attention it received, or the atmosphere prevailing among those present. Among those who gave talks were premier black television journalist Tony Brown, academic scholars like Michael Boskin, and an impressive young man named Clarence Thomas. Even the audience included heavyweights, such as Milton Friedman and Ed Meese.

The most important achievement of the Fairmont conference, to me, was that it brought together blacks who debated their differing viewpoints in an atmosphere wholly free of rancor, of attempts to be blacker-than-thou, and without any charges of "selling out" or the like. Someone in the media called it "a love feast."

"This conference could not have been held on the East Coast," one of the East Coast participants said. The atmosphere in such places as Washington and New York was too intense and too charged, with so many people vying for power, for prominence in the media, or for little empires built on grant money. I was of course gratified that we had held a conference in an atmosphere of mutual respect, though it was sad to think that this had become something to be regarded as a rare accomplishment in a conference on racial issues.

• • •

My transient and tangential relationship to the Reagan administration was in complete contrast with the big role that the media represented me as playing. To read some of the newspaper stories, you would think that I was a black Harry Hopkins, whispering advice into the new President's ear. In reality, I had not seen or talked with Ronald Reagan since sitting in on the luncheon group in August, and had not had even a modestly substantive discussion with him since being in another luncheon group with him in 1977. Yet one news story said, "Sowell is maneuvering within the Reagan administration." Once an idea gets started in the media, it just seems to build up like a snowball rolling downhill.

There was no decent way for me to put a stop to these rumors and speculations. You cannot very well make a public statement that you are not going to accept an offer which the President-elect has not even made to you. Finally, however, a Reagan aide phoned me to ask if I would be interested in being Secretary of Education and I declined. Contrary to later media stories, I did not hang up on the man abruptly but, although I was polite to him, there was not really a lot to say.

By that time, I had resolved in my own mind that I did not have the political skills or temperament to accomplish anything that would justify the aggravation that going to Washington would involve. And if I couldn't really accomplish anything, there was no point being there. My previous experience with being nominated to the Federal Trade Commission during the Ford Administration, and my talks with political pros while considering a campaign for the Senate, were enough to give me lifelong immunity to Potomac fever.

Everyone who knew me well was convinced that I should stay out of politics. Both my wife Mary and my sister Mary Frances felt that way. Birdie said that she could not even *imagine* me in politics. Two women whom I had not seen or heard from in years phoned me long distance from two East Coast cities, because each was alarmed at the stories she had read that I was going to Washington, and each urged me not to do it.

Now that I had been offered and declined a political appointment, I thought that this would end the media speculation. But I was wrong. The media continued to build me up as some kind of new star on the political horizon, and those who disagreed with me painted me as some kind of powerful demon.

Syndicated columnist Carl Rowan warned the President-elect against listening to people like Walter Williams and me, who he said were "supplicants" for the "largesse" of the new administration. Things I had been saying for years were now interpreted in the media as attempts to butter up the Reagan administration, in hopes of getting some political appointment. "Like flies chasing a garbage truck, opportunists of all stripes (and colors) are scrambling to align themselves with the new Reagan administration," one critic said, including among his examples "Thomas Sowell of the notorious Hoover Institution."

These rhetorical flourishes were much less bothersome than the interruptions of my work by media people phoning me at home and at the office. One day, someone knocked on my office door and, when I opened it, quickly stepped inside.

"I'm from NBC News," he said.

"Get out of my office," I said as I turned to walk back to my desk.

"This will just take a minute."

"You didn't hear me. I said *get out of my office.*"

Only when I advanced on him angrily did he decide to beat a retreat.

Eventually, the pestering of the media led to lasting changes in the way I lived and worked. My home phone number was changed and the new number was unlisted. At my request, the Hoover Institution removed my name and room number from the directory in the lobby, and removed the nameplate from my door.

Before this time, anyone could walk in off the street and drop by my office to chat with me, as some Stanford students did from time to time. In the fall of 1980, a local black businessman dropped in and we went out to lunch, later becoming friends and tennis partners. Media hype put an end to this way of life. Afterwards, some in the media referred to me as a "recluse."

• • •

The persistent myth of my influence in Washington led to all sorts of strange things. One professor at a distinguished law school sent me his resume, saying that he would be interested in a federal judicial appointment. He said that he would not accept a district judgeship, but would be willing to serve on an appellate court. The farce in all this was that I could not have gotten anyone appointed as dog-catcher.

This was not the only resume that came in. All sorts of people tried to get me to do all sorts of things. I had to write a form letter, telling everyone who wrote in that I had no way to get anybody anything.

One of the prominent civil rights leaders invited me to an off-the-record lunch at his hotel suite while he was passing through San Francisco. No doubt he too was under the impression that I had some kind of political influence. We had an interesting and pleasant conversation, but I could not help noticing how much more posh his hotel suite was than the one in which I had had lunch with Ronald Reagan during the 1980 campaign.

Instead of dry sandwiches and drinks from styrofoam cups, he had a fancy lunch brought in, complete with fine China, linen tablecloth, and fine wine. What most impressed me, however, was that his suite had an upstairs and a downstairs, with a spiral staircase connecting the two. He knew how to live well, no doubt at the taxpayers' expense and on money contributed to help the disadvantaged.

• • •

The enthusiasm generated by the "Black Alternatives" conference at the Fairmont hotel led several of us to consider holding another conference and to forming an organization where different views on political issues facing blacks could be discussed as an alternative to the positions taken by the established civil rights organizations.

I painfully rediscovered what I had seen before in other situations, that other people's enthusiasm for an idea does not necessarily translate into their willingness to put in the time and do the work necessary to make it a reality. During one conference call, I had to tell the others:

"When I do 90 percent of the work, I don't expect to also have to keep after other people to do their 10 percent."

Some of those who were slow to do their share of the work were all too ready to talk with the media, even though I had warned everyone from the outset that it was crucial that nothing be made public until we had an organization in place and could announce it at the scheduled conference in March. I could not run an organization and do my research at the same time, so we had to get other people to be in charge and in place, so that all inquiries could be directed to them. Unfortunately, one of my colleagues in this venture had an unguarded chat with a reporter for the *Washington Post.* Soon a story went out, coast to coast, describing our organization and the money behind it, both of which were still non-existent. The deluge of demands on my time, which I had tried from the beginning to avoid, was now unleashed.

The phone began to ring almost continuously, with calls from the media, requests for information from people who wanted to join, and comments and suggestions from others. Mail poured in faster than it could possibly be answered. Almost all of this was very positive in tone, but people did not realize that they were killing me with kindness. After my secretary took over answering the phone for me, she could scarcely type a sentence without being interrupted by phone calls—all day long.

Because we could get so little work done during the day, we began to work later and later into the evening. When the galley proofs for *Ethnic America* came in from the publisher, we asked someone at the switchboard to take all our calls, so that we could proofread the galleys. Meanwhile, there were innumerable details to be taken care of for the second "Black Alternatives" conference, scheduled to be held in March at the Hoover Institution.

Week after week of working more and accomplishing less began to take their toll in exhaustion, fitful sleep, and symptoms of cardiovascular problems. Now, my blood pressure went back up to new heights, so that I was put on more and stronger medication than before, and was told to stay home for a couple of weeks. In view of the medical history of my family, I was not about to press my luck. I cancelled the March conference—and never scheduled another one. I wrote another form letter, informing everyone concerned as to what had happened and referring them to two other black organizations that had agreed to distribute material we had planned to hand out at the March meeting.

My wife, Mary, who had always been opposed to any political or even quasi-political activity on my part, was incensed at how I had been done in. More than once, as she gave me my medicine, she said:

"The very idea of your going into politics! *The very idea!*"

The media now had a field day with the cancellation of the conference—and they did not let accuracy cramp their style. One of the black magazines reported that I was hospitalized in Palo Alto. In reality, I had not been hospitalized in more than a decade, and had no idea whether there was a hospital in Palo Alto.

False news can have real consequences, however. Mary Frances, whose cardiovascular problems were much more serious than mine, became worried when she read the magazine story about my being hospitalized—especially since she had heard nothing of the sort from anyone, and thought that I must be so badly off that the family was keeping the news from her. When she phoned me while I was out and received no answer, it seemed to confirm her suspicions. Fortunately, she called back later, after I came home. She seemed reassured when I told her that I had just come back from swimming 500 yards in laps at a local pool.

• • •

There were other commitments to cancel besides the March conference. Meg Greenfield of the *Washington Post* had asked me to write a bi-weekly column for them, and I had agreed to begin in April, but now I had to back out of that as well. I was also on the President's Economic Policy Advisory Committee, which I was told would meet about four times a year. I also resigned from that, after attending the first day of meetings—and after taking my blood pressure afterwards at Dulles Airport. I decided that I was not going to try for the *Guiness Book of World Records* in blood pressure.

The meetings themselves were not stressful, except for how long they went on, but transcontinental flights were very debilitating for me at this time, and then to meet for many hours at a time the next day was too much.

Our committee first met in Blair House, across the street from the White House, and later in the day went over to meet with the President in the Cabinet room. Nothing very momentous was said or done. What I remember most was an anecdote from a White House staffer. When he was over on Capitol Hill, walking down one of the corridors of the Senate or House office building, a Congressman motioned for him to step into his office.

"Next week I am going to make a speech denouncing the President, because of the effect of the administration's policies on my constituents," the Congressman said. "*Pay it no mind.*"

Over at the White House, President Reagan came into the Cabinet room to welcome us all and went around the table, greeting us individually and shaking our hands.

"Good morning, Dr. Sowell," he said, "it's good to see you again."

"Good morning, Mr. President," I said, "it's good to see *you.*"

It *was* good to see him. He had been shot just a few weeks earlier.

That was the sum total of all conversation between me and the fortieth President of the United States, during the eight years he was in office.

. . .

My newly published book, *Ethnic America,* was my main preoccupation during the second half of 1981. I had enjoyed writing it—it was not an intellectual struggle like *Say's Law* or *Knowledge and Decisions*—and I thought others might enjoy reading it. After several months of refusing to speak to anyone from the media, it was now time for me to go out and get some publicity for the book.

From the standpoint of sheer publicity and book sales, the renewed media attention was a big success. *Ethnic America* was reviewed on the front page of the book review sections of *The New York Times* and *The Washington Post,* as well as being reviewed in *Time, Newsweek, Fortune, The Wall Street Journal,* and other publications. I was interviewed on *Meet the Press, Donahue,* and other television and radio programs. The Manhattan Institute held a media luncheon that brought reporters, academics and others, and held a dinner that brought Mike Wallace, William F. Buckley, and other luminaries.

Qualitatively, the story was very different. The merely ignorant and misinformed journalists, such as those on the *Meet the Press* panel, were no real problem to deal with on the air. Print journalists who insisted on attributing things to me that I had never said were another story, because they could not be answered on the spot. *The New York Times'* reviewer depicted *Ethnic America* as a book "to be feared—as a signpost pointing to the probable future direction of the present national administration"—even though not a single policy was recommended anywhere in this book, and it had no connection with the Reagan administration, which did not even exist when it was written. Another writer on the *Times* referred to me as "the Administration's favored black spokesman," even though I literally had not said a single word in public about the Reagan administration since it took office. After months of silence, my first words on the new administration were spoken in answer to a question on *Meet the Press:* "I am not now, nor have I ever been, a spokesman for the Reagan administration."

One of the recurrent themes among critics was the claim that I

NBC News/*Meet the Press*

Taken during my interview on *Meet the Press* in 1981, when I was 51 years old.

had denied the existence of racial discrimination. I have no idea where this crazy notion originated, but it was repeated by many and was impervious to denial. I was phoned by one reviewer of another book of mine—*Markets and Minorities*—which came out at the same time as *Ethnic America*. He wanted to know why I had said that there was no racial discrimination.

"Did you read Chapter 2 of *Markets and Minorities*?" I asked.

"Yes."

"The title is 'The Economics of Discrimination'."

"I know."

"Why would I write a whole chapter on something I did not believe existed?"

When his review came out, he still implied that I did not believe in the existence of discrimination.

The worst of all the reckless misrepresentations came in a broadcast by CBS news reporter Lem Tucker, who said that my position "seems to place him in the school that believes that maybe blacks are genetically inferior to whites." Staggering as it was to suggest that anyone was saying that his own race was genetically inferior, it was still more staggering to suggest such a thing after I had written *against* that argument as often as I had. Two attorneys who had read my writings volunteered to represent me in a lawsuit against CBS, but I knew just enough about the laws on slander and libel to know how unreliable those laws were. I did, however, write to various people at CBS News, listing four books and several newspapers and magazines in which I had written in opposition to what their reporter's innuendoes suggested.

With all the bitter controversy swirling around me, a *Washington Post* reporter who interviewed me in 1981 wrote that I seemed "untroubled, unqualmed by the attacks made on him for all these years." In one sense, he was right. Although I became angry from time to time at the lies being spread about me in the media, that is not the same as being personally hurt—as people are by the truth. I was often as surprised at how hurt other people were by things that I said as some journalists were about how little hurt I was by smears about me. It is the truth that hurts.

The power of a few simple truths to provoke people often caught me by surprise. The worst uproar that any of my writings ever caused followed publication of two op-ed columns of mine in the *Washington Post* in February 1981. They were titled "Blacker than Thou," and their theme was that people who had disdained their fellow blacks in the past were now like reformed sinners who become holier-than-thou. Among the examples were former Carter administration Secretary of Housing and Urban Development Patricia Roberts Harris, who in college belonged to a sorority that would not admit darker-skinned girls. There were other examples cited, but this one seemed to set people off worse than any other.

There was no way to deny it, especially not in Washington, where so many blacks knew about such things from their own personal experience. Denial being impossible, their anger at me for telling this dirty little secret took the form of venomous attacks which took up a whole page of the *Washington Post*—and I was also denounced for these articles in other publications that were likewise unable to deny the truth of what I had said.

Controversy was a passing nuisance, but having my work disrupted by media attention was a more serious problem. My re-emergence in the media to promote my book brought a renewed onslaught on my office by telephone. I told my secretary not to put any phone calls through to me from the media. When she followed these instructions, frustrated reporters became abusive with her. When she hung up on one of them, he phoned right back and resumed his abusive language. I knew that something was going to have to be done when I saw her with her hands trembling and tears welling up in her eyes after dealing with the press on the phone.

"We're going to get an answering machine," I said.

"No, I can handle it, Tom," she said, her voice tense and wavering.

"We're getting an answering machine," I repeated.

After we had an answering machine installed, she loved it. Reporters suddenly became civilized, now that they knew that their words were going on tape, and that nobody had to say anything to them if they didn't behave themselves. Various media stories after that depicted me as a strangely secretive individual who was hard to reach.

None of these stories mentioned the media's own role in causing me to insulate myself and my secretary.

• • •

One day, as I was playing back the tape on my answering machine, I was pleasantly surprised to hear a familiar, mellow voice from the past. It was Ed Gally, the foreman who hired me to work in his machine shop when I was 19. Ed was now retired, and he and his wife were visiting San Francisco. He invited me up to the city to have lunch with them.

Over the years, Ed and I had exchanged an occasional Christmas card and pictures of our families, but somewhere along the way we lost touch. Now there was a lot to catch up on. Ed had gone on from being a foreman to setting up his own business. He told me that one Friday, back in 1976, he came home to find a note in his mailbox from the F.B.I., saying that they wanted to talk with him about Thomas Sowell.

Ed planned to phone them back Monday morning, but he got engrossed in his work. They phoned him.

"Yes, Tom once worked for me," Ed said, "but that was more than 20 years ago!"

"Tell us what he was like 20 years ago," the F.B.I. man said.

All this was in connection with my nomination to the Federal Trade Commission. But who would have thought that a middle-aged man would be investigated all the way back to when he was a teenager? Since then, I have told this story to many young people, to let them know that what they do can follow them for a long time.

• • •

Despite media attempts to make me almost part of the Reagan administration, I remained independent of it throughout its eight years in office, and criticized it severely in print whenever I disagreed with it. The first of these criticisms appeared in a satirical op-ed column in *The Washington Post* of January 26, 1982. One of the liberal writers on the *Post* liked it so much that he offered to buy me lunch the next time I was in town.

When my own long-standing views happened to coincide with

those of the Reagan administration on a particular issue, I of course said so, but there was no attempt to be in step with them. Even in the case of my friend Clarence Thomas, who headed the Equal Employment Opportunity Commission during the Reagan years, I did not hesitate to take opposing positions in print. After the E.E.O.C. lost a lawsuit against the Sears department store chain in 1986, I wrote a column praising the judge's decision.

I also criticized White House chief of staff Donald Regan in at least two columns and attacked one of the administration's foreign policies in a way that brought a nasty note from Secretary of State George Schultz. All the while, the label "Reaganite" was blithely applied to me in the media and I was often described as a Republican, though in fact I have never belonged to that party, and have not belonged to any party since 1972, when I was registered as a Democrat. Facts simply do not seem to matter to many in the media, once they have gotten a stereotype fixed in their minds.

During the Reagan administration, as during the Nixon, Ford, Carter, and Bush administrations, I had a few discussions with high officials on particular policy issues. But there was nothing unique about the Reagan administration in this respect, either in terms of the frequency of the discussions or the level of the officials involved. The idea of my becoming a member of the administration myself was raised more often during the Reagan years than during the Nixon and Ford years, but I declined each time, and I was twice invited to state dinners at the White House, which I also declined. However, the first time a White House staffer had asked me if I were available for a Presidential appointment was back during the Nixon administration, when I also declined.

By and large, I found the economic policies of the Reagan administration effective and I was sufficiently familiar with statistics on taxes and spending to know that it was nonsense to blame the huge budget deficits on the administration, rather than on Congress. In the racial area, the ineptness which I had briefly glimpsed during the 1980 campaign continued to plague the Reagan administration. However, this very ineptness made me doubt that they were a bunch of racists. Real racists would have been more careful to cover themselves.

Almost unnoticed was the fact that the Reagan administration put blacks in non-traditional roles more so than perhaps any other administration before them—at the United Nations, in international economic policy, or in domestic policy positions having nothing to do with race. Those blacks who were in areas dealing with racial policy—Clarence Thomas at E.E.O.C. and Clarence Pendleton at the Civil Rights Commission, for example—attracted more attention, but very able blacks like Alan Keyes and Wendell Gunn were playing important roles in non-racial positions.

The appointment of minorities was nothing new to Ronald Reagan. As governor of California, he was said to have made more minority appointments than in any previous administration. What he lacked was experience in communicating with minority voters or a sense of their psychology which that experience would have given him. By contrast, Governor George Wallace of Alabama, who bitterly opposed equal rights for blacks during the 1960s, was in later years much better able to communicate with the black community and ask for their votes, because he understood how to appeal to them. In politics, as elsewhere in life, sometimes "it ain't what you do, it's the way that you do it."

• • •

I began to travel internationally in 1982, much of it in connection with the writing of a trilogy on race and culture that took place over the next fifteen years. In 1984 and in 1987, Mary and I flew completely around the world. During the latter trip, Mary's commitments as an attorney would not let her leave with me, but she joined me two weeks later. It was our longest separation since we were married and we spent a lot of time on the telephone talking with one another, running up big phone bills across the Pacific.

I had spent several days in Singapore before Mary flew in to join me. We then moved to a larger room in the same hotel after she arrived. When she checked in at the front desk, she mischievously gave ambiguous answers when asked if she were Mrs. Sowell.

Our next stop was Kuala Lumpur. We arrived on July 4th and in our room we found a beautiful bouquet in honor of American Independence Day and of our arrival in Malaysia. It was from a student I had taught at Cornell more than 20 years earlier. I was moved almost to tears, especially since I had been the only member of his doctoral examining committee who held him to strict standards, while the others were prepared to pass him because he was a foreign student and wouldn't be teaching in the United States. It was gratifying to see, after all these years, that he had not interpreted this as harshness on my part but as a matter of concern.

The next evening he sent his chauffeur to pick us up and take us to a posh country club, where he and his wife joined us for dinner.

· · ·

While I was traveling overseas, I was also following very closely the nomination of Judge Robert Bork to be a Supreme Court Justice. I had long been familiar with Bork's writings on anti-trust law, and had assigned some of them in my economics courses, as far back as the 1960s. Moreover, I had also read some of his more recent writings on more general legal issues.

He struck me as one of the leading legal minds of the generation, but I figured that a political ambush was being prepared for him when a long delay was announced before holding confirmation hearings. When the administration asked me if I would be willing to testify for Judge Bork before the Senate Judiciary Committee, I readily agreed, despite my reluctance to testify before other committees on other issues, for this seemed to me one of the crucial legal battles of our time and there was no choice but to fight.

My first misgivings about the way the Reagan administration was handling the Bork nomination came when I read that the White House staffers would not let the Justice Department become involved in the confirmation process. When some group of people think that they know it all, that is usually a prelude to disaster.

Since one of the crucial smear tactics used against Judge Bork was to paint him as opposed to civil rights for minorities, I spent hours in the Stanford law library, looking up civil rights cases in which Bork had been involved as judge, or as an attorney before that. What I learned was that Bork had never voted against a minority plaintiff in a civil rights case as judge, and when he was an attorney he had appeared in more civil rights cases than any Supreme Court nominee since Thurgood Marshall. To look at the cases themselves in the law library, to see Robert Bork's name listed again and again alongside the names of lawyers from the N.A.A.C.P. Legal Defense Fund and other such groups—and then to go home and watch the direct opposite impression being created on television was enough to turn my stomach.

It also raised the question: Where was the Reagan administration and what were they doing to see that the other side of the story reached the public? Full-page ads against Bork were appearing regularly in *The New York Times,* as well as ads on television and elsewhere, picturing him as a menace to all sorts of groups and a danger to the republic. But I looked in vain for any counter-ads.

When my time to testify came, the Senate Judiciary Committee's chairman, Senator Joseph Biden, was out of the room, so Senator Ted Kennedy was in charge. I knew that he would do whatever he could to be a distraction while I was testifying, so I made it a point not to look at him. I fixed my gaze on some other Senator on the panel, even though Kennedy was seated directly in front of me. Before beginning, I asked Senator Kennedy if I had ten minutes for an opening statement, and he said "yes." But eight minutes into my statement, he asked impatiently:

"Can you bring that to a close?"

"I thought I had ten minutes."

"How much more time do you need?"

"Two more minutes."

Because I was not looking at Kennedy during my opening statement, it was not until I saw videotapes later that I saw him yawning and stretching ostentatiously while I was talking. He also coughed loudly, though the microphones were so placed that this did not come through on the television broadcast as much as it did in the room at the time.

Although my opening statement challenged much of what had been said against Bork, both by outside organizations and by members of the Senate Judiciary Committee, the Senators sidestepped all that and began raising all sorts of other issues during the question period. The worst was Senator Arlen Spector, whose invincible ignorance was exceeded only by his pompous certainty. My choices were to get down to his level or simply to let my disgust show. I did not want to become the issue instead of Judge Bork, so after a brief exchange, I just sat there in disgust. Some viewers got that and others didn't, with the result that I later heard the most widely disparate assessments of my testimony and received both enthusiastic congratulations from some and dismayed condolences from others.

Afterwards, I talked with a White House staffer who was involved in this nomination and suggested that someone ought to go over to the Supreme Court to get copies of the briefs that Bork had filed in civil rights cases, and publish some of the things he said in those briefs, so that the public could see the other side. The surprised staffer seemed to think that this was a good idea. Why they had not done it before was what I could not understand. By this time, however, the battle was already lost.

• • •

One Saturday morning, I arrived at the office to find a note left for me by my secretary, Agnes, who had been in earlier. It said that there had been a phone call for me from someone at the White House. I was puzzled as to what could be so urgent as to bring a call from the White House on a Saturday morning. I did not recognize the name of the caller, but phoned back, and received no answer. Shortly afterwards, however, the same man called me again.

Because Secretary of Labor Raymond Donovan had recently resigned to face an indictment, they were looking for a replacement, and wondered whether I would be interested in the job.

"Well, thank you for thinking of me," I said, "but I don't plan to leave my work here. Incidentally, why did you call on a Saturday morning?"

"Donald Regan wanted me to be sure to get in touch with you as soon as possible."

"That's very nice," I said. "Thank you anyway."

Now I was more puzzled than ever. I could not imagine that a pragmatist like White House chief of staff Donald Regan would want someone as controversial as me to be Secretary of Labor, when that would mean not only a tough confirmation battle, but also (if I were confirmed) that Regan would find himself repeatedly being forced to explain away things I had said, or having to put out political brushfires started by my actions. I wrote it off as just one of life's mysteries.

That night, my wife and I went out to dinner with another couple at a restaurant. Even before we sat down at the table, the husband said to me:

"Tom, my phone has been ringing off the hook today, with calls from Washington. You are going to be offered the job of Secretary of Labor. The people who are calling me say that, even if you don't want it, don't say 'no.' Tell them you need a few days to think about it."

"Why?" I asked.

"Donald Regan wants Bill Brock to be Secretary of Labor, but these people don't want Brock. If you want the job, they will throw their support behind you, but if not, then a delay will give them a few days to come up with an alternative candidate."

Now it all fell into place. Donald Regan must have figured out their little scheme and decided to cut them off at the pass by getting me to decline the offer before others could reach me.

"Well, it's too late now," I said, and explained what had happened.

We all sat there speculating as to what would have happened if I had said that I wanted to be Secretary of Labor. We turned it into a game of imagining how the newspaper headlines would have read. Mary came up with the best headline:

ALL CHARGES AGAINST RAY DONOVAN DROPPED

• • •

In May 1991, I stopped in New York on business and stayed at a luxury hotel located very near where I had once worked in the machine shop where Ed Gally was foreman. By now, that whole block had been torn down and replaced by a hospital. Nevertheless, being there reminded me of that struggling period of my life—and of Ed.

I phoned Ed and invited him and his family to dinner. It seemed an appropriate way to express my gratitude for his having lent me money to eat when I was destitute at 19.

In addition to Ed and his wife, he brought his two sons and their wives. All were really fine people. We dined at a restaurant on top of the World Trade Center. Our table had the best view in the house, overlooking downtown Manhattan on a clear spring evening. The food was excellent, the service superb. Others seemed content to let Ed and me do most of the talking, as we ranged from reminiscences of those old days in the machine shop to talk of the world today, our families, and everything in between.

It was one of the most memorable evenings of my life. When time came for parting, Ed and I were both on the verge of tears. He still recalled his trying to warn me away from a young woman who worked in his shop.

"I had no right to say what I did, Tom," he said apologetically, "but I just thought that she was more . . . sophisticated . . . than you were at that time."

"*Everyone* was more sophisticated than I was, Ed," I replied, and we both laughed.

That was the last time I saw Ed. A year later, he died. I felt especially grateful for the opportunity to have spent that evening with him. So many other people who helped me along the way died before I ever had a chance to do anything for them, or even to let them know that all their efforts on my behalf were not in vain. The person I would have most wanted to do something for was Daddy. Even after I was more than half a century old, there were lonely nights when I was working late and would begin thinking of Daddy and how I never had an opportunity to do anything for him, for all the things he had done for me, and sometimes tears would come to my eyes.

· · ·

When my son John graduated from college in 1993, I wrote a newspaper column about him, mentioning that he was nearly four years old before he began to talk. I also noted his remarkable memory and his outstanding abilities in analytical things like mathematics, chess, and computers. His degree was in statistics, with a concentration in computer programming.

This column set in motion an unexpected chain of events that became a major concern of mine over the next several years. First of all, letters began to pour in from around the country, from parents of similar children—similar not just in talking late but also in such things as remarkable memories and unusual analytical abilities. These parents wanted me to tell them why their bright children were years behind schedule in talking and what they should do about it.

Since I could do neither of these things, I wrote back saying that I would see what was available in the literature and let them know. This seemed to me at the time to be something that my research assistant could look up some morning and that I could then mail out the citations to the parents in the afternoon. However, days of searching turned up nothing on bright children who talk late. There were many studies of late-talking children in general, but in the end none of them dealt with the subject of highly intelligent children who were also years late in beginning to speak.

Weeks turned into months. Finally, in September 1993, after four months of futile search through innumerable sources and computer databases, I had to write back to the parents that I had come up empty. Knowing from experience what anxieties they were going through over their children, I could not simply leave them high and dry, so I offered to let them exchange addresses through me so that they could at least share their experiences with one another. Most of them took me up on this offer. Thus began a mutual support group, with parents whose children were grown and doing fine being a reassuring resource for those with younger children whose speech was either nonexistent or much less developed than that of other children their ages.

The group began with about two dozen families, scattered around the country and communicating with one another primarily by mail. Apparently the group meant a lot to parents who had felt completely isolated before and many of them expressed great gratitude to me, though I had done nothing more than sending them each other's addresses.

That might have been the end of the matter, as I thought it was at the time. However, as I read the letters that circulated within our group and sometimes talked with parents on the phone, over a period of months it slowly began to dawn on me that these were not typical people. First of all, the parents seemed to be clearly above average in intelligence. Even more striking were their occupations and the occupations of close relatives that they mentioned. Yet it was mid-April of 1994—almost a year since my column about John appeared—before I finally decided to investigate further by sending out questionnaires to members of the group. What set me off was a mother who mentioned in passing that her husband was a pilot in the Marine Corps. I had just recently heard from other families in the group that included pilots. It seemed to me that this was a lot of pilots for such a small group.

When the questionnaires came back, the first thing that hit me was that more than half of these children had an engineer as a close relative. That had a special impact on me because my younger brother was an engineer. People who played musical instruments were also very common among these children's relatives and included professional musicians. The vast majority of these late-talking children had at least one, and usually more than one, close relative in some highly analytical occupation, such as engineering, mathematics, or science. Most also had more than one amateur or professional musician among their close relatives. As for the children themselves, in addition to being analytical and often having phenomenal memories, many were also musically inclined and most were late in becoming toilet-trained, as my son had been.

I had no idea what all this added up to. But I thought that it was sufficiently remarkable that some professional in the medical, scientific, or related field ought to have this information and be able to pursue the subject. For much of the next year, I began to seek out such people and offer to turn my data over to them and put them in touch with the parents in our group. No one seemed interested. By 1995, it was becoming clear that, if anyone was going to do a study of bright children who talk late, it would have to be me.

After my book *Late-Talking Children* was published in the summer of 1997, a professional specializing in childhood speech disorders contacted me and said simply: "What can I do to help?" He was Professor Stephen Camarata of Vanderbilt University, who began to form his own group of parents of late-talking children. This was an enormous relief to me because I was being inundated with letters and phone calls from more parents of such children. They too had heart-rending stories of gross misdiagnoses and counterproductive treatments of their children. Now, however, I could simply refer them all to Professor Camarata, whose interest in the subject was personal as well as professional. He has a son who talked late and he himself was three and a half years old before he began to speak. I was more than happy to pass the baton to him. Now I could relax and take satisfaction in the fact that a newspaper column of mine had accidentally opened up a whole new area for research on a special set of children whose parents were going through all the anxieties that I had once gone through with my son.

12

Memories

In some ways, my life was much like that of many other blacks growing up in New York during the 1930s and 1940s. In other ways, it was quite different. It was still more different from the lives of blacks growing up in urban ghettoes during a later era. My life has been an even more radical contrast with the lives of many other black intellectuals, activists and political "leaders" and "spokesmen."

Perhaps most important, I grew up with no fear of whites, either physically or intellectually. Had I remained in the South, such fear might have become necessary for survival in adulthood, assuming that I would have survived. But fear is all too often the enemy of rational thought. Many blacks during the 1960s (and later) were inordinately impressed with strident loudmouths whose chief claim to fame was that they "stood up to the white man." As someone who first decked a white guy at age twelve, and who last did it at age thirty-five, I was never really impressed by such credentials—and certainly did not regard them as a substitute for knowing what you were talking about.

With all the vicissitudes of my life, and the long years of living close to despair, nevertheless in retrospect I can see that I was lucky in many ways—not only in escaping permanent harm in many dicey situations, but also in more general ways, both genetically and environmentally. It was clear from meeting my brothers and my sister in adulthood that much of my ability was simply inherited. This was true not only of the general level of ability but also of the particular type of ability—namely, analytical reasoning of the sort found in mathematics, science, chess and economics—as distinguished from the kind of ability required in poetry or politics, where my achievements have been virtually non-existent.

My brother Charles, though valedictorian of his high school class, never had an opportunity to go on to college. Yet he trained himself in electronics sufficiently well to build his own ham radio transmitter and his own stereo systems. Later, after some small formal training in electronics, he became sufficiently knowledgeable about electronic mail-sorting equipment to be made a supervisor in that department in the Washington post office and to be sent around the country by the postal authorities to advise local post offices on the installation and operation of the new system. Of Charles' two sons, one became a mathematics teacher and the other received a Ph.D. in mathematical economics at Princeton.

One of Mary Frances' teenage granddaughters was tested for a program for mathematically precocious children at Johns Hopkins University and also received a summer scholarship, while in high school, for a special program in computer science at Brandeis University. My brother Lonnie became an engineer whose research advanced the development of both rocket and aircraft engines. His sons went on to become engineers as well.

My own children have tested consistently higher for mathematical ability than for verbal ability. My son was on his high school chess team that competed for a national championship and he graduated from college with a degree in statistics, with a specialty in computer science.

Mathematics was always my best subject throughout my school years. Unfortunately, a whole decade away from math eroded my skills and denied me the foundation needed to develop much further in this field, so environment obviously had its influence as well. Nevertheless, when I was a graduate student at the University of Chicago, Milton Friedman said to me: "Although you don't have that much mathematics, you have a mathematical kind of mind."

I didn't learn chess until I was in my thirties, which is much too late to develop your full potential. I could beat other duffers who played an occasional game at lunchtime, but not many tournament players. Checkers was a different story because I played checkers as a child. When I first met my brother Lonnie, when we were both young men, we spent the evening playing checkers—each being astonished whenever the other won a game. At that time, I usually had only victories and draws. Judging from his reactions, apparently his experience was similar.

Some remarkable similarities in personality traits also showed up as between me and my siblings, even though we were raised in separate households hundreds of miles apart. The most common characteristic was that most of us were loners. This was brought home to me when I passed through Washington on my way out to California in 1969. We stopped at the home of Charles' former wife, and waited there for him to come over and join us. Meanwhile, my son went outside to play with kids in the neighborhood. When Charles arrived, I said:

"Let me take you outside to meet my son."

"I've already met him," Charles said. "We've had a long conversation."

"How did you know who he was?" I asked.

Charles smiled indulgently.

"Tommy," he said, "when I see a dozen kids, all doing the same thing, and in the midst of them is one kid who is doing something entirely different, I don't have to guess which one is our mother's grandson."

Charles himself was a prime example of a similar pattern of marching to his own drummer. During one of the ghetto riots of the 1960s, Charles was out in the midst of the rioters, asking them such questions as: "After you burn down this man's store, where are you going to shop?"

It never occurred to Charles that a riot is not the place for a Socratic dialogue. Apparently there is no gene for politic behavior in our family.

Although marching to your own drummer has its down side, both personally and professionally, it also made me no stranger to controversy, decades before my controversies became public. Without already being pre-hardened against vilification, my research and writings on racial issues would not have been possible.

Although the environment in which I grew up was very deficient in the kinds of things measured by sociologists and economists, it nevertheless provided some of the key ingredients for advancement. I was, for much of my formative period, an only child in contact with four adults who took an interest in me, even if they were not all under the same roof all the time. Contrast that with being one of several children being raised by a single woman—or, worse yet, a teenage girl. The amount of adult time per child was many times greater in my case.

Although none of these adults had much education, and certainly no knowledge as to what was good or bad education, Birdie and Lacy cared enough about my development to see to it that I met another boy who could be a guide to me. Meeting Eddie Mapp was another remarkable—and crucial—piece of good fortune.

The luck of passing through particular places at particular times was also on my side. Some of my happiest times were spent in the South, though I was very fortunate to leave before I would have fallen irretrievably far behind in the inferior schools provided for Southern blacks—and before I would have had to confront the corrosive racism faced by black adults. In New York, I passed through the public schools at a time when they were better than they had been for the European immigrant children of a generation earlier and far better than they would be for black children of a later era.

Once, when my niece in New York was lamenting that she had not done more with her educational opportunities, she said:

"I went to the same school you went to, Uncle Tommy."

"No," I said. "You went to the same *building* I went to, but it was no longer the same school."

The family in which she was raised was also no longer the same family that it was when I was growing up. Her parents were no longer a carefree young married couple, with time and money to spare, and an upbeat outlook on the new world of New York. They were now care-worn parents, preoccupied with trying to cope with multiple hardships, punctuated by tragedy. Although my niece came ultimately to live in the same apartment in which I had grown up a decade before her, the life in that apartment was now even more bitter than that which had sent me out into the world at seventeen.

My early struggle to make a new life for myself under precarious economic conditions put me in daily contact with people who were neither well-educated nor particularly genteel, but who had practical wisdom far beyond what I had—and I knew it. It gave me a lasting respect for the common sense of ordinary people, a factor routinely ignored by the intellectuals among whom I would later make my career. This was a blind spot in much of their social analysis which I did not have to contend with.

With all that I went through, it now seems in retrospect almost as if someone had decided that there should be a man with all the outward indications of disadvantage, who nevertheless had the key inner advantages needed to advance.

The timing of that advance was also fortuitous. My academic career began two years before the Civil Rights Act of 1964 and I received tenure a year before federal "goals and timetables" were mandated under affirmative action policies. The books that made the key differences in my career—*Say's Law,* whose manuscript was crucial to my receiving tenure at U.C.L.A. and *Knowledge and Decisions,* which brought an offer of appointment as Senior Fellow at the Hoover Institution—were both books on non-racial themes. Altogether, these facts spared me the hang-ups afflicting many other black intellectuals, who were haunted by the idea that they owed their careers to affirmative action or to the fact that writings on race had become fashionable. I knew that I could write for a whole decade without writing a single book or article on race—because, in fact, I had done that during the 1960s.

Timing was on my side in another way. I happened to come along right after the worst of the old discrimination was no longer there to impede me and just before racial quotas made the achievements of blacks look suspect. That kind of luck cannot be planned.

Crucial pieces of good fortune like these would have made it ridiculous for me to have offered other blacks the kind of advice which the media so often accused me of offering—to follow in my footsteps and pull themselves up by their bootstraps. The addiction of the intelligentsia to catchwords like "bootstraps" has made it all but impossible to have even a rational discussion of many issues. As for following in my footsteps, many of the paths I took had since been destroyed by misguided social policy, so that the same quality of education was no longer available to most ghetto youngsters, though there was never a time in history when education was more important.

Most of my writings on public policy issues in general, and on racial issues in particular, were directed toward the public or toward policy-makers, and tried to show where one policy would be better than another. These writings were not advice directed toward less fortunate people as to how they could cope with their misfortunes. I am not Dear Abby. My hope was obviously that better policies would reduce those misfortunes. Nevertheless, clever media interviewers insisted on asking me such questions as:

"But what do you say to the welfare mother or to the ghetto youth?"

I cannot imagine what would have led anybody to think that I was writing handbooks for welfare mothers or ghetto youths, or that either would be reading them, if I were. Even worse were suggestions that I thought that too many benefits were being given to minorities, whether by the government or by other institutions. Yet, from the very beginning, I have argued that many of these "benefits" were not in fact beneficial, except to a relative handful of middle-class people who ran the programs or who were otherwise in some special advantageous position. Whether or not I was correct in my analysis or conclusions, that was the issue raised—and the issue evaded by red herrings about "bootstraps" and the like.

By and large, my books on racial controversies attracted more media attention and had larger sales than my books on economics, politics, or the history of ideas. However, the books on racial issues were not written as an intellectual outlet, but because there were things I thought needed saying and I knew that other people were reluctant to say them. More than one colleague has suggested to me that I would be better off to stop writing about race and to return to the things in which I did my best professional work—books on economics like *Knowledge and Decisions* or books on ideas like *A Conflict of Visions* and *The Quest for Cosmic Justice*.

What, if anything, will endure from what I have written is of course something that I will never know. Nor is what I have said and done enhanced or reduced by my personal life, however fashionable amateur psychology has become. What has been done stands or falls on its own merits or applicability.

The whole point of looking back on my life, aside from the pleasure of sharing reminiscences, is to hope that others will find something useful for their own lives. Justice Oliver Wendell Holmes said it best:

> If I could think that I had sent a spark to those who come after I should be ready to say Goodbye.

On the Stanford University Campus at age 68, as a Senior Fellow at the Hoover Institution, where my best work was written.